CINO NIGHTS

edited by
Daniel Talbott & Addie Johnson

foreword by
Todd London

Published by The New York Theatre Experience, Inc.
P.O. Box 1606, Murray Hill Station, New York, NY 10156
www.nyte.org
email: info@nyte.org

ISBN-13: 978-0-9794852-6-8

Cino Nights is made possible, in part, with public funds from the New York State Council on the Arts, a state agency.

Cino Nights is made possible, in part, with public funds from the New York City Department of Cultural Affairs.

Cino Nights is made possible, in part, by support from piece by piece productions.

Photos by Daniel Talbott.
Book and cover designed by Nita Congress.

PERMISSIONS

Dedicated to all the original writers of the Caffe Cino. And to Jimmy Carbone, the memory of Doric Wilson, and to Joe Cino himself.

CONTENTS

FOREWORD

Todd London

I miss Joe Cino. I miss his theater, which was a café. I miss the moment of Caffe Cino, a moment when Judson Church welcomed playwrights under the wide communitarian wings of Reverend Al Carmines, when writers sought to begin a cultural revolution at Theatre Genesis, when Ellen "Mama" Stewart first rang her little bell, signaling curtain time at the global art pushcart called La MaMa Experimental Theatre Club. I miss the sound of that bell, the tinkle-tinkle-tink that rang on East 4th Street in lower Manhattan and reverberated around the world. Yeah, I miss what I never had.

I caught the originating bells as echo and the Ur-tumult in after-shock. Caffe Cino started serving coffee and food on Carmine Street in 1958, with poetry on the side, and added plays to the menu in '61. I entered high school ten years later to find teen-aged longhairs rocking Megan Terry's *Viet Rock*, N. R. Davidson's Malcolm X play *El Hajj Malik*, and one-acts by John Guare and other children of Cino. Among the first lines I spoke as a fresh-man actor was "Blah blah blah blah blah blah hostile. Blah blah blah blah blah blah penis" from Jean-Claude van Itallie's *America Hurrah*. My first semester in college—middle of Iowa—I discov-ered that preeminent Cino writer Lanford Wilson by getting cast in *Rimers of Eldritch*. These crazies had been blowing minds in downtown Manhattan since the sixties were still the fifties. They blew my mind after the fact, but it stayed blown. And so the explosion that began in Joe Cino's bohemian coffeehouse—walls plastered with posters, torn photos, glitter stars, balls of foil, and a motley of memorabilia almost a foot thick—and changed the shape of our theater, changed the course of my one Midwestern life as well. It led me, a millennium later, to sit down and write this to you, introducing a collection of plays by another bunch of retroactively blown minds, from yet another generation, plays produced by Rising Phoenix Repertory in a series called *Cino Nights*.

Just to be precise: I miss what I missed, but I'm not nostalgic for that other time. Nostalgia is a tribute band, opening the graveyards of our imagined youths, so the dead can walk the earth in Peter Max clothes. They were magical and painful times, those first days of Off-Off-Broadway, but the pain was as real as Joe Cino's suicide in '67. Who wants the madness that went with that particular moment of searching? No, I'm not nostalgic for the rats and roaches, not for the poverty, the raw street and drug life, for the hallucination, the bacchananihilation that was the underbelly of so much beautiful dreaming.

I'm nostalgic for an urgency of impulse, a driving drive to make theater for some pressing, if still indiscernible, reason, the reason you have to discover by doing. I'm nostalgic for art that tastes like freedom. I'm nostalgic for theater that smells like fun.

I can't remember who said that theater is either easy or impossible. Whoever it was, was right. The easy is what we know; it confirms what we know. I want the impossible kind, exploration without end, the challenge to make miracles in minutes with a figurative gun to your head. This isn't to suggest that great theater can only happen when it's thrown together under duress. Astonishing theater (who wants any other kind?) can be, in the making, fast or slow.

Slow is Peter Brook, The Wooster Group, Andre Gregory—all diamond, impact and edge, the brilliant earthen density made of pressure over time. Fast means propulsive, the burst and flood of energy that drags the unconscious with it, meaning made on purpose and by happy accident. Overnight play festivals are fast. Weekend intensives are fast. Plays improvised before your eyes are fast fast fast. Fast can be a way to the vital and communal, a way to pack the intensity of years together into mere evenings. Theater fails in the middle ground between fast and slow—the three-and-a-half-week rehearsal, for example, which gives you time to learn lines, get your moves down, and run cue to cue. It's hard, in the middle, to release bursts of the unconscious that happen under pressure, or to drill down the way you can in the long haul.

Rising Phoenix Rep's *Cino Nights* are fast: a week's rehearsals starting on Monday and culminating with a throw-it-up tech on Sunday afternoon and a single performance that same night. Theater in the blink of an eye. And the blink of it confirms—no, celebrates—the theater's ephemerality, its now-you-see-it, now-it's-gone-ness.

The original Caffe Cino was an amateur enterprise with professionals. Joe Cino chose artists by instinct or, famously, by astrological sign. His Caffe was part playground and part destination for the devoted. This, I think I believe, is the best way to make theater: with professionals engaged in amateur activities. In the first Greenwich Village experimental age, in the nineteen-teens, theater folk were fond of reminding everyone that the Latin root of the word amateur is love. In other words, amateur theater is love sport. Amateur theater with professional artists is a double blessing, because it reconnects with the *amour* that gives us our first reasons to create—the love of self at play, the love of imagining, the love of singing/dancing/pretending with others. And it draws on the finest attuned sensitivities of the dedicated artist—the expressive body, the resilient voice, the emotional/creative intelligence, and human insight that expands with practice. We say professional theater artists have "chops," a term that comes from Jazz. You need chops to hit the high notes on the horn. To play in the *best* way, though, you need to want to hit those notes *in the worst way*. You want magic? You want astonishment? You want theater? You want music that hasn't been heard before? Try mixing professional virtuosity with amateur hunger.

God, I love that Daniel Talbott and the Rising Phoenix gang came up with *Cino Nights*. Yes, it's homage and nostalgia, but out of the longing for what you missed altogether comes something else again. They aren't recreating Caffe Cino. To do that you'd need to resurrect Joe Cino, give him a broom and a coffee machine, dial the Village back to 1961, bring back the young Ellen Stewart, Al Carmines, and all of them, including Lanford Wilson, Doric Wilson, H. M. Koutoukas, Leonard Melfi, and Tom Eyen. We'd need to make John Guare, Robert Patrick, Terrence McNally, Maria Irene Fornes, and Sam Shepard kids again (which has its appeal but isn't possible even in the impossible theater). But no, *Cino Nights* are after that elusive grail of the theater: Something else again. The new thing that reminds us. The new energy that reignites us. The speed that unearths that which might take a lifetime to investigate and fully express. Something else again and again and again.

Something else again is the back room of the East Village restaurant Jimmy's No. 43, where *Cino Nights* happen and which gets tricked out anew for every show. Jimmy's became, for example, the underground headquarters of a cult dedicated to the Russian poet Anna Akhmatova in Kristen Palmer's *The Stray Dog*. Something else again is Gary Sunshine's *The Best Sex Ever*, in which an ambitious soldier sets out to marry his prematurely old kindergarten teacher on a cruise ship, only to encounter his "butt-boy" from ROTC, the pharmaceuticalized nebbish with whom he had, yup, the best sex ever. Something else again is Adam Szymkowicz's *Clown Bar*, a noir play with a bar full of gangster clowns in full red-nose regalia and an ex-clown cop trying to get to the bottom of his junkie brother's murder. Courtney Baron's *Here I Lie* is something else again, too, a pas de deux of loneliness, illness, and, finally, death, which appears to be the only perfect thing in life. As is Lucy Thurber's *Named*, where the unspoken and spoken each define love's desire in their own way, and Mando Alvarado's *(O)n the 5:31*, which folds what happened, what might have happened, and what's remembered into a fluid ten-year love triangle. Jessica Dickey (*Row After Row*) dresses a New York woman in a "farbing" (you gotta look that one up) Civil War uniform, so she can mingle with Gettysburg re-enactors, and, so, makes something else again out of the past. In *The Upstart*, Emily DeVoti tracks down Hitler's Irish sister-in-law and finds her living out on Long Island, and Brigid Hitler's story becomes a twisted lifeline for a struggling writer and for an aging actress at the end of her hope. Each of these plays—eight of the seventeen *Cino Nights* plays to date—is its own kind of new, its own kind of something else again. Some were written fast, some slow, some for all time, some for the blink of an eye. They may recall another moment, but they all live in the theater present or, as Szymkowicz says of the clown play, "Right fucking now."

You didn't see them? Read them then. Stage them in your own theater, in the middle of your own café. Mount a marathon—all these plays and all the ones you can find from the original Caffe Cino. You may just hear the tinkle-tinkle-tink of a bell you thought had fallen silent long ago.

Todd London has been the artistic director of New Dramatists since 1996. He's the author of The Artistic Home, Outrageous Fortune: The Life and Times of the New American Play *(with Ben Pesner) and of* The World's Room, *a novel; he is editor of* An Ideal Theatre: Founding Visions for a New American Art, *due out in the summer of 2012. In 2009, he became the first recipient of Theatre Communications Group's Visionary Leadership Award for "an individual who has gone above and beyond the call of duty to advance the theatre field as a whole."*

PREFACE

Ever since we began publishing plays in 2000 (with *Plays and Playwrights for the New Millennium*), it has been both our goal and our privilege to share the works of emerging, talented dramatists with a wide audience, so that they may begin to assume their rightful place within the canon of contemporary American drama.

In August 2011, we took a giant step in enlarging the scope of our publishing program with the launch of Indie Theater Now, the digital theater library for the 21st century (online at www.indietheaternow.com). It's a website that readers immediately christened "iTunes for plays," providing a virtual home for playwrights, theater professionals, audiences, and lovers of new drama, where the latest works from America's vibrant and ever-growing independent theater scene can be discovered, explored, and read online. At this writing, Indie Theater Now's library encompasses some 350 plays, written by more than 200 playwrights...and counting. I hope that readers of this volume will take a moment to visit Indie Theater Now and become acquainted with the next generation of play publication for this increasingly connected, paperless world.

I still love books, and we're proud to continue our print publication program with this collection of new works from Rising Phoenix Repertory's remarkable, audacious, and entirely admirable *Cino Nights* series. The eight playwrights whose works appear within these covers—Mando Alvarado, Courtney Baron, Jessica Dickey, Emily DeVoti, Kristen Palmer, Gary Sunshine, Adam Szymkowicz, and Lucy Thurber—possess strong, compelling, individual voices and by any measure are among the leading theater artists of their generation. I hope you will enjoy sampling their work here and on Indie Theater Now.

I am indebted to Daniel Talbott and Addie Johnson of Rising Phoenix for all of their hard work, dedication, and vision in bringing this volume to fruition; to our book designer/copy editor Nita Congress for applying her usual excellence to this project; to NYTE's Managing Director Rochelle Denton for shepherding this book to completion; and to piece by piece productions for their particular support of *Cino Nights*.

Martin Denton
Executive Director, The New York Theatre Experience, Inc.

ACKNOWLEDGMENTS

Rising Phoenix Rep would first off like to thank every artist, family member, and friend who gave their time and their heart to making this whole project happen. From acting in the back room to writing the gorgeous words that bounced off the tight and extremely intimate walls of Jimmy's No. 43, to the countless friends who guarded the doors, took the tickets, and shouted "The house is open! Grab your beers and come on in," there's not nearly enough room in this book to thank all of you enough here, and please know you forever have our love and respect—huge thanks and we know none of this would've ever been possible without all of you.

Special thanks to Wendy vanden Heuvel, piece by piece productions, and Distracted Globe. David Van Asselt, Brian Long, the whole Stick family, and Rattlestick Playwrights Theater. Stephen Willems and MCC Theater. Brian Mertes and Melissa Kievman and the whole Chekhov at Lake Lucille crew. Todd London and everyone at New Dramatists. Morgan Jenness, Beth Blickers, Leah Hamos, and everyone at Abrams Artists Agency; Peter Strain, Bill Timms, and everyone at Peter Strain & Associates; Kathy Hood, Joe Kraemer, Michael Kahn, James Gregg, and everyone at the Juilliard Drama Division. Martin and Rochelle Denton, The New York Theatre Experience, nytheatre.com, and Indie Theater Now. All the writers of the Caffe Cino, including: Doric Wilson, Robert Patrick, John Guare, Sam Shepard, Lanford Wilson, and William M. Hoffman. Larry Kramer, Patricia Bosworth, Estelle Parsons, Amy Potozkin, and George Maguire. Berkeley Rep, Solano College Theatre's Actor Training Program. Robert and Louise Rosen. Jimmy Carbone, Pixie, Georgia, Nik Bullit, and everyone at Jimmy's No. 43. Tessa LaNeve and everyone at ESPA/Primary Stages. Dan Bacalzo at TheaterMania; Robert Diamond and BroadwayWorld. com; Kenneth Jones, Michael Gioia, and Playbill.com; Micheline Auger and her *Theatrespeak* blog; Zack Calhoon and his *Visible Soul* blog, J. Stephen Brantley and his blog. Evan Caccioppoli, Brad Peterson, Janie Bullard, Laura Ramadei, and Erin Kennedy-Lunsford.

Cino Nights has been made possible with the support of piece by piece productions, the Distracted Globe Foundation, The Alpert Foundation, and through the donations of many wonderful individuals.

INTRODUCTION

Daniel Talbott

When I showed up at La MaMa a couple years ago to see a bunch of the original writers of the Caffe Cino speak about their work and their experiences there, I was pretty down. I felt, at the time, like most of the theater folks I loved and respected were being forced to think less and less about work, and more about career, fiscal reports, marketing, networking, audience-building strategies, and fundraising, and that theater artists were being dwarfed by administrators all over the country. I felt like most of the conversations I was having were not about work, or creating theater, or that wonderful balls-out/tits-out play we had just seen at New York Theatre Workshop, Rattlestick, the wonderful 13P folks, The Amoralists, or in some shit-hole bathroom on the Lower East Side. I felt like if I heard the word "networking" or the phrase "we really need to get a name" or anything else like that one more time, I was going to rip my eyes out and vomit.

Not that I didn't want to work, not that I didn't want to make a living as a theater artist, or think that theater artists should be paid a living wage for their insanely, insanely hard work, of course we should. I just felt that things had been deeply skewed to the wrong side of the equation, and that things were looking more like the corporate plague that had taken over our country and our institutions with a capital "I" instead of places that were there solely to support work, artists, risk taking, failure, and change. I was in desperate need of some blood in my heart; I was in a bad way and deeply down.

I walked into La MaMa and, first off, was so happy (as I am every time I go in there) about how wonderfully funky, chaotic, and human that place is. I saw this incredible, hysterical, loud, eclectic, grumpy, and completely mesmerizing group of people filling the lobby and the theater. I knew almost no one that day except Doric Wilson (whom I miss incredibly since he passed away) and a couple of other folks, and I felt so lucky to be there—like I had been given a ticket to travel back in time and see how explosive and messy and wonderful so much of the theater must have been in the sixties and seventies. I watched Robert Patrick's grainy and exquisite documentary, and got to listen to Doric, William Hoffman, and a group of other theater folks talk and laugh and share stories about the Caffe Cino. I loved the idea of a place where the person in charge asked about your zodiac sign instead of reading your play, and then trusted you to show up and do your work. I loved that Joe Cino believed you were important and that he should give you a space, a floor, simply because you had come to him and felt you had something to say through a play—that in itself was reason enough.

I know it sounds totally corny, but I sat there in the dark, in the back of the theater, listening to all those folks, and cried. It was the shot in the arm I really needed, and I went home and wrote a crazy, rambling, profanity-ridden, grammatically suicidal, and probably equally cheesy email to a bunch of friends and folks I love and admire. I said, "I want to do this project to honor the work of the original writers of the Caffe Cino and to try to create something together that has nothing to do with our careers, with reviews, with money, or with anything other than the work and the play itself. If you want to be a part of this, write whatever you want for the back room of Jimmy's No. 43, and each month we'll put it up, fully produced, warts and all, no matter what it is. Whoever responds to this and wants to do it, we're on and we'll do your play, and we'll do one each month 'til all the plays have been worked on, produced, and have gotten to put down the book and jump up off the page and start to run around some, wild, buck naked, and free." We stole the week-long, fully produced rehearsal model from the brilliant Brian Mertes and Melissa Kievman and their luminous and extraordinary work up at Chekhov at Lake Lucille—some of my favorite theater I've ever seen has been up on that beautiful lake, rehearsed in a single week. We chose the order based on the order folks wrote us back. Everybody donated their time, and most importantly, as much as possible, we wanted to see if we could produce all these plays for free—to do the highest quality theater possible for as little money as possible, and let the limitations be the inspiration.

Almost two years later, I'm sitting here writing this and we're about to start rehearsal tomorrow on Brooke Berman's wonderful play, *Casual Encounters*. I can't even begin to say how lucky and blessed I feel to have gotten to be a part of this with all the Rising Phoenix Rep-ers and the rest of the insanely talented, huge-hearted, generous, and exceptional artists involved. I still feel like the whole world is way too obsessed with money, fame, and corporate structure. I still feel like theatrical institutions should only exist for the work and the theater artists who dwell there, and that they should form around the plays that are being developed and put on, not expect the work to form around them and their growth. I still feel that the number of artists at a theater should dwarf the number of administrators, and that corporations and institutions are not people, and they are not work.

That day at La MaMa was a brilliant reminder of what I hope for. That talk is cheap if it isn't acted upon, that "the play's the thing," and that truly great theater can happen anywhere, and under any budget, and in any space, big or small. Joe Cino had a space and he shared it and great, even magic, things happened down on Cornelia Street. He didn't discriminate, or attempt to be the ultimate tastemaker, or waste any energy slumming around in empty hierarchies, review whoredom, or popularity pageants. He simply trusted artists to do their work, announcing the show by saying, "It's magic time." Caffe Cino was where, as Edward Albee put it:

> We were all very young; we were all innocent; we knew nothing. We lived in a kind of Eden called Greenwich Village—this was a long time ago. Greenwich Village then was the center of all the new arts, and everyone was talented, and no one was famous, and we all spent our time with each other's work, learning and cribbing. And one of the theatre centers was Caffe Cino, where young playwrights who knew nothing about what they were supposed to be doing made exciting work, and the failures were as exciting as the successes. It was Eden. I miss it.

Daniel Talbott is an actor, director, playwright, producer, and artistic director. He is a graduate of Juilliard, and is one of the literary managers at Rattlestick Playwrights Theater and the artistic director of Rising Phoenix Rep.

BEST SEX EVER

Gary Sunshine

GARY SUNSHINE has been the recipient of an NYFA fellowship and a Helen Merrill Award for Emerging Playwrights. His play *Sweetness* was produced in the Summer Play Festival (SPF); *Mercury* was produced at HERE in association with Eve Ensler; *The Names of Foods* was produced by the eXchange; other recent productions include *Kahn & Kant* (Drama League Directors Project), *Al Takes a Bride* (Actors Studio; Sydney Mardi Gras Festival; King's Theater) and *My President* (Echo Theater Company). His work has been seen/developed at the Royal National Theatre Studio, New York Stage & Film, Playwrights Horizons, NYTW's Just Add Water Festival, Theatre of Note, P73 Productions, Rattlestick, the New Group, the New Company (London), Underwood Theater, MCC Theater, and the Actors Studio. His one-act play *Al Takes a Bride* was published in *The Best American Short Plays of 2001* (Applause), and by Playscripts, Inc. Gary wrote, co-created, and co-produced the documentary *What I Want My Words to Do to You* (Freedom of Expression Award, Sundance Film Festival; Audience Award, Lake Placid Film Festival; Crystal Award, Heartland Film Festival; HBO Audience Award for Top Documentary, Provincetown International Film Festival), which premiered nationwide on PBS's *P.O.V.* He has been a staff writer on HBO's *Hung* and CBS's *As the World Turns* (WGA Award nomination). He received an AB from Princeton and an MFA from NYU's Dramatic Writing Program. He is a member of Rising Phoenix Rep and an alumnus of New Dramatists.

VISIBLE SOUL INTERVIEW WITH GARY SUNSHINE
Conducted by Zack Calhoon, October 28, 2010

How did you get started in theater? What made you start writing plays?

I started at Maplewood Day Camp in a production of *The Wizard of Oz*. I was ten, a really tiny kid with a huge head and a big voice. I played the Scarecrow, and the drama counselor, for some reason, gave me an extra song—"No Time at All," from *Pippin*, usually belted out by a cantankerous old lady. He gave me a microphone and put me on the lip of the stage to start the slow verse, and then directed me to slink my way up when the peppy vamp started, and then he had me go out into the audience to sing the chorus—"Oh, it's time to start living/ Time to take a little from the world I'm giving…" I got hooked.

I didn't start writing plays until after college. I had acted and directed all through school, but I knew I just didn't have what it took to pull off a career as an actor—I was crazily self-conscious and had no connection to my body—I was way too stuck in that previously huge head of mine. But a year after I graduated, my father died—he had prostate cancer for six years. And I sucked at mourning, and I was even worse at communicating with myself about what I was feeling. But I knew I needed to say something about and maybe even to my family. So I wrote a "death of the father" play called "Scenes from a Condo," pulled together some friends in an apartment and had them read it out loud. We all had a really fun time, and for a little bit, I felt like I was revealing something about myself I'd never be able to do in a regular, human conversation. So I kept going.

Tell me about your play, *Best Sex Ever*. What was the process like? How do you think the play went?

Best Sex Ever is basically the story of two really neurotic, really fashion-challenged guys approaching middle age who love each other like crazy, and whose relationship supports each other's craziness. One of the guys is trying to stop his high school fuck buddy from marrying their kindergarten teacher, while the other guy thinks he's latched onto a way to turn him and his boyfriend into "adventurous" people. All on a rickety old cruise ship. There's some farce, some sex, a tiny bit of camp, and, I think, an attempt to look at monogamy and marriage in a heightened but honest way.

I can't tell you how happy I was when I got the email Daniel Talbott sent around asking a bunch of us for plays. Daniel Talbott and Addie Johnson, and Denis Butkus and Sam Soule, and Brian Roff, and Julie Kline—all of them—they're such good and wise eggs and when they say they want to work with me, my gut tells me, whoa, that's a smart place to go. I had just spent the previous seven months in LA writing for *Hung*, and I needed to get back to my own voice. It was really important to me to take pleasure in the writing of whatever I was going to come up with for *Cino Nights*. I needed to have fun—so I set out to write a full-on comedy, something I've never done before.

Getting the play ready for its *Cino Nights* performance was an insane process. The director, the very brilliant and preternaturally calm Moritz von Stuelpnagel, worked with all of the Rising Phoenix people to assemble this very game, very talented cast, who just jumped in and somehow convinced themselves they could put up a full-length play in a week. In the basement of a bar—with a guy hauling five dead pigs through the space during a rehearsal one day (Jimmy of Jimmy's No. 43 was orchestrating a barbecue on Governor's Island, I think). But these actors—Jimmy Davis, Jeffrey Nauman, Mike Doyle, Cathy Curtin, and Stephen Bel Davies—are wildly talented and so generous—and I think everyone just got off on the impossibility of the task in front of them. There was no time to think—they just did it. That manic energy really serves this particular play.

What was it like working at the National Theatre of Great Britain?

I was so, so lucky to get to go to London and work at the National Theatre Studio on two of my plays, *Sweetness* and *Reasons to Wake Up*. The opportunity came about through SPF, where *Sweetness* was produced back in 2004. The National set me (and Brooke Berman) up with a terrific bunch of people and made me feel very much at home in someone else's city and country, and for that I'll always be grateful to Arielle Tepper Madover and Rachel Neuburger. But to be honest, probably the best part was the free theater tickets they had set up for Brooke and me. All that theater, lots of West End stuff, including *The History Boys* and *Buried Child* and *Sweeney Todd* and this breathtaking *Romeo and Juliet*…and something involving an autopsy beneath a Tube station by London Bridge…it made me feel more alive within and connected to the world of theater than I think I'd ever felt up to that point.

What kind of writing inspires you?

It changes and it's varied. At this point, as an audience member and a writer, I'm looking to anything that can transport me, take me someplace that is in some way unfamiliar. There's so much great TV writing going on right now, as everyone keeps saying in the press…but I'm realizing how different fantastic theater writing is from fantastic TV writing. It has something to do with size, expansiveness, working with ideas and language that can fill up a public, shared space. An electricity and an energy that can only happen in a theater, that's what I'm looking for. I felt it when I saw Rajiv Joseph's *A Bengal Tiger at the Baghdad Zoo*, and David Adjmi's *Stunning*, and anything by Anne Washburn, or Lucy Thurber, just to name a very, very few of the playwrights I deeply admire. And Daniel Reitz has this play called *Studies for a Portrait* that's been produced in London but not here yet. I heard it in a Naked Angels reading and it shook me and lacerated me and busted my gut with biting comedy—those are the kinds of plays that make me want to be a bigger theater fan and a better writer.

Who or what has been the biggest influence on your work as a playwright thus far?

Eve Ensler, one of my grad school teachers at NYU and someone who has literally found a way to change the world with her work—told me early on that she had to learn that being funny was the best way to get her point across, to win or earn an audience's attention. But she's also the person who taught me not to write something unless, on some level, I could explicitly determine how important it was to me. To be a responsible writer—not necessarily in the service of a specific, concrete political or social goal, but at the very least to take responsibility for what I put into the world. These ideas have stuck with me for a long time.

Best Sex Ever, directed by Moritz von Stuelpnagel, premiered October 3, 2010, at the Seventh Street Small Stage at Jimmy's No. 43.

CAST LIST

Kraatz .... Jeffrey Nauman
Jeremy .... Jimmy Davis
Miss Alice Smith/Lolly/Waitress .... Cathy Curtin
Lieutenant Colonel Delgado .... Mike Doyle
Burt .... Stephen Bel Davies

CHARACTERS

KRAATZ, mid-30s. Emigrated from an Eastern European country. Very loving with no sense of style. Not conventionally attractive but not ugly either.

JEREMY, mid-30s. KRAATZ's longtime boyfriend. Also no sense of style. Similarly not unattractive but no one (except KRAATZ) would call him a looker. On a lot of psychopharmaceuticals that don't seem to work all that well.

MISS ALICE SMITH, early 50s. Prematurely old. In constant kindergarten-teacher mode.

Lieutenant Colonel DELGADO, mid-30s. MISS ALICE SMITH's fiance. One very hot, very repressed man.

BURT, mid-30s. A wedding videographer with cowboy roots. Also a bit sexy.

LOLLY, any age, BURT's lighting person.

WAITRESS, any age.

NOTE: One actress should play MISS ALICE SMITH, LOLLY, and the WAITRESS.

PLACE

Aboard the *Icy Maiden*, a very, very low-rent, cramped, and dark cruise ship.

TIME

Now.

SCENE 1

(Main deck of a very low-rent cruise ship. JEREMY and KRAATZ, a hopelessly unstylish couple, drink from tall fruity glasses.)

KRAATZ: Remember first time?

JEREMY: Absolutely.

KRAATZ: We were on our way to...

(Pause.)

JEREMY: We were on our way to...

(Pause.)

KRAATZ: Sun, it was—

JEREMY: —It was yellow.

KRAATZ: Ya, ya, yellow.

JEREMY: Definitely yellow.

KRAATZ: And circumstances, circumstances was—

JEREMY: —Very trying.

KRAATZ: No! Holiday! Fun!

JEREMY: We were broke.

KRAATZ: Still, was sweet.

JEREMY: No, our second vacation, that was sweet.

KRAATZ: Really? Where did we go?

JEREMY: Oh, that's an easy one. We went to...

KRAATZ: ...On roof of tongue...

JEREMY: ...Tip of the tongue, mine too...

KRAATZ: ...We went to...no, that was vacation third.

JEREMY: Where?

KRAATZ: Hershey Park.

JEREMY: I would never go to Hershey Park.

KRAATZ: Ya. Hershey Park. Big hotel. Loud family in next room. They laugh at television program, laugh come through wall, you cry.

JEREMY: No way.

KRAATZ: Fine, I was with my imaginary boyfriend of many many years.

(Pause.)

JEREMY: I'm sorry.

(Silence.)

KRAATZ: Maybe it was Minnesota.

JEREMY: No, it was Hershey Park.

KRAATZ: Yes, no, maybe not.

JEREMY: Hershey Park!

KRAATZ: We want to go to Hershey Park, but we never make it.

JEREMY: It was Hershey Park!

KRAATZ: Okay. *(Pause.)* Are you on the edge?

JEREMY: No.

KRAATZ: That is good.

JEREMY: Are you?

KRAATZ: No no no. A little. Yes.

(Silence.)

JEREMY: It's a beautiful sea.

KRAATZ: It is beautiful sea. But this ship, it is shit.

JEREMY: It's the darkest, dingiest, tiniest cruise ship in the world.

KRAATZ: Utter shit.

(JEREMY gently puts his arm around KRAATZ's shoulder.)

JEREMY: Good thing we brought our Kodak Easy Share Point and Click.

KRAATZ: Yah, yah, very smart of us. *(Pause.)* I forgot our Kodak Easy Share Point and Click.

JEREMY: So did I.

KRAATZ: So what do we do?

JEREMY: I don't know. *(Takes out a bottle of pills.)*

KRAATZ: Let us not be scared.

JEREMY: But we always have a camera.

KRAATZ: What is worst thing that happens?

JEREMY: We wind up with no pictures.

KRAATZ: So?

JEREMY: And we get back home and it's like we were dead the whole time we were away.

KRAATZ: Is that what it is like for you?

JEREMY: A little. Sometimes. Maybe.

KRAATZ: We are not dead. We are just. You know. Heavily medicated.

(JEREMY produces two tiny bottles of water and hands KRAATZ a pill, and one to himself. They take their pills. They look out at the sea.)

KRAATZ: Remember first time...

JEREMY: ...First time we took pills?

KRAATZ: No. First cruise!

JEREMY: Oh. Yeah. Not really.

KRAATZ: Oh.

JEREMY: I love you.

KRAATZ: I love you.

JEREMY: I really love you.

KRAATZ: I really love you.

(Silence.)

KRAATZ: I love you.

JEREMY: You just said that.

KRAATZ: Ya, ya.

JEREMY: Because Dr. Opel says repeating ourselves is fine. As long as we're *conscious* of it.

KRAATZ: I remember important stuff!

JEREMY: And nothing's more important than the "I love you's."

KRAATZ: I love you I love you I love you I love you I love you. Nobody will forget nothing. Now, do you want to make some sex?

(Pause. JEREMY starts to hyperventilate. KRAATZ rubs his back in small circles, until he calms down. KRAATZ then pulls a flower from his throat.)

JEREMY: Oh God, no.

KRAATZ: Sorry. Is compulsive.

(MISS ALICE SMITH, prematurely old, appears and speaks to a small unseen crowd that gathers around JEREMY and KRAATZ.)

MISS ALICE SMITH: Shhhh...shhh...hands over mouths, hands over mouths and one...two and...LISTEN TO ME NOW!!! *(Beat.)* There, that's so much better. Thank you for joining us. I've attended fifty-eight weddings over the years. I never dreamed I'd have my own. My dear mother used to say I was born to be someone's elderly aunt. Mother's dead now.

(An extremely loud foghorn startles her.)

MISS ALICE SMITH: EYES UP FRONT!! (Beat.) Now...the Icy Maiden may be compact, but it's a genuine pleasure cruiser! It has a wading pool! And a Ping-Pong table! And a salad bar! And a jukebox! And free towels! And I hear tomorrow there might even be a little sun! Lieutenant Colonel Delgado and I encourage you to drink alcoholic beverages, but please exercise caution and good judgment. Do not attend the wedding ceremony if you are covered in sick. That would just be rude! And insulting! And terribly immature. As a matter of fact, let's not chance it. No drinking at all, for any of you. I will go tell the cruise director...

(Canned music begins to play.)

MISS ALICE SMITH: Oh, my...

(LIEUTENANT COLONEL DELGADO, in full uniform, enters and holds his hand out. They dance. As they wind down, KRAATZ pushes JEREMY, who crashes into the couple.)

MISS ALICE SMITH: Oh, my!

DELGADO: What's the big idea?!

JEREMY: Sorry sorry sorry.

MISS ALICE SMITH: Jeremy? Is that you?

JEREMY: Yes, Miss Smith, it's me.

MISS ALICE SMITH: He's just as dainty as he was when you were five years old.

DELGADO: I don't remember him.

MISS ALICE SMITH: It's Jeremy! Your very best friend since you were both in my kindergarten class!

DELGADO: Jeremy?

JEREMY: Hi there.

MISS ALICE SMITH: I invited him as a special surprise.

JEREMY: (To DELGADO.) ...Surprise?

(Beat. DELGADO salutes JEREMY.)

JEREMY: I don't know what that means.

MISS ALICE SMITH: Shake his hand, dear.

JEREMY: Oh. Okay.

(JEREMY puts his hand out to shake. DELGADO shakes his hand, cold and formal.)

MISS ALICE SMITH: I'm sure you two have so much to catch up on. So why don't I go back to the cabin and wash out my unmentionables, while you boys... (Leaves.)

DELGADO: (Calling to MISS ALICE SMITH.) I brought the Woolite! (Leaves.)

JEREMY: (Looks at the unseen crowd, then:) We go way back.

SCENE 2

Cruise ship cabin. KRAATZ and JEREMY are on the bed, post-coital.

KRAATZ: That was very good. Very good. Very. It was good?

JEREMY: Yup.

KRAATZ: You like it when I...you know?

JEREMY: Yup.

KRAATZ: Because I never—

JEREMY: —You think he remembers me?

KRAATZ: Who?

JEREMY: Delgado.

KRAATZ: You are on his wedding cruise.

JEREMY: He left me out of his first three weddings. If Miss Smith didn't send us an invite—

KRAATZ: —His eyes, they had sparkle when he see you.

JEREMY: A sparkle?

KRAATZ: Sparkle of oh, the past!

JEREMY: Really. Sparkle.

KRAATZ: Like when you see old stray cat on street years after you give it milk.

JEREMY: So I'm a begging cat?

KRAATZ: Delgado's eyes, they say, "Hello cat!"

JEREMY: Why can't I just be a guy to him—

KRAATZ: —"Nice Cat!"—

JEREMY: —or a man—

KRAATZ: —"Cat, I missed you so!"—

JEREMY: —Why can't I just be the ROTC water boy he used to queer out with?

KRAATZ: "Queer out"? Where you get this term from?

JEREMY: During the ceremony...when they ask if anybody has a reason to object? I might not say anything.

KRAATZ: Nobody really asks that.

JEREMY: Or I might say a lot.

KRAATZ: Dreamy—

JEREMY: —It might seem a little brutal. But in the end, honesty...what is it they say about honesty?

KRAATZ: Is thing that go bump in the night.

JEREMY: No, I don't think that's what they say.

KRAATZ: Will create trouble.

JEREMY: Yes.

KRAATZ: Will cause heartbreak.

JEREMY: Possibly.

KRAATZ: Was what you two did...what you had...was it that much of a spectacular?

(Beat. JEREMY smiles. KRAATZ smiles.)

JEREMY: Yes you have.

KRAATZ: Yes I have what?

JEREMY: The pinkie-thumb-mouth bit. You've done it before.

KRAATZ: No, I never, not like that.

JEREMY: I thought you did.

KRAATZ: Oh. I am sorry, then. It felt like new idea. Hmmph.

JEREMY: No, you're right. It was new. And I was...surprised.

KRAATZ: You were?

JEREMY: Completely.

KRAATZ: Did I hurt you?

JEREMY: No. A little.

KRAATZ: Oh no! Oh no!

JEREMY: I'll be fine.

KRAATZ: Do you need ice pack?

JEREMY: No.

KRAATZ: Should I call ship's doctor?

JEREMY: I'm okay.

KRAATZ: Would be hard to explain to ship's doctor. But I would do that. I would take blame.

JEREMY: Dude. It's fine.

(KRAATZ sits up in bed. Stares at JEREMY.)

JEREMY: What?

KRAATZ: You call me "dude."

JEREMY: So?

KRAATZ: You do not never call me this.

JEREMY: Yes I have.

KRAATZ: No. Never.

JEREMY: You're just forgetting.

KRAATZ: You never call me "dude" because you are not young enough to call me "dude."

JEREMY: I am so totes young enough to call you dude, dude.

KRAATZ: "Totes"? It is unseemly.

JEREMY: Are you saying I'm *old*?

(Loud knock on door.)

JEREMY: Oh my God it's Delgado!

KRAATZ: So?

JEREMY: Don't answer it!

(Knock on door. Another knock on door. Another. Another. A note slides toward them from under the door. JEREMY and KRAATZ don't know what to do. Finally, KRAATZ gets up and picks up the note. He studies it.)

JEREMY: Get your glasses!

KRAATZ: Oh. Right. *(Grabs his reading glasses from the night stand, puts them on, and reads.)* Ahhh. Ohhhh. Hmmmm.

JEREMY: What does Delgado want?

KRAATZ: No, not Delgado.

JEREMY: Not Delgado?

KRAATZ: No...no...no...ya. I see. Ya.

JEREMY: What?!

KRAATZ: It appears we have been... observed.

JEREMY: Doing what?

KRAATZ: This person...this man...

JEREMY: How do you know he's a man?

KRAATZ: His handwriting, it is very masculine. And the smell of the paper... *(Sniffing the page.)* ...Old Spice Body Wash.

JEREMY: You're just speculating.

KRAATZ: And the way he signs his note with name "Burt."

JEREMY: Oh. What does he say?

KRAATZ: He saw us ask room steward for extra towels. He says "You guys remind me of sushi." What does this mean, to remind someone of sushi?

JEREMY: I don't know.

KRAATZ: He wants to meet us.

JEREMY: Delgado's wedding is stressful enough. No meetings with men named Burt.

(KRAATZ reads the note again.)

KRAATZ: He says to meet him for a late-night drink on the Latino Deck.

JEREMY: Well there you go. That's just impossible.

KRAATZ: Why?

JEREMY: Our pills. They knock us out by nine.

KRAATZ: True. True. *(Beat.)* Jeremy?

JEREMY: No.

KRAATZ: Just this once?

JEREMY: Once becomes twice becomes three times—

KRAATZ: —No, I promise—

JEREMY: —Schedules keep the buses running on time.

KRAATZ: We are not buses. We are men.

JEREMY: If our pills can't count on us, how can we possibly count on each other?

(Pause. JEREMY takes out a bottle of yellow pills and a tiny bottle of water. He gives a pill to KRAATZ. They both swallow their pills. JEREMY kisses KRAATZ, then gets into bed, gesturing

for KRAATZ to join him. KRAATZ gets into bed with him. They turn out the lights.)

JEREMY: I love you, Creamy.

KRAATZ: (Garbled.) Lohh yuhhh.

(Beat. Beat. JEREMY snores. KRAATZ carefully gets up and out of bed. He spits out his yellow pill, kisses JEREMY on the head, and leaves.)

SCENE 3

The Latino Deck. KRAATZ sits at a table. Salsa music plays softly. A WAITRESS appears.

WAITRESS: What would you like to drink, por favor?

KRAATZ: A soda. No. A scotch and soda. No. A scotch. No. A double scotch, no ice. Yes. No. I should not drink because I take pills. No. I would like to drink because I am in uncomfortable situation. I am meeting man for first time. No. Not a man like that. I am married. No. Not married. Where I live we cannot be married. So we are not married. No. We are not married because we do not go to place where we can be married. Because we wait until we can be married where we live. Is political statement. No. Is not. Is more like we are lazy. Because to get married in other place means to make phone calls to government and fill out papers. Is hard enough to call for pizza. So we are not married. I am not married. Would like to be married, yes, of course. Show of love. Show of determination. Show of...is hard. Life, it is very very hard. You understand?

WAITRESS: Sprite?

KRAATZ: Ginger ale.

WAITRESS: Sprite?

KRAATZ: Ginger ale?

WAITRESS: Fresca?

KRAATZ: Ginger ale?

(WAITRESS leaves.)

(KRAATZ takes out a toothpick and picks his teeth. He accidentally pricks his gum. He puts a napkin to his mouth and it turns bloody.)

KRAATZ: Goetz's pidinski!

(He puts the bloody napkin down and applies a clean one. And then another. Until a pile of bloody napkins accumulates on his table.)

SCENE 4

Upper deck, outside, under the moonlight. MISS ALICE SMITH, carrying two large sketch pads and crayons, runs in, pursued by DELGADO, who holds pieces of paper.

DELGADO: Just look at these emails and faxes! "Atta boy, Delgado...Lieutenant Colonel Michael T. Putnam." "Welcome back to the Ol' Ball and Chain Club... Colonel George T. Washington." "Hold onto your football!...Brigadier General Thomas T. Vikenberry." I am the man!

MISS ALICE SMITH: That must make you feel very proud.

DELGADO: I should have you. Now!

(DELGADO turns her around and grabs her from behind.)

MISS ALICE SMITH: We're getting married tomorrow afternoon!

DELGADO: And then I'll take you to the Officers' Ball. And you'll sit with the officers' wives, just like my other wives did. And talk about how strong your men are. How strong...and manly.

MISS ALICE SMITH: Let's enjoy the moon.

DELGADO: One last point?

(MISS ALICE SMITH makes a reprimanding face. DELGADO sheepishly raises his hand.)

MISS ALICE SMITH: Yes, Lieutenant Colonel?

DELGADO: Does your belly sweat?

MISS ALICE SMITH: Sometimes when I'm running after children in the playground, yes.

DELGADO: I have imagined your belly sweating. Dots of sweat. Tiny blond hairs. The cutest little belly button. I even gave it a name... "Miss Smith's Knockhole."

MISS ALICE SMITH: That's very sweet.

DELGADO: I should make love to Miss Smith's Knockhole.

(MISS ALICE SMITH hands him a sketch pad and crayons. She takes one herself. She points to the moon.)

MISS ALICE SMITH: Make the prettiest picture.

DELGADO: This never ends well.

MISS ALICE SMITH: Let's both draw the prettiest moon ever!

(MISS ALICE SMITH and DELGADO both draw, looking to the moon for inspiration.)

MISS ALICE SMITH: Let's see what a pretty picture you've drawn.

DELGADO: (Looks at his drawing and grows disturbed.) You first.

(MISS ALICE SMITH reveals her drawing—a childlike depiction of a moonlit sky and ocean.)

DELGADO: That's very...very pretty, Alice.

MISS ALICE SMITH: Why thank you, Lieutenant Colonel. Now it's your turn!

(DELGADO, panicky, doesn't move.)

MISS ALICE SMITH: Batter up and that batter is Y-O-U!

(DELGADO shakes his head "no.")

MISS ALICE SMITH: Come on, I'm sure it's wonderful!

(MISS ALICE SMITH reaches for his sketch pad. DELGADO holds it tight. MISS ALICE SMITH applies all her strength and rips it out of his hands. She looks at it.)

MISS ALICE SMITH: My. My. This is...my.

DELGADO: Do you like it?

MISS ALICE SMITH: I do! I'm just not sure...

(MISS ALICE SMITH turns the sketch pad around to show DELGADO [and the audience], revealing his picture of a human body featuring two small breasts and a ridiculously large penis.)

MISS ALICE SMITH: ...Where is the moon here?

(DELGADO, now very embarrassed, turns away from her, like he's going to cry.)

MISS ALICE SMITH: You clearly have a much more sophisticated head for drawing than I do!

DELGADO: Maybe if I try again?

MISS ALICE SMITH: Rather than that, I think you should go see that nice Jeremy.

DELGADO: Don't wanna.

MISS ALICE SMITH: Ask him to be your best man!

DELGADO: Don't remember him.

MISS ALICE SMITH: He's your dearest friend in the entire world!

DELGADO: He stinks. Make him leave.

MISS ALICE SMITH: We're in the middle of the Atlantic.

DELGADO: I don't care!

(MISS ALICE SMITH raps DELGADO on the head. DELGADO instantly salutes her. She salutes him back.)

MISS ALICE SMITH: When a guest goes to such trouble to attend your party, you must pay him extra attention.

DELGADO: Yes ma'am.

(She kisses him on the cheek.)

DELGADO: I wish I had a better tan.

MISS ALICE SMITH: What?

DELGADO: Huh? Oh. Nothing. Where were we?

MISS ALICE SMITH: You were going to go see your old friend Jeremy.

DELGADO: When I'm tan in this uniform, my face really pops.

MISS ALICE SMITH: Lieutenant Colonel?

DELGADO: Sorry, sorry. You're wonderful.

MISS ALICE SMITH: Me, or the idea of me?

DELGADO: The whole package.

MISS ALICE SMITH: So you're marrying me out of love?

DELGADO: With a wife like you, I'll make colonel by Christmas!

MISS ALICE SMITH: But you're not just marrying me for all the best reasons, right?

DELGADO: It's just You and Me Equals We.

MISS ALICE SMITH: That has a lovely lilt. Now go ask Jeremy to stand by your side. We can't do this alone, can we?

(DELGADO exits. MISS ALICE SMITH looks at his drawing, tears it off the sketch pad, and shreds it.)

SCENE 5

(The Latino Deck. As before, KRAATZ nurses his gum wound, with bloody napkins in front of him. A FRIENDLY MAN, devilishly handsome, takes a
clean napkin, dips it in water, gets behind KRAATZ and, before KRAATZ can argue too much, slides it into KRAATZ's mouth, applying firm, direct pressure. KRAATZ squirms, but FRIENDLY MAN presses on the top of KRAATZ's head, both keeping him in place and oddly relaxing him. KRAATZ melts. The bleeding stops.)*

FRIENDLY MAN; All gone.

KRAATZ: Thank you.

FRIENDLY MAN: My pleasure.

KRAATZ: Sometimes that will go on for hours.

FRIENDLY MAN: Hemophiliac?

KRAATZ: *(Shaking his head "no.")* No flossing in formative years.

FRIENDLY MAN: As a matter of principle?

KRAATZ: Where I come from, we have floss shortage, due to constant invasions. Others in village, they floss with the hay, but I had the, the hay fever. So I do not floss. Now I pay price.

FRIENDLY MAN: When I was in dental school, they used to say, A man's history is etched in his gums.

KRAATZ: Is true, is true. You dentist?

FRIENDLY MAN: No. Filmmaker.

KRAATZ: Oh. But you just say—

FRIENDLY MAN: —Wish we could get that waitress over here.

KRAATZ: She is kind woman. Remind me of Father.

(FRIENDLY MAN reaches over and takes KRAATZ's water, drinks it down, slams the glass down on the table.)

FRIENDLY MAN: Burt here.

KRAATZ: Ohh. Burt. From the note, Burt?

BURT: Where's your other half?

KRAATZ: He is in room.

BURT: He looked shy at the steward's desk.

KRAATZ: Very shy, very shy. Still, I love him.

BURT: Sure about that?

KRAATZ: I am here on cruise, am I not?

BURT: Whose idea was it?

KRAATZ: Is his. There is wedding.

BURT: Yes, the Delgado-Smith wedding. I'm the videographer.

KRAATZ: Ohhhh!

BURT: Friends of the bride or groom?

KRAATZ: Both. Not me. Jeremy. The groom. Bride was their kindergarten teacher.

BURT: That happens all the time.

KRAATZ: Bride pay for us to come. Otherwise we cannot come.

BURT: She's gone all out.

KRAATZ: Groom and Jeremy, they never see each other no more. But we come. We ride the waves, we eat the pineapple, we get dizzy and nauseous. We are old.

BURT: Old?

KRAATZ: So you go on lots of cruises?

BURT: Every chance I get.

KRAATZ: Is my first. Or maybe my second. Third, maybe. We argue over this.

BURT: You guys argue a lot?

KRAATZ: Oh, same as anyone else.

BURT: Bet the making up is top notch.

KRAATZ: Top notch?

BURT: Bet you argue and fight and fight some more, but then you fall into each others' arms and, well, you know...

KRAATZ: ...Oh. Yes. Well. Sometimes.

BURT: How many years you guys been together?

KRAATZ: Ten. Or twelve. Fourteen. More than ten.

BURT: Bet you don't do a lot of anal.

KRAATZ: Is not something we discuss.

BURT: But when you do anal, you finish up and you say to each other, "That wasn't as hard as we thought!"

KRAATZ: Oh...well...hah hah...hah hah hah...

BURT: Are you tense?

KRAATZ: Yes.

BURT: Why?

KRAATZ: Is my natural state.

BURT: So Jeremy, he's the laid back one?

KRAATZ: No, he is more tenser than me.

BURT: Fascinating!

KRAATZ: He is like electric bug and I am like the rock bug sits on. You understand?

BURT: Perfectly.

KRAATZ: We do not hide from each other. Is too hard.

BURT: That's what marriage is all about.

KRAATZ: Exactly. We, uh, we hug each other's anxiety. Even as it grows bigger each day.

BURT: What are you anxious about?

KRAATZ: Oil in Gulf.

BURT: Well, life is full of twists and turns.

KRAATZ: For you too?

BURT: Nah. Got cowboy blood in me. Tend to look at the world as one big dusty trail.

KRAATZ: Dust get in lungs, cause scarring and cancers.

BURT: *(Lustily.)* You are hot.

KRAATZ: No no.

BURT: Seriously. I knew it from the first time I saw you with the room steward.

KRAATZ: You say I remind you of sushi.

BURT: Yes. Slick. Raw. Clean. Tightly wrapped. One mouthful of perfection.

KRAATZ: Oh. Well. Thank you. Thank you for your kind words. One mouthful. Okay. Probably right, give or take mouthful. But anyway...well... *(Rises.)*

BURT: Where are you going, Kraatzy?

KRAATZ: My beloved, I did not kiss him good night, it make him cry.

BURT: Crying's sweet. Sit down.

KRAATZ: I kiss Jeremy good night and then I do some word search puzzles, is good for my English.

BURT: Have I made you uncomfortable?

KRAATZ: Yes. Very.

BURT: That's the last thing I wanted, Kraatzy. Let me make things better.

KRAATZ: If you make things better... maybe I make things worse.

(BURT puts his hands on KRAATZ's shoulders.)

KRAATZ: You are housebreaker?

BURT: Huh?

KRAATZ: Housebreaker. You come in to other people's houses and steal one from other, rip apart what God has stitched together.

BURT: Oh no, I have no interest in that.

KRAATZ: Oh. *(Beat.)* I just thought. *(Beat.)* Oh. *(Beat.)* Ohhh! You want threesome?

BURT: No.

KRAATZ: Because Jeremy and me, we try it once, back many many years ago, we bring in baker from down street, he make good marble rye, but not so good in bedroom, Jeremy cry, so after that we get bread from supermarket.

BURT: I have no penis.

KRAATZ: No penis?

BURT: Well, I *have* one.

KRAATZ: Good. Is necessary organ.

BURT: Mine looks normal. I wash it every day. Urine passes through it. But nothing else.

KRAATZ: I am so sorry.

BURT: I've made my peace.

KRAATZ: Still, I cannot imagine, life without penis, without...

BURT: ...I like old cars. I work weddings, retirement parties. And I also make movies.

KRAATZ: Movies.

BURT: Yes, many people are excited by my movies. And that makes me happy.

KRAATZ: Is good for work to make you happy.

BURT: Nourished. That's what I aim for.

KRAATZ: Nourished?

BURT: At the end of the day, I want everyone involved in my work—from the grips to the actors, all the way to my users—

KRAATZ: —Users?

BURT: My audience. I want every single person to feel like they've just eaten a full meal, like they've eaten so much that they're about to throw up, but then, out of nowhere, they belch, and they experience relief and satisfaction at the same time.

KRAATZ: You aim high.

BURT: I aim for the stars. And sometimes I catch 'em.

KRAATZ: Is admirable.

BURT: Would you like to be in one of my movies, Kraatzy?

KRAATZ: Excuse me?

BURT: It'll change your life.

KRAATZ: Not so good at changes.

BURT: Oh, you'll love this one.

KRAATZ: I am no actor.

BURT: I saw the way you handled the room steward.

KRAATZ: Is movie about getting extra pillows?

BURT: Could be. If you want. I'm very collaborative. I crave input.

KRAATZ: I would be no good at memorizing lines.

BURT: You can make them up as you go along. Just use your imagination.

KRAATZ: I do not have one of those.

BURT: Between the two of you, you'll come up with the perfect things to say—

KRAATZ: —Two of us?

BURT: Of course! You and Jeremy, you're a team.

KRAATZ: We are team. But he cannot do thing like this.

BURT: Haven't you ever wanted to be in a movie that other people watch? And they see you, being you, but you at your very best? And then they know you, only it's you at your very best? You and the great love of your life, showing the world just who you are...the essence of you...without ever having to explain a word... Doesn't that make you...hot?

(KRAATZ considers this. BURT takes out a money clip filled with bills. He counts off ten bills, then slides them toward KRAATZ. KRAATZ picks up the cash, then BURT snatches it back.)

BURT: No free rides here.

KRAATZ: Right.

BURT: Gotta be in it to win it.

KRAATZ: Of course.

BURT: Money, it makes the world—

KRAATZ: —This movie...what will be its subject area?

(BURT smiles big-time. Lights go down on them, loud cruise music plays, as BURT and KRAATZ whisper in each others' ears. The more whispering, the more appalled and fascinated and appalled and fascinated KRAATZ grows. Suddenly, sound goes out, lights bump back to normal.)

BURT: Mull it over. See how it feels. Could be one of those milestones you look back at. Could be important. Or just a heckofa lotta fun.

SCENE 6

(Cruise ship cabin. DELGADO stands over JEREMY, who sleeps in his bed. DELGADO kicks the bed. JEREMY sits up.)

JEREMY: *(Very groggy.)* Oh, hello.

(DELGADO doesn't answer.)

JEREMY: You wanna play Risk?

(DELGADO doesn't answer.)

JEREMY: I'll give you North America if you give me Southern Europe.

(DELGADO doesn't answer.)

JEREMY: Madagascar for Kamchatka?

(DELGADO doesn't answer.)

JEREMY: Am I asleep?

(DELGADO grabs JEREMY by the throat and squeezes. JEREMY gasps for air.)

DELGADO: Keep. Your mouth. Shut.

(JEREMY nods in agreement.)

DELGADO: For the duration of this cruise. And then until you die.

(JEREMY makes a hard rattling sound.)

DELGADO: And then after you die, no haunting. You understand that?

JEREMY: No...haunting...sir.

(Pause. DELGADO releases JEREMY.)

DELGADO: You all right?

JEREMY: No!

DELGADO: What's wrong?

JEREMY: My trachea's cracked and hemorrhaging. And I'm having stroke-like symptoms.

DELGADO: You're not old enough.

JEREMY: You can have a stroke at any age—

DELGADO: —Why did you have to come?

JEREMY: Miss Smith said you wanted me here.

DELGADO: She's pre-pre-Alzheimers.

JEREMY: Then why are you marrying her?

DELGADO: The army doesn't discriminate!

JEREMY: I wish you well.

DELGADO: Thank you. *(Starts to leave.)* Keep. Your mouth—

JEREMY: —Shut. Yes, I know, I know. But can you tell me one thing?

DELGADO: We'll adopt.

JEREMY: That's not what I was going to ask. But since you're bringing it up, I think adoption would be a giant waste of your gene pool. But I guess it would be hard—

DELGADO: —Are you trash-talking my fiancée?

JEREMY: No, no, never—

DELGADO: —Because I won't stand for that.

JEREMY: She taught me phonics and I am grateful! *(Pause.)* Look, Kraatz is the dip on my chip, and he'll be that for the rest of my life...but you...for those four years...every afternoon after Junior ROTC...you'd still be in uniform... And I'd be wet from all that water I served...and all the water the guys would dump on my head...and my mom would be at work at the snack cake company...and my dad would be off on the road with the other dancers...and we'd go straight up to my bedroom... and I'd pull back Green Blankey...and I'd get into bed, on my stomach...and wait for you...I'd hear each of the buttons of your uniform popping open...and those big black shoes hitting my floor... and your brass belt buckle jiggling... and I'd slide my underpants down, and then...then...

DELGADO: ...And then?...

JEREMY: You were the best I ever had.

DELGADO: The best...?

JEREMY: ...The best sex ever. Over and over. In and out, and in and in and in, and...I've missed that. And...was I that for you? *(Beat.)* I know that sounds kinda needy, but...well, it *is* kinda needy, and that's okay, because I'm a very needy person.

(The door flings open. It's KRAATZ.)

DELGADO: ARRGHGHHH!!

KRAATZ: ARRRGHHHH!!

JEREMY: ARRGHHHH!!!

KRAATZ: Why we scream like this?!

JEREMY: Guilt!

DELGADO: No sex happened here, sir.

KRAATZ: Who said anything about sex?

DELGADO: I'll go now. A little self-control, guy. Especially during a man's wedding cruise.

JEREMY: Come on! Stop that! Make him tell you the truth!

(KRAATZ, uneasy, blocks the door.)

KRAATZ: Why you drop him when you are young, so long ago?

DELGADO: He made too many demands on me. Demands I couldn't possibly fulfill.

JEREMY: *You* were the one with the demands! I was just your little butt boy—

KRAATZ: —And these demands? What was the nature of them?

DELGADO: Sexual, sir. But I could not comply. Because it wasn't in my makeup.

JEREMY: But you were all up in *my* makeup, every chance you got—

DELGADO: —He just told me I was the best sex he ever had. And I think that included you.

KRAATZ: Ya? You say this, Jeremy?

JEREMY: Context! Context!

DELGADO: The only thing is, we never *had* sex. Not today, not ever.

JEREMY: Oh don't do this—

KRAATZ: —Jeremy tells me you two have supersexy past. Are you saying he is liar?

DELGADO: I don't want to say that. But back in school, we had a nickname for him.

KRAATZ: What was nickname?

DELGADO: Jeremy the Liar.

JEREMY: That is such a fallacious piece of—

KRAATZ: —No no, my Jeremy, he think if he tell lies he will get caught and sent to ovens.

JEREMY: You came here and you pounced on me, in my bed, which could only mean you wanted to pick up where we left off back at 6693 Marigold Avenue...oh my God, CRAMPS! CRAMPS!

(JEREMY runs off to the bathroom. KRAATZ and DELGADO look each other over. Finally:)

DELGADO: (To KRAATZ.) It must be hard for you.

KRAATZ: What is hard?

DELGADO: To live with somebody who's lied for so long that he believes he's never told a lie at all.

KRAATZ: No, no, Jeremy is difficult, but I too am difficult—

DELGADO: —You must be...some kind of saint.

(Pause. A very charged, oddly erotic moment between DELGADO and KRAATZ. Like they're going to kill each other or go to bed. Then DELGADO leaves. After a moment, JEREMY returns.)

JEREMY: Some people wear their emotions on their sleeves. I guess I just wear mine on my bowels.

KRAATZ: Drink some ginger ale.

JEREMY: Did you throw him out on his ass?

KRAATZ: He left.

JEREMY: I just can't fucking believe that.

KRAATZ: It's okay.

JEREMY: It's *not* okay. He's trying to wipe me out.

KRAATZ: Of course he is.

JEREMY: And for what? So he can marry our kindergarten teacher?

KRAATZ: He is scared boy. And in army.

JEREMY: So you believe me?

KRAATZ: Of course I believe you.

(JEREMY runs into his arms and they kiss.)

KRAATZ: He claims you said best sex you ever had was with *him*. That makes him liar. Because my Dreamy would never say that. Or even think that. Right?

(Pause.)

JEREMY: Tell me something, anything, anything. Just take my mind off that terrible person.

KRAATZ: Oh. Okay. Well, this Burt, from note. I meet him.

JEREMY: How did you stay awake?

KRAATZ: I spit out pill.

JEREMY: Oh. Well.

KRAATZ: Please be okay with my spitting.

JEREMY: Okay? Sure I'm okay. *(Beat.)* You might as well have killed my mother.

KRAATZ: She is difficult woman, but no, I would never...I speak to Burt. He tells me of...possibility.

JEREMY: What would you say Delgado is for you, like a five? Six?

KRAATZ: He is handsome man. Don't you want to know about Burt and his possibility?

JEREMY: Yeah, totes. Sorry.

KRAATZ: So this Burt, he make proposal.

JEREMY: When you say "handsome," do you mean like if we were the kind who went to bars, you'd want to go home with him? Or handsome like an Aaron Copland piece?

KRAATZ: This Burt has business proposal. He put all money in. And he use initial capitalization to fund us. So we can participate. Fully.

JEREMY: Fully?

KRAATZ: Fully...fully...

JEREMY: ...Fully what?

KRAATZ: Fully present. In the flesh, you could say.

JEREMY: Oh. Will we have to travel?

KRAATZ: No.

JEREMY: I can't get any more time off, and I'm planning to catch something on the flight home.

KRAATZ: We do here.

JEREMY: Here? It's so small in here. So small and cramped and dark and...

(BURT enters, carrying a video camera. He is followed by LOLLY, who is hauling lights.)

JEREMY: ARRRGHHHH!

(KRAATZ grabs him protectively.)

BURT: Light it!

(LOLLY rushes to plug in her lights. Light smacks the embracing JEREMY and KRAATZ harshly. BURT starts to shoot them.)

JEREMY: What are they doing, Creamy?

BURT: Tighter, guys! Like you mean it!

KRAATZ: I did not give the okay yet!

BURT: No hay problema! We'll take care of releases later.

JEREMY: I'm scared, Creamy.

KRAATZ: Nothing to be scared of. It's just Burt. Burt from note.

JEREMY: Make him leave, Creamy.

BURT: Okay, that's good, that's good. Now I want you to brush your teeth.

JEREMY: I already brushed my teeth.

BURT: How about a quick floss job? Kraatzy, you better floss Jers, because this ain't no *True Blood*!

(JEREMY starts to cry. BURT waits, then motions for LOLLY to cut the lights. LOLLY cuts the lights. BURT puts the camera down.)

BURT: Those guys out there. They don't want to see you crying.

JEREMY: What guys?

KRAATZ: Is hard to cry with all medications he is on, so we encourage it.

JEREMY: What guys?

BURT: Your fans.

JEREMY: I don't have fans.

BURT: You will soon.

JEREMY: I'm moving into a negative space.

BURT: You didn't tell him, Kraatzy?

KRAATZ: Not entirely.

LOLLY: You got any cookies?

KRAATZ: No. Sorry.

LOLLY: Fuckers. *(Leaves.)*

BURT: Okay, Jers. Here's the straight poop. I'm going to make a movie about you two—

JEREMY: —But why?

BURT: Because you're exactly what I'm looking for.

JEREMY: But why?

KRAATZ: I know this is crazy crazy, but is kind of cool, no? To be in movie? To be

seen by peoples, and they will know us, eh, top to bottom, eh, and remember us, *remember* us, right, but we do not have to talk to them.

JEREMY: We are not movie stars! Or actors, even!

BURT: I don't want actors. They tend to be attractive. I'd much rather have guys like you.

JEREMY: But we're intensely private people.

BURT: And that is so motherfuckin hot. Hot! HOT!

(JEREMY tries to push BURT out. BURT doesn't budge.)

KRAATZ: Dreamy, you're not being a good host.

JEREMY: Host? I'm the *invaded*. I'm a Falkland Island, I'm Gaza!

KRAATZ: Why don't you hear him out—

JEREMY: —He's making some sort of reality show, right? For the gay network, right?

BURT: No no no—

JEREMY: —Because I don't watch the gay network. All those handsome gays with so many friends, laughing and loving together.

BURT: That can be very oppressive.

KRAATZ: See? He understands us!

JEREMY: If it's not a reality show, then what the hell do you want us for?

BURT: I'm a pornographer, Jeremy. A fetishist, specializing in real-life homosexual couples who don't put a lot of stock in how they look. Now, you guys don't wax, do you?

KRAATZ: Once, before we visit Jeremy's mother in Arizona, we use Nair for Men. Long time ago.

JEREMY: Stop having this conversation!

BURT: I know, I know. You hear "pornographer," and you think, wow, he's an "artist." How do I act around an artist? He's probably temperamental and exacting.

JEREMY: Not what I'm thinking.

BURT: Let me assure you, I'm just a working man with a job to do. Yeah, sure, I have an aesthetic, and it's finely honed—

JEREMY: Did you study with Godard or Truffaut?

KRAATZ: Maybe you should pour sarcasm in jelly jar and store for winter.

JEREMY: Maybe you should stop pretending we're adventurous people.

KRAATZ: Maybe you should stop taking so many pills.

JEREMY: (Gasps.)

KRAATZ: (Gasps.)

(Beat.)

Kraatz: I'm sorry, Dreamy.

JEREMY: No, I'm sorry, Creamy.

KRAATZ: No, me, I just feel so bad—

JEREMY: —I love you—

KRAATZ: —I love you—

JEREMY: —I love you.

BURT: Oh man, I gotta shoot some of this before we move to the full-on action—

JEREMY: —I am going to the bathroom!

KRAATZ: More cramps?

JEREMY: I'm not sure yet. But when I'm done, please have him gone! (Exits to the bathroom.)

KRAATZ: (Loudly, so JEREMY can hear.) We are not interested in your pornography. Please leave our cabin room at once. (Winks at BURT.)

BURT: (Smiling.) Sure, sure. I get it. Well, guess I'll be on my way. Nice meeting you fellas.

KRAATZ: (Whispering.) Please do not change mind about us.

BURT: As long as you don't become any less...you.

KRAATZ: Is deal.

(BURT leaves. JEREMY emerges.)

KRAATZ: You do okay in there?

JEREMY: Totes.

KRAATZ: Good, good.

(Awkward silence.)

JEREMY: You take your yellow pill?

KRAATZ: What? Oh. I will.

JEREMY: Because if you take it too late, then you'll sleep too late, and then you'll be a wreck for the wedding.

KRAATZ: Right. Can't have that.

JEREMY: Especially if I start to do something terrible at the ceremony. I need you to stop me. Or encourage me. Either way, I need you alert.

KRAATZ: I always on lookout for you.

JEREMY: I count on that. (Pause.) You don't really want to do this, this film, do you?

KRAATZ: No.

JEREMY: Because it's crazy, we're not, you know—

KRAATZ: —We don't take off clothes—

JEREMY: —Not on camera!

KRAATZ: Not in public. Maybe at Y.

JEREMY: Not even.

KRAATZ: Well, actually, lately, I have been doing that.

JEREMY: You have?

KRAATZ: At lockers. I start taking pants off and people see my underwears.

JEREMY: What do they say?

KRAATZ: Nothing. Oh, except once. Old man say, "Get out of my way." Because I was in his way.

JEREMY: What else have you been doing without telling me?

KRAATZ: Nothing! I swear it! Except, maybe I forget to tell you I buy raw milk on black market.

JEREMY: What?!

KRAATZ: Yes!

JEREMY: How could you?

KRAATZ: Lady at work, she tell me, "Drink it, will make you better person." So I follow steps. I make secret calls. I meet man behind alley. He give me bottle. I take one sip. I am hooked.

JEREMY: You are a total stranger.

KRAATZ: No, I am your Creamy.

JEREMY: I want to break up.

KRAATZ: Over raw milk and under-wears?

JEREMY: We have a commitment to the truth!

KRAATZ: And I am very full of it. The truth.

JEREMY: I'm full of it too.

KRAATZ: Of course you are.

JEREMY: You believe me, don't you? About what Delgado and I had together all those years?

(Pause.)

KRAATZ: Film would be good thing for you. And for me. For us.

JEREMY: On what planet?

KRAATZ: Step into unknown. Out of usual.

JEREMY: But I like the usual.

KRAATZ: But usual with me is not "best ever" for you.

JEREMY: A, don't be jealous, and B, do you want a pop tart?

KRAATZ: No, too close to bed.

JEREMY: Right. And C, if *you* think I make shit up, then where's my touch-stone to reality? Where's the one place I go to assure myself I am not a crazy lunatic?

KRAATZ: Touchstone will be in this cabin tomorrow morning with erection, hopefully full-fledged. Touchstone will smile for camera. Touchstone hopes you will join him.

JEREMY: And if I don't?

KRAATZ: Nothing.

JEREMY: Nothing?

KRAATZ: Nothing.

(Beat.)

JEREMY: You've still never mastered the whole "threat" thing—

KRAATZ: —I mean *nothing will change.*

JEREMY: Oh. Stasis is bad now? (Beat.) What if my mother sees me giving you head?

KRAATZ: Does your mother watch a lot of gay fetish porn?

JEREMY: Well, she *is* in a book club now.

KRAATZ: Is movie! No violence, no cruelty, no negatives. Just fun and pleasure and some love. How could that be bad? Can you tell me this? How could any show of love between us be bad?

(Silence. JEREMY reaches for a bottle of pills, takes out a yellow one, takes out a tiny bottle of water, hands them both to KRAATZ. KRAATZ takes the pill and swallows it with the water. He puts on a nightlight, turns off the overhead lights, gets into bed and spoons JEREMY. After a few moments, KRAATZ starts to snore. JEREMY stares, unable to sleep.)

SCENE 7

(Upper deck. Under the moonlight, MISS ALICE SMITH, crying, looks out at the waves. BURT, carrying his camera, walks by, sees her, stops, and starts shooting her.)

MISS ALICE SMITH: What are you doing?

BURT: My day job.

MISS ALICE SMITH: How is this your day job?

BURT: Don't you want to look back and remember exactly what made you so happy?

MISS ALICE SMITH: These aren't tears of joy.

BURT: It all looks the same in digital.

MISS ALICE SMITH: I am profoundly sad.

(She cries hysterically. BURT, surprised and caught, puts down his camera and attempts to hug her. She pulls back.)

MISS ALICE SMITH: No touching the teacher!

BURT: You're not my teacher.

MISS ALICE SMITH: I'm *everyone's* teacher.

BURT: I never went to kindergarten.

MISS ALICE SMITH: What kind of savage are you?

BURT: My mother wanted me at home. She bought me my first camera. I took pictures of her all the time, in so many different positions.

MISS ALICE SMITH: None of them compromising, I hope.

BURT: Do you take me for some kind of pervert?

MISS ALICE SMITH: No, no, no! I am a terrible person!

BURT: Maybe, but you're a very nice lady.

MISS ALICE SMITH: The filth that runs through my head!

BURT: Your head's not filthier than anyone else's.

MISS ALICE SMITH: Oh, you don't know the half of it.

BURT: Really? How else are you filthy?

MISS ALICE SMITH: I think about...sex... all the time.

BURT: Tell me all about it.

MISS ALICE SMITH: Sex with my principal, sex with the fruit man at the supermarket, sex with the president of the PTA—

BURT: —Why don't you just get some from your fiancé?

MISS ALICE SMITH: I've never once imagined that.

BURT: Wait...you're not a virgin, are you?

MISS ALICE SMITH: Well, technically...

BURT: Not that I'd judge you. I just never met one before.

MISS ALICE SMITH: (Whispering.) There was someone else before the lieutenant colonel. Someone...big.

BURT: Big?

MISS ALICE SMITH: Big. Very big. Big hands. Big feet. Big fingers. A captain in the United States Marines.

BURT: You really like your uniforms.

MISS ALICE SMITH: He was *married*. To the mother of my most innocent student, Candace Ashoki.

BURT: Candace? Who names their kid Candace anymore—

MISS ALICE SMITH: —Candace was a darling, but I kept finding fault with her. And then I started setting traps, like stealing another child's sandwich and hiding it in Candace's bag. Or slipping caffeine pills into her juice cup so that she would run wild and eventually eat sand. Anything to get her parents down to that school. Anything to see that father of hers. One day Captain Ashoki came alone, as his wife was out of town at a Mary Kay convention. After we finished speaking about Candace, a silence fell upon us. Captain Ashoki reached over, took my chin and pointed my face toward his. "Look at me," he said. "Look at me."

BURT: What did you see?

MISS ALICE SMITH: His blue eyes. His button nose. But most of all? His tongue. It came to a perfect point. And the next thing I knew, he applied his tongue to me. Right here, and here, and here...

BURT: That must have been very pleasurable.

MISS ALICE SMITH: Licking turned to nibbling, and nibbling turned to rubbing, and there were screams that made dogs bark and cats sing. And my head exploded through my ears and the vein on his temple burst and we both died, we *died*, but then we came back to life, in each others' arms, over and over, for three hours! Three glorious, perfect hours!

BURT: That sounds like heaven!

MISS ALICE SMITH: You understand me, yes! It was heaven.

BURT: I had you pegged all wrong.

MISS ALICE SMITH: If they did an autopsy on me right now, they'd label me a virgin. But when I think back to Captain Ashoki, I don't feel like a virgin. I feel very...wet. Wet with hope for my future.

BURT: Your passion makes me wet with hope.

MISS ALICE SMITH: Really? Where are you wet?

BURT: My lips.

MISS ALICE SMITH: You have nice lips.

BURT: Don't I?

(BURT *sweeps MISS ALICE SMITH up in his arms and kisses her. She kisses back, but then pushes away.*)

MISS ALICE SMITH: I'm about to be married!

BURT: Those things never work out.

MISS ALICE SMITH: Mine will. I'll love Lieutenant Colonel Delgado.

BURT: He's not real enough for you.

MISS ALICE SMITH: He's a fine man and a patriot. And by marrying him, I'll be serving our country.

BURT: That just makes me want to kiss you again.

MISS ALICE SMITH: Are you a patriot too, Burt?

BURT: I'm the Yankiest Doodle who's ever dandied.

MISS ALICE SMITH: Ohhh... We shouldn't be talking like this. What if the Lieutenant Colonel were to hear?

BURT: Screw the army. *I'm* winning *this* war.

MISS ALICE SMITH: That's impossible.

BURT: Can you imagine being with a man who has no sexual needs of his own? All of his attention would be devoted to you.

MISS ALICE SMITH: Ohhhh.

BURT: The tips of his fingers, his lips, his tongue...

MISS ALICE SMITH: Ohhh.

BURT: ...touching every inch of you and making you yell words a kindergarten teacher isn't supposed to know...

MISS ALICE SMITH: Like, "Ride 'em."

BURT: Excuse me?

MISS ALICE SMITH: Ride 'em...ride 'em cowboy...ride 'em. *(Beat.)* I really need my shawl.

(She starts to leave. He grabs her arm.)

BURT: You just need the right guy to tap into your barrel and make it spew fun all over the floor—

MISS ALICE SMITH: *(Suddenly ferocious.)* —Enough!

BURT: It's never enough, baby.

MISS ALICE SMITH: I am about to become Mrs. Lieutenant Colonel Delgado!

BURT: But there's something better out there for you. For both of us.

(MISS ALICE SMITH breaks away from BURT and runs off. MISS ALICE SMITH runs back on, kisses BURT on the lips, smacks herself once in the face, then kisses him again, then slaps herself, then slaps herself again, and then runs off.)

SCENE 8

(MISS ALICE SMITH alone in her cabin, on her knees.)

MISS ALICE SMITH: May the Lord shine his light upon my path and illuminate the right way to go.

May the Lord flood me with wisdom.

May the Lord insert his...fill me with his goodness until I too am good.

(Lights up on DELGADO, doing crunches.)

DELGADO: Two thousand seventy two... Two thousand seventy-three...

MISS ALICE SMITH: May the Lord lay me down gently under the tree of knowledge and spread my...may the wings of angels spread and flutter over my...

DELGADO: Two thousand seventy-seven...Johnny Depp seventy-eight...

MISS ALICE SMITH: May the angels sing a song into my ears, a song of love that reminds me I am a committed woman...

DELGADO: Two thousand eighty one... Jake Gyllenhaal eighty-two...

MISS ALICE SMITH: ...A woman of strength and dignity. A woman worthy of God, angels, the tree of knowledge, and the United States Army.

(DELGADO lifts his legs in the air, comes up for a crunch, then spreads them ridiculously far apart, and repeats.)

DELGADO: Two thousand eighty-five... Taylor Lautner eighty-six.

MISS ALICE SMITH: *(Pulls a vibrator out from under her dress and holds it up to God.)* Zap it, please!

(DELGADO's crunches become more elaborate, his legs furiously twisting around like a helicopter propeller.)

DELGADO: Matt Damon eighty-eight... Mike Huckabee eighty-nine...

MISS ALICE SMITH: Free me!

DELGADO: Me and my boys ninety...me and my boys ninety-one!

SCENE 9

(JEREMY and KRAATZ's cabin. They sleep on their bed, snoring and

spooning. Sunrise light gives way to hot morning sun.)

JEREMY: *(Bolts up.)* ARRRGHHHHH!!!

(KRAATZ pets JEREMY.)

JEREMY: I dreamed you left me!

KRAATZ: That would never happen.

JEREMY: You didn't think I loved you enough.

KRAATZ: That would cause sadness.

JEREMY: But I do love you enough.

KRAATZ: If only there was measuring stick for love.

JEREMY: You need proof?

KRAATZ: Most of time, no.

JEREMY: I'm too freaked about Delgado.

KRAATZ: Really.

JEREMY: Yeah. Dude—

KRAATZ: —Dude.

JEREMY: Baby. For every guy like him who pretends he's straight, that's one more of us who gets beaten up in the park.

KRAATZ: You do not even vote for president.

JEREMY: Well, maybe it's time I became political. Maybe it's time for me to cast my voice into the choir of freedom-lovers everywhere.

KRAATZ: I need my juice.

JEREMY: Don't you see? Delgado and I were each others' first and only for four years. He loved every second of it. But then he joins the army and marries three women before he marries his kindergarten teacher, and all throughout he pretends what we had never existed—

KRAATZ: —I think I will make it a double—

JEREMY: —That lie, it erases me. It's ethnic cleansing. He's Hitler, he's Pol Pot, he's a Hutsi or a Tutsi and I'm the Tutu. Or the Hutu. Whatever. I have *got* to stand up and ruin his wedding or else I'm what? What? *Invisible. I cannot be invisible anymore!*

(Banging on door.)

JEREMY: *(Ducking under the covers.)* Delgado's coming to kill me! Hide!

(KRAATZ reluctantly hides with JEREMY. More banging on the door. Followed by:)

BURT: *(Offstage.)* Fellas! You're late for your call!

KRAATZ: *(Popping up from under the cover.)* What do we do?

BURT: *(Offstage.)* I got props for ya.

KRAATZ: I could tell him to go away.

BURT: *(Offstage.)* My camera's sploogin' all over ya.

KRAATZ: Or we could maybe...I don't know...be historic?

(Beat. JEREMY uncovers himself, looks at KRAATZ, gets up, and opens the door, letting BURT and LOLLY in. BURT hands over a sack to JEREMY. LOLLY immediately starts lighting the room.)

BURT: Go ahead. Look inside.

(JEREMY looks inside the sack. He looks at BURT, then KRAATZ. Lights out.)

SCENE 10

(JEREMY and KRAATZ's cabin, a little while later. BURT films and LOLLY lights as KRAATZ, wearing an eye mask, pastes photos into a large book and JEREMY, also wearing an eye mask, reads from the bible.)

JEREMY: *(Stilted, reading.)* "In the beginning, God created the heavens and the earth."

KRAATZ: *(Stilted.)* Hey, dear. That is Book of Genesis.

JEREMY: *(Stilted.)* Yes it is, sweetheart.

KRAATZ: *(Stilted.)* That is good book to read on a Sunday night at home.

JEREMY: *(To BURT.)* Nobody spends their Sundays like this!

BURT: Maybe not in New York City. But there's a whole world between the coasts, Jers. And a fuckofalotta bible-reading and scrapbooking goes on there.

KRAATZ: Is true, we see country through very narrow lens.

BURT: Stick to the script, boys. Makes it easier in post. Roll 'em.

JEREMY: Uhhh...*I miss our twins.*

KRAATZ: *Caleb and Aron are having great time at soccer camp.*

JEREMY: *I miss making their waffles.*

KRAATZ: *I miss them too. But at least we have place to ourselves.*

(KRAATZ looks to BURT, who nods encouragingly. KRAATZ then leers at JEREMY. JEREMY looks to BURT, who nods even more encouragingly. JEREMY forces himself to leer back at KRAATZ.)

SCENE 11

(A few minutes later. BURT films, LOLLY lights as JEREMY and KRAATZ, still masked, stiffly make out on the bed. They butt heads/bang teeth.)

LOLLY: *(Whispering.)* What year do you think they forgot how to kiss each other?

JEREMY: We can hear you.

BURT: Then show us you still got all your moves.

(JEREMY and KRAATZ try to amp up the passion in their kissing.)

JEREMY: You taste like blood.

KRAATZ: You know my gum problem.

JEREMY: It's like you're giving me a transfusion.

KRAATZ: Bitch bitch bitch.

BURT: Guys, please...stay focused...open his shirt, Jers.

(JEREMY carefully unbuttons KRAATZ's shirt. He pops a button.)

JEREMY: Oh, don't worry, I'll go get my sewing kit. *(Starts to walk away.)*

BURT: *(Scarily forceful.)* FUCK THE BUTTON! LICK HIS CHEST!

(JEREMY, scared, returns to KRAATZ and, very tentatively, licks his chest once.)

BURT: Again.

(JEREMY licks again.)

BURT: Again.

JEREMY: I feel like Mariel Hemingway in *Star 80.*

BURT: Say the line, Jers. Say the line.

JEREMY: Oh. *Fifteen years have passed since our first date, and your pecs still fill me with passion.*

KRAATZ: *Oh, yes. Lick them, dear. I enjoy it.*

SCENE 12

(A few minutes later. BURT films from far away. LOLLY lights, as JEREMY kneels between KRAATZ's legs, trying to give him a blowjob.)

KRAATZ: *Ahhh yes. That is the way to do it, dear.*

JEREMY: *(All garbled.)* Eeeeh nahh aaaahhh.

KRAATZ: What?

BURT: *(Whispering.)* This is the master shot. Great composition.

JEREMY: Ohh naahh aaaahh.

KRAATZ: What?

BURT: *(Whispering.)* Moving in for the closeup.

(BURT moves in close, and LOLLY follows.)

JEREMY: Ohhh nahhh... *(Jumps to his feet.)* Why aren't you hard?

BURT: That's not in the script.

KRAATZ: *(Pulls up his boxers. To JEREMY.)* I did not think you would notice.

JEREMY: What's that supposed to mean?

BURT: Loll, give Kraatzy a little assistance.

(LOLLY reaches into her pocket and takes out a bottle of pills. As she's opening it:)

JEREMY: I thought you wanted to be historic.

KRAATZ: I do, I did.

BURT: Move it, Loll.

JEREMY: Then what's the problem?

KRAATZ: Stomach is full of French toast and beans.

BURT: Feel free to fart on film.

JEREMY: That's disgusting!

BURT: It'll make you seem even *more* ordinary. Loll!

(LOLLY sticks a blue pill into KRAATZ's mouth.)

KRAATZ: What is in mouth?

BURT: Pornographer's little helper.

(He spits it across the room.)

JEREMY: Pills like that are bad for his blood pressure.

BURT: Lookee lookee. This happens, okay? But you have to separate the real

middle-aged somewhat flaccid couple you are from the make-believe flaccid couple your fans want to see.

JEREMY: Don't I make you excited anymore, Dreamy?

KRAATZ: *(Barely audible.)* Feeling is gone.

JEREMY: Dreamy?

KRAATZ: I am sorry, Jeremy. But is true. We walk together all these years but now we hit Berlin Wall and we have no wire cutters, and pack of mad dogs bite our ankles and we bleed, we bleed all over Germany—

JEREMY: —Breathe deep—

BURT: *(Putting down his camera.)* —Who wants poppers? Huh? Gays love poppers. Lolly, get me the goddamned poppers.

LOLLY: They're with my Oreos.

BURT: Why?

LOLLY: Oreos are cream-filled. Poppers make gay guys shoot their cream. It's a mnemonic—

BURT: —GO GET THE POPPERS!

(LOLLY runs out.)

JEREMY: Stop shooting.

BURT: I did, there's no light.

JEREMY: *(Takes his mask off.)* Take your mask off, Dreamy. We need to connect.

(KRAATZ takes his mask off.)

JEREMY: This movie seemed so important to you, so I said yes. The least you could do is *respond*.

KRAATZ: Why should I when I know you would rather be making sex with your "best ever"?

BURT: We could arrange that.

JEREMY: You can't be mad about something Delgado said I supposedly said. I mean, come on, he's in the *army*.

KRAATZ: I am not mad.

JEREMY: Good.

KRAATZ: I am doomed. Is much worse.

BURT: When Lolly gets back, why don't we aim a little lower and shoot some handwork.

JEREMY: How are you doomed, Dreamy?

KRAATZ: You love sex with Delgado. And you never love it with me.

JEREMY: Of *course* I love our sex!

KRAATZ: You never moan.

JEREMY: I moaned last month.

KRAATZ: That was from picking up recliner. No. I am cheap substitute. And Delgado, he know it. He hold you at distance and this is power. A soldier's brutality. I cannot compete. Goodbye, *mon amour.*

(KRAATZ leaves. JEREMY and BURT look at each other. KRAATZ comes back, grabs his pants, shoes, and a suitcase, and leaves again.)

JEREMY: What am I going to do, what am I going to do?

BURT: How about a solo shoot?

JEREMY: I don't care about your stupid movie! I care about my Creamy.

BURT: I thought you called him Dreamy.

JEREMY: They're interchangeable.

BURT: That's convenient.

JEREMY: He's gone, and it's all because Delgado has me under a spell.

BURT: You love him so much.

JEREMY: Jesus Christ, what's so hard about this? I DO NOT LOVE DELGADO. I don't even like him. I just...I just...I want his sex. Our sex. Proof. Evidence that it happened. That I am a person who actually has a "best sex ever."

BURT: And that's all you need?

JEREMY: That's all I could hope for.

BURT: Hmmm. It's funny, I happen to hate Delgado.

JEREMY: You do?

BURT: Sure. He's marrying my girl.

JEREMY: Miss Smith and you...but I thought you were...

BURT: ...In love with Miss Alice Smith? I am. I don't know if it's her porcelain skin or how much she reminds me of the softest Q-tip, but she's got this cowboy all roped up. Feels so strong like I got a tumbleweed wrapped around my heart and all my blood's flowed down into my boots.

JEREMY: That sounds very uncomfortable.

BURT: I *hate* being uncomfortable!

JEREMY: What are you going to do about it?

BURT: Only Lieutenant Colonel Nancy Pants is standing in my way.

JEREMY: Same guy who's standing right smack in my way too.

BURT: Oh well. Love's a soiled saddle you just can't clean. *(Picking up his camera.)* Now take off your clothes and give yourself a handy.

JEREMY: *(Way loud.)* Wait!

BURT: What?

JEREMY: What if I were to come up with a plan that got me my best sex ever and you a great movie?

BURT: I need to make me some art, Jers, but how's that gonna get me the lovin' I crave?

JEREMY: Oh Pornographer, if you've got sex and you've got art, maybe love'll just poke you from behind.

BURT: I love that.

JEREMY: Now come on, we've got a wedding to wreck!

SCENE 13

(The Latino Deck. MISS ALICE SMITH, wearing a life jacket, whistling "Ave Maria," looks both ways, then starts to climb overboard. KRAATZ enters, dressed, carrying his suitcase, sees her and tries to pull her away from the edge.)

KRAATZ: No!!!

MISS ALICE SMITH: Yes!!

KRAATZ: Is bad luck to kill self on wedding day!

MISS ALICE SMITH: I'm not killing myself.

KRAATZ: You jump in icy water!

MISS ALICE SMITH: I'm a member of the Polar Bear Club. I can swim in anything.

KRAATZ: But you will ruin hair before ceremony.

(Pause. MISS ALICE SMITH starts to cry.)

KRAATZ: There there, is okay, is okay.

MISS ALICE SMITH: I am a disgrace.

KRAATZ: No no, you are just nervous wreck.

MISS ALICE SMITH: Another man has declared his feelings for me.

KRAATZ: So?

MISS ALICE SMITH: So? I'm poisoned now!

KRAATZ: No no. Is like jelly you put on toast after it has already been buttered.

MISS ALICE SMITH: But I never asked for jelly.

KRAATZ: But jelly is good tasting, no?

MISS ALICE SMITH: ...I *love* jelly.

KRAATZ: Ya. Is good. As long as you remember that jelly is just sweet distraction. Butter is substance, is warmth in winter, coats insides.

MISS ALICE SMITH: Butter is queer.

KRAATZ: What?

MISS ALICE SMITH: I didn't say anything.

KRAATZ: I thought you said—

MISS ALICE SMITH: —Why are you carrying around a suitcase?

KRAATZ: Oh. This. Ya.

MISS ALICE SMITH: Are you abandoning one of my students?

KRAATZ: He is not your student no more.

MISS ALICE SMITH: The bond between teacher and student lasts a lifetime.

KRAATZ: Bonds we think are forever, turn out they have expiration date.

MISS ALICE SMITH: So does life.

KRAATZ: Oh, you want to go that way, huh?

MISS ALICE SMITH: No, no. I don't. I'm just a very confused kindergarten teacher.

KRAATZ: Confusion is not worst thing in world.

MISS ALICE SMITH: What is?

KRAATZ: Losing love! *(Breaks down crying.)*

MISS ALICE SMITH: Shh...there, there... Tell me, what's your favorite dinner together?

KRAATZ: Jeremy and me?

MISS ALICE SMITH: Jeremy and you.

KRAATZ: We like the eggs. I scramble a Heineken into them, ya? We eat the eggs, some ketchup. Some salt, some pepper...paper napkins with the flowers on them...

MISS ALICE SMITH: Imagine sitting at the table and that's all in front of you.

KRAATZ: Mmm, is making me hungry.

MISS ALICE SMITH: Now imagine Jeremy's seat is empty.

KRAATZ: Oh!

MISS ALICE SMITH: Or worse, you look across, and in Jeremy's seat sits a big mean stranger you met last night at the local pub. Maybe he's wearing dark reflector sunglasses, and a leather band around his upper bicep, and a motorcycle cap. And he snarls.

KRAATZ: I would not like that!

MISS ALICE SMITH: Or maybe he's a young, fey gentleman who expects you to buy him a Lady Gaga record and some marijuana.

KRAATZ: No, that would be terrible.

MISS ALICE SMITH: Think how many years it would take to turn either of those fellows into familiar people... men you could trust with your eggs.

KRAATZ: But my man has betrayed me.

MISS ALICE SMITH: Did he steal your money?

KRAATZ: No.

MISS ALICE SMITH: Did he tell the CIA to deport you?

KRAATZ: No, I am citizen.

MISS ALICE SMITH: Then there's no betrayal.

KRAATZ: Is sexual problem. You would not understand.

MISS ALICE SMITH: My dear, we are all living on the weakest shoot of the weakest limb of the weakest tree. This just isn't the time to let your pee-pees push you off into the void.

KRAATZ: But what if my pee-pee isn't enough for him?

MISS ALICE SMITH: Then you help him get whatever else he needs.

KRAATZ: And what if he leaves?

MISS ALICE SMITH: Repeat after me. Gratitude glues.

KRAATZ: Gratitude glues.

MISS ALICE SMITH: Resentment wrecks.

KRAATZ: Resentment wrecks.

MISS ALICE SMITH: Again.

KRAATZ: Gratitude glues. Resentment wrecks.

MISS ALICE SMITH: One more time, with music.

KRAATZ: I don't know the tune.

MISS ALICE SMITH: (Singing.) Gratitude glues, resentment wrecks.

KRAATZ: (Singing.) Gratitude glues, resentment wrecks.

MISS ALICE SMITH: Wonderful. Now go back to your cabin and prove me right.

KRAATZ: Yes ma'am! (Turns and starts to leave. Then stops.) Are you still going to jump?

MISS ALICE SMITH: I'm not sure.

KRAATZ: You want to be married, no?

MISS ALICE SMITH: Very much so.

KRAATZ: Is lifelong dream, no?

MISS ALICE SMITH: Is lifelong dream.

KRAATZ: You have corsage?

MISS ALICE SMITH: Corsage? Why, I didn't think of that...

(KRAATZ reaches for MISS ALICE SMITH's life jacket and pulls a small *bouquet of carnations from it, then hands it to her.)*

MISS ALICE SMITH: How did you do that?

KRAATZ: Cannot help it. Is compulsive. You take.

(MISS ALICE SMITH takes the corsage, truly touched.)

KRAATZ: May lifelong dream be dream no more.

SCENE 14

(KRAATZ and JEREMY's cabin. JEREMY sits on the bed, extending a small gift-wrapped box to DELGADO, who stands near the door.)

DELGADO: Did you call me here to give me a bomb?

JEREMY: Why would I give you a bomb?

DELGADO: Hurt feelings.

JEREMY: It's just a wedding present.

DELGADO: Give it to Miss Smith.

JEREMY: But it's for you.

DELGADO: That's not how weddings work.

JEREMY: Did I ever get you a gift you didn't like? Huh, Vincento?

DELGADO: Nobody ever calls me that anymore.

JEREMY: It's a good name. Now go on. Open it.

(Pause. DELGADO takes the box and opens it. He removes a pair of men's superhero underpants.)

JEREMY: Try them on.

DELGADO: They're not regulation.

JEREMY: Give 'em a shot.

DELGADO: Why?

JEREMY: Because you want me to see them on you.

DELGADO: Where's your gay lover?

JEREMY: My "gay lover"? He dumped my ass.

DELGADO: Oh. Too bad. I wouldn't worry.

JEREMY: How come?

DELGADO: You people always find somebody else pretty fast.

JEREMY: Yeah. Hey. Guess what? You've got new underpants!

(Pause.)

DELGADO: I like underpants.

JEREMY: Good. Go on.

(Pause. DELGADO goes into the bathroom. BURT sneaks out from the closet with his camera. JEREMY races to him.)

JEREMY: *(Whispering.)* Are you getting everything?

BURT: Yeah, yeah. But there's a formula to this. Six lines of dialogue to one sex act.

JEREMY: That sounds very schematic.

BURT: Unshaped art is like cabbage your grandma's gotten too senile to stuff…a depressing reminder of beauty that could have been.

JEREMY: I'll keep that in mind. Now go—

BURT: —Make sure you don't block my money shot!

(JEREMY pushes BURT back into the closet. DELGADO emerges, still in his shirt, but now wearing the Superhero briefs.)

JEREMY: That looks so…

DELGADO: Ridiculous.

JEREMY: No. Handsome.

DELGADO: Nahh!

JEREMY: But you've always been handsome.

DELGADO: I had a few awkward years.

JEREMY: I don't remember them.

DELGADO: My back used to break out, as did my shoulders.

JEREMY: I don't remember that.

DELGADO: Dr. Engel gave me that medicine. Those creams. I couldn't reach. And you...

JEREMY: I don't remember that.

DELGADO: You helped me.

JEREMY: I don't remember that.

DELGADO: You put the creams on my back.

JEREMY: Long time ago.

DELGADO: It was disgusting.

JEREMY: As disgusting as everything else we used to do?

DELGADO: We didn't do much.

JEREMY: But we did something?

DELGADO: Kids experiment.

JEREMY: Like playing Doctor.

DELGADO: Yes, kids are curious. Especially teenagers.

JEREMY: So to satisfy their curiosity—

DELGADO: —To figure out who they are—

JEREMY: —They fuck each other exclusively for four years.

DELGADO: It wasn't four years.

JEREMY: How long do you think it was?

DELGADO: However long I make it.

(JEREMY approaches DELGADO and tries to remove his shirt. DELGADO blocks him. JEREMY tries harder. This goes on, until DELGADO finally pushes

JEREMY away and takes his shirt off himself.)

JEREMY: That army sure knows how to mold a fella.

DELGADO: I do six thousand crunches a day.

JEREMY: And your back. It's smooth like you could skate on it. No creams necessary.

DELGADO: We all grow up.

JEREMY: *(Gasps.)* I just remembered something.

DELGADO: What?

JEREMY: How much you liked this...

(JEREMY takes DELGADO's head in his hands and kisses him passionately. DELGADO kisses back. They make their way to the bed, crazy sexy.)

(JEREMY suddenly stops, towering over DELGADO.)

JEREMY: How many years did we go at it?

(DELGADO pulls JEREMY toward him, but JEREMY does not budge.)

JEREMY: Tell me how long and I'll let you do whatever you want.

DELGADO: What the hell does it matter?

JEREMY: Just guesstimate.

DELGADO: I don't know, a few weeks...a few months...okay, okay, four years.

JEREMY: And did you love it?

DELGADO: Yes.

JEREMY: A little louder?

DELGADO: Huh?

JEREMY: *(À la the military.)* Did you love having sex with me for four years, Lieutenant Colonel?

DELGADO: Yes sir!

JEREMY: Was it the best sex you ever had, Lieutenant Colonel?

DELGADO: Yes sir.

JEREMY: Do you think sex with anyone else will ever come close, Lieutenant Colonel?

DELGADO: I don't know.

JEREMY: I can't hear you!

DELGADO: If I answer "yes," then I'll most likely offend you.

JEREMY: You've been offending me for years.

DELGADO: And if I answer "no," then I'm doomed to a life of bitter disappointment. Either way, I can't win!

JEREMY: And that's hard for you.

DELGADO: Just look at me! Doesn't everything about me spell "Winner"?

JEREMY: If you spell winner "F-A-G."

DELGADO: You're a threat to my track record of unparalleled success, and that...that just makes me want to...

(DELGADO flips JEREMY onto the bed and starts to mount him from behind. KRAATZ enters, sees the two of them going at it, starts to leave, then turns around and goes to them.)

KRAATZ: If this is what you need...

JEREMY: Ah, Vincento!

KRAATZ: ...then I say take it, Dreamy, because I LOVE YOU.

(DELGADO, scared at first, tries to get away.)

JEREMY: No no no don't...

KRAATZ: Don't go anywhere!

DELGADO: But you two are a gay-lover couple!

KRAATZ: If my man get what he want, then I have lived a good day.

DELGADO: You serious?

JEREMY: I love you so much, Creamy.

KRAATZ: I love *you* so much, Dreamy.

(JEREMY reaches for KRAATZ, who takes his hand and joins him on the bed. They look at each other, and then both put their arms around DELGADO.)

DELGADO: What are you guys doing?

(JEREMY kisses DELGADO gently. KRAATZ kisses DELGADO.)

DELGADO: You should both know...I'm really...just not that kind of guy...

(The three of them duck under the blankets and go at it, rough and tough and wild, with a lot of sound. As they do:)

JEREMY: This is so much better than the guy who made the marble rye—

KRAATZ: —So much better—

JEREMY: —Oooohh—

KRAATZ: —Ahhhh—

DELGADO: —THIS IS WHAT I WANTED—

JEREMY: —So much—

DELGADO: —JUST GUYS—

KRAATZ: —My Creamy is hot man, no?—

DELGADO: —GUYS, ALL GUYS—

JEREMY: —My Dreamy has a hot accent, doesn't he?—

DELGADO: —GUYS ALL THE TIME!!—

JEREMY: —GUYS ALL THE TIME!!—

KRAATZ: —GUYS ALL THE TIME!!

ALL THREE: I'm commmmmming! I'm shooting! Fucccckkkkk! It's huuuuge!! Ahhhh!! *(Etc.)*

(All three climax. Then there is silence. Finally, KRAATZ sits up.)

KRAATZ: Did you stop the mail while we are away?

JEREMY: I thought you did.

KRAATZ: No, that is your thing.

JEREMY: Sorry.

KRAATZ: Is okay.

DELGADO: *(Sits up.)* Please don't tell anybody.

KRAATZ: Is nothing to be shamed by.

DELGADO: I have a career in the United States military.

KRAATZ: We will not stand in way of that.

DELGADO: I'm getting married today.

KRAATZ: Is strange choice, but is your own.

DELGADO: I trust *you*. But Jers?

JEREMY: Did you and I have sex for four years when we were teenagers?

(Pause.)

DELGADO: Yes.

JEREMY: And was I...at the very least... one of the most important relationships in your life?

DELGADO: Yes.

JEREMY: I missed you so fuckin much.

(Pause. Finally:)

KRAATZ: Good good, so we are all fair and squared. See what little squirt-squirt between friends can do? Now. Let us be on our ways.

(The door flings open, and in walks MISS ALICE SMITH, in her wedding gown, unzipped in the back down to her waist. She sees the three of them on the bed.)

MISS ALICE SMITH: Zip me? *(Covers her mouth, staring at them.)*

DELGADO: I'm not supposed to see you before the wedding.

MISS ALICE SMITH: Sorry.

DELGADO: It's very bad luck.

MISS ALICE SMITH: I've never done this before.

KRAATZ: Miss Teacher, someday you will make laughs about this.

JEREMY: We were helping Vincento get dressed—

MISS ALICE SMITH: —Who is Vincento?

JEREMY: Your fiancé.

MISS ALICE SMITH: Is that your first name, Lieutenant Colonel?

DELGADO: Yes ma'am.

MISS ALICE SMITH: It's very Italian.

(JEREMY goes to her and zips up her gown.)

MISS ALICE SMITH: Thank you, thank you, Jeremy. You were always such a helpful boy. All rightee.

(MISS ALICE SMITH swoons. BURT leaps from out of the closet, with his camera, and saves her from falling.)

DELGADO: ARRRGHHHH!

KRAATZ: AARRRGHH!!!

DELGADO: What are you doing here?!

JEREMY: It's my fault.

DELGADO: Were you *filming* us?

KRAATZ: Dreamy?

JEREMY: Aww, Creamy. I know. I'm bad.

BURT: Wake up, Miss Smith. Wake up.

DELGADO: Why would you do this to me? After all we've been through.

JEREMY: I just wanted a record. To prove what I remembered was true.

DELGADO: That's all?

KRAATZ: Is that all, Dreamy?

JEREMY: Yes. Except the part where I was going to show this movie at your wedding.

DELGADO: I'll beat you up! And then I'll shoot you! And then I'll sue you!

(DELGADO swoops MISS ALICE SMITH up in his arms.)

MISS ALICE SMITH: Where am I...where am I?

DELGADO: You're aboard the Icy Maiden.

MISS ALICE SMITH: Oh. Did I get seasick?

DELGADO: No, just a little nervous. All of my wives get nervous before they marry me.

MISS ALICE SMITH: That's very reassuring.

BURT: You got sickened by the way the gays have treated you.

MISS ALICE SMITH: But the art teacher is gay. We buy yams together at the farmers market.

JEREMY: Look, this wedding has clearly pushed a few buttons for me.

(BURT grabs at MISS ALICE SMITH but DELGADO won't let go.)

JEREMY: But it's really been a teachable moment. I've learned so much about myself and my gay lovers, and I've learned a lot about sexual shame.

(DELGADO and BURT engage in a tug of war over MISS ALICE SMITH.)

JEREMY: I've learned that sexual shame turns us into monsters. And that the more we try to hide our sexual truth, the more we rob ourselves...and each other...of our humanity.

(BURT finally succeeds in yanking MISS ALICE SMITH out of DELGADO's arms.)

MISS ALICE SMITH: Why are you stealing me from my fiancé?

BURT: Because you can't marry him!

DELGADO: He's a sneaky lowlife who tried to entrap me!

KRAATZ: Dreamy...

JEREMY: And I completely own my part in this—

BURT: —The audio alone's gonna sell this baby bigtime—

DELGADO: —He's lying, let's get married—

MISS ALICE SMITH: —Burt. I know exactly what you're doing here.

BURT: Yeah, look, I really didn't want you to get caught in the crossfire—

MISS ALICE SMITH: —You're trying to save me from a certain army officer who can never love me the way I should be loved.

BURT: In a way...yeah...I sure am!

MISS ALICE SMITH: And in my classroom, I would call that a Super-Duper Whipper Whopper.

BURT: A what?

MISS ALICE SMITH: Say it with me, Burt. A Super—

BURT: —Super—

MISS ALICE SMITH: Super Duper—

BURT: Super Duper—

MISS ALICE SMITH AND BURT: Whipper Whopper.

MISS ALICE SMITH: You have a way with words, Burt.

(Pause. BURT gets down on one knee and takes MISS ALICE SMITH's hand.)

MISS ALICE SMITH: Are you hoping to make You and Me equal We?

BURT: If you would.

MISS ALICE SMITH: But I'm still affianced.

BURT: Can't you take care of that?

MISS ALICE SMITH: It seems so fast, so rash, so cruel...but I'll try. *(To DELGADO.)* Lieutenant Colonel, I'm sorry I can no longer be your wife. But I wish you well. I wish... May your most painful dreams be the ones you most easily forget...You closet-case gaylord. *(To BURT.)* There, that should cover it. Now, Burt. Ride 'em. Ride 'em right down the aisle of love.

(She and BURT leave.)

DELGADO: I've been dumped.

KRAATZ: You are very different people.

DELGADO: How am I going to explain this to the men and women who serve under me?

KRAATZ: Just say it did not work out and you wish her well.

DELGADO: But they're counting on me to be a role model.

JEREMY: Then tell them the truth.

DELGADO: That she got seduced by our videographer? Do you know how humiliating that would be?

JEREMY: No, I mean the other truth.

DELGADO: What other truth?

KRAATZ: I think what he means, what my husband, partner, and lover is trying to say...

DELGADO: That my kindergarten teacher was weak-willed. An easy mark. Not worthy of my uniform.

JEREMY: No, more like she didn't have a dick big enough to satisfy you.

DELGADO: That's not the truth.

KRAATZ: You are only with us, Lieutenant Colonel. You can be calm and you can be honest.

DELGADO: I've never felt calmer or more honest.

JEREMY: Really? I mean...really?

DELGADO: Your version of honesty isn't necessarily mine.

JEREMY: Okay, just go now, run along.

DELGADO: I plan to. But while you're being so smug and righteous, just remember this. I'm out there fighting for your right to be as honest as you want. Placing my body in harm's way. So does your life have any more integrity than mine? Because you're "honest"?

JEREMY: Have you ever even stepped foot out of the country?

DELGADO: Yes.

KRAATZ: Iraq? Afghanistan?

JEREMY: Manitoba.

KRAATZ: The one in Canada?

JEREMY: He did active duty there for six months before he requested and received a transfer back home to Kentucky. *(To DELGADO.)* Your mother told me. So unwrap that big flag you're hiding in and God, save yourself.

(DELGADO slowly begins to crumble. And cry. KRAATZ goes to him and holds him.)

KRAATZ: Is okay, is okay.

DELGADO: I can't be alone.

KRAATZ: Is okay.

DELGADO: I've tried for two, three weeks at a time, but I get so scared.

KRAATZ: Shhh, we all get scared. *(Gestures for JEREMY to join him.)*

DELGADO: And the army, they like their men to be men. And I like being a man. I don't want to be anything else. And I know this is a different time and I'm not one of the *Boys in the Band*—

JEREMY: —You've seen *The Boys in the Band*?

DELGADO: I've seen every gay film ever made! But nothing changes me into a good gay. And I don't have a Jeremy or a man with a funny accent. All I ever have is me and whatever wife I happen to be married to. What am I going to do?!?

KRAATZ: Do you...do you want a Jeremy and a man with funny accent?

JEREMY: What?

KRAATZ: Because if you want them... you can have them.

JEREMY: How's that going to work?

KRAATZ: We like you. We like being with you.

JEREMY: Creamy—

KRAATZ: No, is good, is good. You come live with us. Like high class of pet at first. Then you grow into it, become equal partner.

JEREMY: You want him to live with us?

DELGADO: Live with the two of you? What would that make us?

JEREMY: Shouldn't we discuss this first?

KRAATZ: Dreamy. He is your best sex ever. That is hard for me to swallow, but at same time, a little exciting. And it give me some comfort. Because at least it is in front of my face and I am not waiting for it around every corner.

JEREMY: Sex with you is really good, Creamy. Really, really good, I swear.

KRAATZ: Bet he could be good for me too. He just need a little love. Which we can both give him. In our home. Right, Jeremy? Right, Delgado?

(JEREMY and DELGADO look at each other. Good and hard. Very tentatively, DELGADO salutes JEREMY. JEREMY salutes DELGADO. KRAATZ whips out a magic flower and presents it to them both.)

(LIGHTS UP on BURT filming himself kissing MISS ALICE SMITH while she whips out her vibrator, turns it on lovingly, and they kiss in wedded bliss.)

(Lights fade to black.)

(END OF PLAY.)

(O)N THE 5:31

Mando Alvarado

MANDO ALVARADO is a playwright, screenwriter, and an actor from South Texas. His first feature film, *Cruzando*, which he cowrote and codirected with Michael Ray Escamilla, has was won praise and accolades and has screened at such notable festivals as HBO New York International Latino Film Festival, Newport Beach International Film Festival, and London Latino International Film Festival and will be distributed by Vanguard Cinema. His play *Post No Bills* received its Off-Broadway premiere at Rattlestick Playwright's Theater in November 2009. His play Splitting Mama was selected to participate at the Black Swan Lab at Oregon Shakespeare Festival. He was a Hispanic-Playwright-in-Residence at INTAR and is currently a company playwright for Theater 167. He also participated in the Freight Project, where he developed *(O)n the 5:31*. His play *Rear Exit* was presented at INTAR's NewWorks Lab in an evening of shorts entitled *One Night in the Valley* and as a part of The Atlantic Theater's Latino Theater Festival. His play *Throat* was developed at The Field ArtWard Bound Residency Program and was produced by Allison Prouty at the 45th Street Theater. It went on a three-city tour to Washington, D.C., McAllen, Texas, and Minneapolis, Minnesota, and had its closing run at INTAR's NewWorks Lab. His plays have received developmental support from the Kennedy Center, Rattlestick Playwright's Theater, INTAR, The Lark, Naked Angels, Mixed Company, Sonnet Rep, Theater Alliance, Woolly Mammoth Theater, and the Round House Theater. He is currently developing *Basilica* with Rattlestick Playwright's theater. He is a graduate of North Carolina School of the Arts. www.cruzandothemovie.com, www.tgtgfilms.com.

VISIBLE SOUL INTERVIEW WITH MANDO ALVARADO
Conducted by Zack Calhoon, October 26, 2010

How did you get started in theater?

In 8th grade. I wasn't doing well in Drama class. In Texas, they have a no pass no play rule in order to play sports. So I needed to do extra credit to play football. An actor in the spring production of *You Can't Take It With You* had quit, and my best friend at the time, Cesar Cantu, was in the play. He convinced my drama teacher to let me do the play for that extra credit. I did it. I was horrible but I loved it. In fact, my best friend now, Michael Ray Escamilla, saw me in that production and thought, "If that football player can be that horrible and people still like him, maybe I should do drama to." And we've been in this crazy world ever since.

What made you start writing plays?

My first real attempt at writing was in college. We have this student-run event called Intensive Arts where the students can produce, write, or direct whatever they want. I wrote a sketch comedy piece entitled "Chiclets and Tortillas." Then, when I got to New York in 2005, I was looking for representation as an actor. So I thought, "Maybe I should write a play that I can star in, present it, and get an agent." I was temping at the time and it was so slow and boring. So I cranked out a play. We had a reading of it, at a back of a bar in Brooklyn. Michael was directing it and he asked a friend of ours, Raul Castillo, to read my part so I can focus on the play. Two things happened that night, one, I fell in love with writing, and two, Raul was better than me so he ended up doing the part.

Tell me about your play, *(O)n the 5:31*.

The play is about two people learning to move on after the death of the woman they both loved. It takes place in a bar and it snakes in and out of the need to deconstruct memory and time.

What was the process like?

You know, I wrote the play in a week in late August in a writer's retreat in upstate NY at The Freight Project in Cambridge. It was an intense week. Trying to come up with the story in such short time. There were a lot of discussions, improvs, late night writing, and drunken philosophical sharing. But at the end of the week, we had a play. The process for *Cino Nights* was very similar. Again, an intense week. Feels like we had a lifetime in a week. The actors, Bernardo, Jolly, and Sarah were amazing. Really threw themselves at the play and really tried to figure out every minuet detail. It's a hard play because if fluctuates between five realities—present, past moment, thoughts in the moment, in between, and could have been. So we had to be very specific on how and where we were at so the audience could follow.

How do you think the play went?

I was very proud of the work everyone did. Again, I was really moved by the dedication from the actors and my director, Taibi. They really committed to doing the best work possible. One of the downers of doing work in NY is that most of the time, you face a lot of judgment. Its a hard town and its tough to be really honest in the work and its even tougher to be allowed to fail so, at times, you fight the need to play it safe. There was nothing safe about this play and the process so I was really grateful to have the opportunity to work in the way we did. It was one of those rare theatrical nights that keeps giving you the juice to keep going.

What kind of writing inspires you?

I'm still playing around with that. Right now, I love what the Mexican playwrights are doing. Playing with narrative and construction of what a play is. But I love being a fan, an audience member where the work really knocks me off the block. I love plays that challenge me emotionally and intellectually. Plays that take me on a journey.

Who or what has been the biggest influence on your work as a playwright thus far?

Starting out, I was plugged into Stephen Adly Guirgis. Loved the urgency in his work. Admire the work that Craig Wright is doing, really loved *Lady*. I'm inspired by what Matt Olmos writes, love the worlds he creates, Andrea Thome, Raul Castillo, Cyn Canel Rossi, and I'm hyped to see the work of young writers like Fernanda Coppel and Mariah MacCarthy. As far as people that really challenge me as a writer and shaped how I approach the work, I got to say these three people really cracked the prose in my head. Eduardo Machado, really made me challenge my self and what I want to say in my work. David Van Asselt, he gave me a chance, gave me blind faith in a world where product is valued over substance, and Lue Douthit from OSF. She's the Lit. Manager there and she gave me the bones. She opened up the confidence to finally allow myself to feel like a writer.

(O)n the 5:31, directed by Taibi Magar, premiered on October 24, 2010, at the Seventh Street Small Stage at Jimmy's No. 43.

CAST LIST

Gina Morgan .... Jolly Abraham
Benny Maldonado .... Bernardo Cubria
Sandra Kertz-Maldonado .... Sarah Baskin

CHARACTERS

GINA MORGAN
BENNY MALDONADO
SANDRA KERTZ-MALDONADO

TIME

Present
Past moment
Thoughts in the moment
In between
Could have been

PLACE

Bar.

RE(VISIT)

(A back section of an old bar. For now, it's closed. GINA comes in carrying a bus tub. She puts out candles on the tables. She picks up some dirty glasses.)

GINA: Routine.

When all else fails, that's what you got.

What you can come home to.

You sign in.

Go over your section. Over the drink specials. How many kegs. Wood. Mirrors. The deer head.

Don't have to think.

Empty. *(Goes into the back of the bar.)*

(BENNY walks in. He wears a black suit and carries a rolling suitcase. He looks around. A small shiver shoots up his spine. He's been here before. GINA comes out of the back. She sees him. They lock eyes. Shift.)

BENNY: When it happens,

When you sit back and think about what you saw,

What you felt,

When you close your eyes and you try to recall the memory,

There are only two things that you can rely on.

What you remember and what really happened.

And they're not the same thing.

GINA: Can I help you?

BENNY: Huh?

(Shift to Present.)

GINA: You need something?

BENNY: Hi.

GINA: Hello.

BENNY: Bathroom?

GINA: In there.

BENNY: Thanks.

(He goes in. She begins to clean. She takes a peak in the direction of the bathroom. After a moment, the door opens and she goes back to work. He returns.)

BENNY: I like the way it smells in there.

GINA: It's a bathroom.

BENNY: No. The scent. It reminds me of Hawaii.

GINA: It's passion's fruit.

BENNY: Nice. So? You're still working here?

GINA: Excuse me?

BENNY: I used to come to this bar.

GINA: I don't remember you.

(She walks back into stockroom. BENNY's mind shifts.)

BENNY: She doesn't?

You enter places.

Lots of places and sometimes you remember the people you come across and sometimes you don't.

Meaningless connections turning into something, nothing.

What the hell am I doing here?

(Shift.)

THE B(LIND) DATE

(SANDRA walks into the bar. She looks around. Checks her phone. She's nervous. Calls her sister.)

SANDRA: Liza I don't want to do this. It's too soon. I'm overwhelmed. I don't like blind dates. They make me feel icky. What's his name again? Benny. What kind of name is Benny? Sounds like he's hairy. A hairy Jewish man. He's Mexican? Great. Why do you do this to me? Okay. Okay. Okay. I'll text you from the bathroom.

(Hangs up. GINA spots her. She walks up. She's softer than before.)

GINA: Can I get you something?

SANDRA: Have you seen a guy, brown hair? Waiting for someone?

GINA: Nope.

SANDRA: What time is it?

GINA: Eleven after.

SANDRA: Yeah. I'll wait.

GINA: Okay. Just let me know if you need anything. *(Walks off and picks up some glasses at another table.)*

(Shift. SANDRA stares at her phone.)

GINA: I'm a product of a divorce.

Now I don't blame my unsuccessful attempts at love on my parents. They did the best they could.

But they did leave an impression.

You can go two ways.

You can run, protect yourself. Never really invest in someone because you don't ever really want to feel pain. Disappointment.

Or.

You can do what I do.

Be honest.

Go full in.

Swan dive into love and let the chips fall where they may.

(Shift.)

You sure you don't want a drink?

SANDRA: Um. I'll take a...is it rude to order a drink before the person?

GINA: He's late. You can drink.

SANDRA: Right. I don't know. Vodka? I don't really like vodka. I hate beer.

GINA: I'll get you a bourbon. There's a chill in the air.

SANDRA: Thank you.

God I hate waiting.

It's suffocating.

(GINA comes back with bourbon. Places it on the table.)

GINA: How late is he?

SANDRA: Twelve minutes. It's rude.

GINA: It's not so bad.

SANDRA: Puts me at his mercy.

GINA: I've never had a guy that's been on time.

SANDRA: That sucks.

GINA: Tell me about it.

SANDRA: How's your day going?

GINA: Peachy.

SANDRA: Been working here long?

GINA: Actually this is my first week anniversary.

SANDRA: Well, congratulations.

GINA: Yes. Applaud me for keeping employment for a week.

SANDRA: That's not what I meant.

GINA: Don't worry. I got this thing. I turn everything into a negative.

SANDRA: I can't believe he's still not here.

GINA: It happens.

SANDRA: You wanna have a drink with me? Celebrate your week.

GINA: You gay?

SANDRA: No.

GINA: Just a little bit?

SANDRA: Funny. No.

GINA: Okay.

SANDRA: I'm on a blind date.

GINA: Seems to be the flavor.

SANDRA: Huh?

GINA: Fourth blind date this week.

SANDRA: How did they turn out?

GINA: You know, it was a coin flip. It worked out for some and not for others.

SANDRA: It's not gonna work out for me.

GINA: I see that you got the negative thing too.

SANDRA: It's not that. I don't deserve love.

GINA: Don't say that.

SANDRA: Karma.

GINA: Karma?

SANDRA: You know, you hurt someone. Someone that didn't deserve it. They were nothing but good to you. And they gave you unconditional love or the closest thing to it. But you couldn't accept it. Because you're a selfish bitch who's too scared to let anyone in. So you shit on them. You rip them apart because you can. But it'll come back to you. What you did. You did some horrible shit. And you know the wrath of God will strike you down. Because you deserve it.

GINA: You're a complicated woman.

SANDRA: I'm a coward. What's your story?

GINA: It's short.

SANDRA: Do you have a somebody?

GINA: A significant other?

SANDRA: Yes.

GINA: Who has time? Come home smelling of beer, cigarettes. Who wants to put up with that?

SANDRA: There's someone.

GINA: Eh, I've been down that road before and it's always a letdown. I don't know about karma. It just feels like this is how it is. How it's gonna be. I'm not doing anything with my life. Working at a bar. Wah. I'm trying to figure it out. Hoping I have some of that good side of karma heading my way.

SANDRA: Have you ever gone on a blind date?

GINA: No.

SANDRA: I got an idea. Let's trade places.

GINA: That's a horrible idea.

SANDRA: No it's perfect.

GINA: Are you serious?

SANDRA: Wait. What's your name?

GINA: Gina.

SANDRA: Sandra.

GINA: Nice to meet you.

SANDRA: You take my life and I'll take yours. You go on the blind date and I work the bar.

GINA: You don't want that. Trust me.

(BENNY enters. He's soaking wet. He looks around.)

SANDRA: Oh shit. I think that's him. Here he comes. Please.

BENNY: Sandra?

(GINA and SANDRA look at each other.)

GINA: Yeah?

SANDRA: Can I get you something to drink?

BENNY: Sorry I'm late. I missed the 5:31. Then I got caught in the rain. And now my underwear's all wet. I probably shouldn't have said that. Can I have a bourbon? Neat.

GINA: Me too.

SANDRA: Coming right up.

(SANDRA and GINA give each other a look. SANDRA goes to the back, watching from a distance. BENNY and GINA sit.)

BENNY: You come here often? Oh man that was horrible.

GINA: I've been here before.

BENNY: It's a cool little spot.

GINA: It's got some interesting characters.

BENNY: I like it.

GINA: It's not bad.

BENNY: So. Tell me about yourself.

GINA: Not much to tell.

BENNY: Where you from?

GINA: Around here.

BENNY: Local?

GINA: Yup.

BENNY: That's different.

GINA: In what way?

BENNY: This is such a transient town. It's rare to meet someone who was actually born here.

GINA: Well...

BENNY: You have any dreams?

GINA: Dreams?

BENNY: Yeah, you know, what do you want to be when you grow up?

GINA: That's a scary thought.

BENNY: What is?

GINA: Adulthood.

BENNY: You know, and I don't want to be weird about this although by saying "I don't want to be weird" already makes me weird but, you're really pretty.

(She looks at him. Then looks at SANDRA. She gets up.)

GINA: I'm not Sandra.

BENNY: What?

DIS(COMFORT)

(A shift. GINA looks at SANDRA.)

GINA: I met her first.

She walked in.

Sat at my table.

She was wearing all black, a red scarf, unsure of herself.

I shared a drink, a moment with her...

First.

(SANDRA drifts off. GINA goes back to cleaning the table. Shift.)

RE(VEAL)ING

(Back at the bar.)

GINA: Look, it's closed.

BENNY: Excuse me?

GINA: This section. It's closed.

BENNY: Can I sit here for a moment?

(Silence.)

BENNY: She looks at me.

Like she hates me.

She knows who I am.

GINA: What do you want?

BENNY: You sure you don't remember me?

GINA: Come on man, it's been a long week. I'm tired. This is my fourth double this week. I just want to set the room up and get on with it.

BENNY: Do you mind if I stay?

GINA: Yes. I mind.

BENNY: Please?

GINA: I have work to do.

BENNY: I'll help you set up. Please?

GINA: Light the candles.

BENNY: Okay. I'll go find a lighter. *(Goes to the back.)*

(Shift.)

GINA: Fucking men.

They think they know everything.

That look that he was talking about?

It's not hate. It's indifference.

My face represents what I have become.

Alone.

I don't give a damn about him.

He's like every man in my life.

(RE)CALL

(BENNY enters again, but there's something different. As GINA recalls her memories, he takes on the shape of all her ex-boyfriends.)

BENNY: Come here.

GINA: No.

BENNY: Goddamn it, Regina. Come here.

GINA: Don't call me that. Only my daddy's allowed to call me that.

BENNY: I am your daddy.

GINA: My daddy pays the bills. My daddy takes care of the house. MY DADDY HAS A JOB!

BENNY: Does your daddy love you like this?

(Kisses her neck.)

GINA: Only when he was drunk.

BENNY: GINA. Not funny.

GINA: Then you shouldn't tread on ground you don't have traction for.

BENNY: What time you get off work?

GINA: Late.

BENNY: Want me to wait for you?

GINA: What for?

BENNY: For you and me and Mr. Happy.

GINA: Mr. Happy's gonna be disappointed. Ms. Buttercup's got a visitor.

BENNY: It's that time again?

GINA: Every month junior.

BENNY: I miss you.

GINA: Get off me. I have to work.

BENNY: Come on Gina. I miss you.

GINA: So.

BENNY: Doesn't that mean anything to you?

GINA: No.

BENNY: You still pissed at me?

GINA: Go home Bobby.

BENNY: Tomas.

GINA: Frank. Just go home.

BENNY: You know I love you.

GINA: Yeah, you loved the hell out of me the last time.

BENNY: I'm sorry.

GINA: No. You're not sorry. You're never sorry. Cause if you were sorry. You wouldn't behave like that.

BENNY: I love you so much it hurts. My arms hurt without you.

GINA: Bullshit.

BENNY: Give me another chance.

GINA: I'm not gonna be your punching bag every time the mood suits you. What about me?

BENNY: What about you?

GINA: Don't you think I have bad days? Don't you think that I don't want to wake up? Just lie in bed and not work. Don't you think I wish my arms didn't hurt? Because they're not wrapped around someone that really loves me.

BENNY: I do love you.

GINA: Stop it. I'm not buying what you're selling Frank.

BENNY: Tony.

GINA: Juan. I've been down this road too many times, making the same mistakes. I'm not doing it again.

BENNY: Not even if I promise?

GINA: Empty. That's what I hear from you. Empty.

BENNY: Give me another chance to prove you wrong.

GINA: Why?

BENNY: Cause you know what we have is true. When we're in bed, talking, drinking, laughing. It's the good stuff. I know I make you happy.

GINA: You wanna know the last time I felt really happy with you?

BENNY: When?

GINA: I came across this short story. About a lady who lived in the country or some farm or something. And every morning, her husband would take the train into the city for work. One of those mornings, she was watching the news and she saw that there had been a train wreck. No survivors. The train was the 5:31...her husband's train. A flood of *relief* came over her. Not sadness, relief! And she started dancing around her living room, dreaming of all the things she would do—now her life would really begin! Then the doorbell rings. She opens it. And standing there is her husband. Sadness washes over her and she begins to sob. He assumed it was for him, for being lucky he didn't get on the 5:31. But it was for herself. For the death of her soul. And I think about that. About her. And then I think about you Juan—

BENNY: Larry—

GINA: Jim. I think about you. And what you're doing to me. Killing my soul. And I imagine that you were on that train. And that thought. Your body smashed to pieces. Limbs ripped apart. Face mangled, unrecognizable. That brings a small smile to my face. Because I have my soul back. Just for a moment. Do you understand what I'm saying to you?

BENNY: You're a real bitch.

GINA: I need you to get on the five fucking thirty-one.

(SANDRA enters and sits. GINA turns.)

(2)ND DATE

(Shift.)

SANDRA: That was divine.

GINA: It was stupid.

SANDRA: No way. That guy was an asshole.

GINA: He might have been the last.

SANDRA: What's that?

GINA: Never mind. Drink?

SANDRA: Yeah. Can I have a bourbon?

GINA: What kind?

SANDRA: I don't know.

GINA: You want single malt?

SANDRA: You pick.

(GINA goes and pours a bourbon. Comes back.)

GINA: Here you go.

SANDRA: Are you alright?

GINA: I'm fine. It just sucks.

SANDRA: I think you did the right thing.

GINA: Not looking forward to going home alone again.

SANDRA: Wanna have a drink with me? Celebrate your freedom.

GINA: I hate being single.

SANDRA: Sometimes it's needed. Self-reflection.

GINA: That scares me.

SANDRA: You look like the kind of woman that kicks that kind of fear in the balls.

GINA: (Laughs.) It's all a show.

SANDRA: Let's get out of here.

GINA: That would be nice.

SANDRA: I'm serious. Come have a drink with me.

GINA: I don't know. I got to finish my shift.

SANDRA: When's the last time you did something outrageous?

GINA: When I pretended I was you.

SANDRA: Let's get out of here. Go get into some trouble.

GINA: Now that sounds really scary.

SANDRA: It's supposed to. What does the little voice inside your gut say?

GINA: She says fuck it. Close out.

SANDRA: You should listen to her. *(Gets up.)* I'll wait for you outside.

GINA: This is how it starts.

(SANDRA smiles. She leaves.)

RE(KINDLE)

(BENNY flicks a lighter. Present.)

BENNY: Where do you want me to start?

GINA: What?

BENNY: Start? Candles? Which table?

GINA: Over there. Start there.

BENNY: *(Begins to light candles.)* I like lighting candles.

GINA: Mmmm.

BENNY: Focused light. For the darkness to live around it.

GINA: I see couples, huddle around it. Kissing. Nibbling on each other. Laughing. Makes me want to puke.

BENNY: I think it's romantic.

GINA: You would.

BENNY: What does that mean?

GINA: You look like the type.

BENNY: Maybe once, long ago.

GINA: Yeah, me too.

BENNY: You still like working here?

GINA: No.

BENNY: Then why do you do it?

GINA: It pays the rent.

BENNY: I like my job.

GINA: You're one of those happy people aren't you?

BENNY: Closet optimist is what I prefer to be called.

(Shift.)

GINA: I hate optimism.

It's pointless.

Hope. Faith.

Just a bunch of nonsense that keeps you from facing the truth.

BENNY: And what's that?

GINA: Excuse me?

BENNY: What's the truth?

GINA: You heard that?

BENNY: What?

GINA: Did you hear what I just said?

BENNY: About you calling me an optimist?

GINA: You traveling somewhere?

BENNY: I'm moving.

GINA: And you stopped in for a beer?

BENNY: I used come to this bar. I was on my way out and I saw it. Had to say goodbye. I met my wife here.

GINA: Really?

BENNY: Yeah.

FRAGMENT OF (TRUTH)

(Shift. SANDRA enters.)

SANDRA: It was a blind date.

GINA: We traded places.

BENNY: But I ended up with her.

(SANDRA sits.)

GINA: Can I get you guys something to drink?

SANDRA: Bourbon.

GINA: It's on me. Sorry about.

SANDRA: It's not her fault.

(GINA leaves.)

BENNY: It's funny what you remember.

What you hear. Are memories true?

Can any of it be taken as a fact? Like this table.

SANDRA: It's our table.

BENNY: Right. It's our table.

SANDRA: Where it all started.

BENNY: But was it even this table?

SANDRA: Yeah. Right here.

BENNY: You know, at the end of the night, they move all the tables to the side so they can mop the floor. And in the morning, they put the tables back. But it's not always the same table that goes back to its original position. So our table, the actual table, could be sitting over there.

SANDRA: That's not the point.

BENNY: What's the point?

SANDRA: It's not the spot that's important but what happened at the spot.

BENNY: Then why am I here?

SANDRA: To remember.

BENNY: Sandra would like for me to believe that it was worth it. That this pain I feel inside was worth it.

SANDRA: Benny would like for you to believe that he's become jaded. But I know what he was.

BENNY: And what was I?

SANDRA: Raw. Fresh. Gentle.

(BENNY sits. Shift.)

(1)ST GO OF THE 2ND

(We're back at their first date. BENNY fidgets. Nervous. A long silence.)

BENNY: So *you're* Sandra?

SANDRA: Yeah. Sorry about that.

BENNY: Okay. So. I'm Benny. Why did you do that?

SANDRA: You were late. I got nervous. If you want—

BENNY: No. I thought it was pretty cool.

SANDRA: Sometimes I like to play pretend.

(Awkward, but good awkward.)

BENNY: So, you're a temp?

SANDRA: Yeah. Till I finish school.

BENNY: You like temping?

SANDRA: No one likes work.

BENNY: I do. I like working.

SANDRA: Really? What do you do?

BENNY: I'm a copywriter.

SANDRA: What's that?

BENNY: For commercials. Like, "No one beats a Honda like a Honda." Or "It's not just a burger, it's a Whataburger."

SANDRA: You wrote those?

BENNY: No. Just wanted to give you an example of good copy. I generally crank out useless material. But I like what I do. Makes me feel like I'm doing something.

SANDRA: Like you're earning your keep?

BENNY: Exactly. I'm from a migrant family. We used to go up north. Well, not me but my dad and my older brother. They would go to Wisconsin or Michigan and pick. Work. You could see it in their faces, their hands, the way they moved. They earned every penny. So I feel like I owe it to them. To like what I do cause they didn't have that choice.

SANDRA: You were the chosen one.

BENNY: I was the baby.

SANDRA: They're proud of you.

BENNY: I don't know. My dad died when I was in high school and my big brother resents me. So.

SANDRA: I'm sure your dad was.

BENNY: What?

SANDRA: Proud of you.

BENNY: Maybe. So Liza's your sister?

SANDRA: Now, Benny's probably thinking, "How come we've never met and why did we have to meet on a blind date?" Too much expectation.

BENNY: I hate blind dates. So much expectation.

SANDRA: See.

Isn't that part of the excitement?

BENNY: No. It freaks me out. I've been a mess all day. I wanted to come in early, scope it out. You know, switch places with the waitress.

SANDRA: I'm really sorry.

BENNY: It's okay. Just messing with you. I guess I wanted to see, witness the disappointment right at the moment you saw me.

SANDRA: I'm not disappointed.

BENNY: Oh. No? Well. Neither am I.

SANDRA: You're blushing?

(He shifts.)

BENNY: I know this girl. I mean, we just met. But I know her. And for the record, what she did. Fucking cool. I like her. Shit.

(They both shift.)

BENNY: I like//her—

SANDRA: I like her.

BENNY: I don't want to mess//this up—

SANDRA: I don't want to mess this//up—

BENNY: Got to play this//cool—

SANDRA: Got to play this cool—

BENNY: I really like you.

SANDRA: What?

BENNY: I mean, that I think you're cool. You know, a pretty cool person, a kind of person that I like to be around. You know, hang with the homies with.

SANDRA: So I'm like one of your homeboys?

BENNY: Yeah, but with benefits.

SANDRA: I don't fuck homeboys.

(SANDRA gets up. GINA brings in two bourbons.)

GINA: Messed it up already?

(Shift.)

BENNY: I get up. And I go after her.

GINA: You convince her to stay.

SANDRA: I give you another chance because you're an idiot.

BENNY: But what if I don't go? What if I'm too scared and I stay back?

SANDRA: Then this place wouldn't mean anything.

GINA: And we'd be strangers.

BENNY: Isn't that better?

GINA: I don't know.

SANDRA: You can't run away from pain. Come after me.

(He gets up and goes after her.)

GINA'S (L)OVE (L)IVES

(GINA follows but is left behind. She watches them leave. Again, she stands alone.)

GINA: You only get like four great loves in your life. And there's nothing you can do about it. You will love them and they will mark you forever. My first one, when I was a kid. His name was Alan. He lived in a gated subdivision. A fancy gated subdivision. We would play tether ball after school. I'd let him win. One day in lunch, our pictures were up on the wall. School pictures. And we were staring at them. And he said, "Your picture came out good." "Really," I say. "Yeah, who knew?" And he walked off. Hand in hand with Linda, the class whore. Second time, I was nineteen. I was engaged to Pete Garcia. He was the manager at Best Buy. Which was a great perk. Lots of great electronic equipment. He got me a job working with him. Loved that jerk. At night, he would ask me to take home stuff, left over stuff he said. Customers never picked them up. So I did. About six months later, I'm in front of a judge, getting probation for theft, I lose my scholarship to school and he walks off hand in hand with Debbie, the Best Buy whore. The third time. That was Jeff. More about him later. And the last time. I didn't have a choice. She was my fourth. Ladies and Gentleman, Mr. and Mrs. Benny Flores.

B(RING)ING IT BACK

(She walks off. BENNY and SANDRA enter. She's in a wedding dress. Their song comes on. They embrace, lock hand in hand. And begin to dance. At first it's a nice dance but then they break into fun choreography. The song ends. They sit at their table.)

BENNY: Are you having fun?

SANDRA: Yeah.

BENNY: You want a drink?

SANDRA: No.

BENNY: What's the matter?

SANDRA: Nothing.

BENNY: *(Stares at her finger.)* How come you're not wearing your ring on that hand?

SANDRA: It's weird.

BENNY: You think it looks it weird?

SANDRA: *(Takes it off.)* It's my new friend. Meet Permanent Patty. This is my husband. Weird. Do you feel funny saying I'm your wife?

BENNY: A little. I'm getting used to it.

SANDRA: You're getting used to it?

BENNY: I mean, I look forward to saying it. Where I don't find it weird. And where I don't mind wearing our rings on our left hand. Can I put it back?

SANDRA: You did it a few hours ago.

BENNY: Yeah but that was for everyone else. This will be for us. Can I?

(He slowly takes it off her hand and tries to put it back on. She yanks away.)

SANDRA: Do you love me?

BENNY: Yeah, that's why I married you.

SANDRA: What if we can't live up to our vows? I was standing there, and these words were coming out of my mouth. And then I heard yours, they were so epic. It's unrealistic.

(BENNY shifts.)

BENNY: Sandra's freaking out.

Now I'm freaking out. What should I do?

I can be a total douche and make it about me. Put up a front.

Do you think this was a mistake?

SANDRA: I'm not saying that.

BENNY: Fuck, Sandra. Why did you go through with it if you didn't want to get married to me?

SANDRA: I'm not saying that. God, you're such an asshole.

BENNY: That's not going to work.

What did I say?

SANDRA: You didn't say anything. You held my hand, looked into my eyes, and you kissed me.

BENNY: You thought you were gonna fail me.

SANDRA: You thought I didn't want you.

BENNY: I thought you wanted someone else.

SANDRA: I thought this is too good to be true.

BENNY: I thought this is it.

SANDRA: I was scared.

BENNY: So was I.

(He places the ring back on the proper hand. He sits.)

SANDRA: Did you know you were gonna marry me when you first saw me?

BENNY: I liked you. A lot. You?

SANDRA: I knew but I had to be convinced.

BENNY: Anyone who makes me dance to Celine Dion and I like it has my heart.

SANDRA: Celine is fierce but emotional.

BENNY: That's why I love you.

SANDRA: But what if in ten years you stop loving me? You wake up one morning and you think to yourself, I hate this woman. I have wasted, wasted ten years of my life with her.

BENNY: Well let's skip ahead. Ten years.

IN THE DEVIL'S (DEN)

(BENNY stands at the doorway of the bar.)

GINA: Back at my bar.

SANDRA: I shouldn't have come here.

GINA: It hurts. I'm helpless.

BENNY: It's our ten-year anniversary.

SANDRA: And we should see where it all began.

GINA: I bring you two drinks.

BENNY: Maker's on the rocks.

SANDRA: White wine.

GINA: Coming right up.

SANDRA: You're running late. Again. You walk in and think, "Crap. She looks pissed. How am I gonna get out of this one?"

BENNY: Actually, I thought, she looks sad. Did I do something wrong?

SANDRA: You didn't do anything wrong. I did.

BENNY: I sit down.

SANDRA: You're wearing your crisp black suit.

BENNY: I want to tell you that I got a promotion.

SANDRA: I want to tell you that I've just come back from the doctor.

A.DOC S(UPPOR)T

(Shift. GINA comes in. She's flustered. SANDRA sees her and she gets up and throws herself into GINA's arms.)

SANDRA: Where were you?

(SANDRA just continues to hold her.)

GINA: I have the late shift today. You knew that.

SANDRA: I called you dammit.

GINA: I'm sorry. I was running errands. What's the matter?

SANDRA: ...

GINA: Baby, you're freaking me out. What the hell is going on?

SANDRA: *(Does a small ironic smile.)* Karma.

GINA: *(Steps back.)* Karma?

SANDRA: I was misdiagnosed. The doctor thought it was ulcers. And I kept fooling myself. Didn't take it seriously. And. It cut into my stomach lining. Now it's spread.

GINA: Does he know?

SANDRA: Not yet. We're supposed to meet here for dinner.

GINA: Shit. What are you gonna say?

SANDRA: I don't know. Nothing.

GINA: You're not gonna tell him?

SANDRA: That would be one hell of ten-year gift.

GINA: It's not funny.

SANDRA: I don't want it to be one of those memories. Not tonight.

GINA: I don't know what to say.

SANDRA: Me neither.

GINA: What did the doctor say? This is treatable right? With chemo, pills—

SANDRA: Six months.

GINA: Excuse me?

SANDRA: He gave me six to eight. That's all.

GINA: He's wrong. That motherfucker is wrong.

SANDRA: Gina.

GINA: That's ridiculous. We'll get another opinion. There's no way. It's

2010 for god's sake. There's some method or new alternative whatever. Something. There's something out there that will fix this.

SANDRA: I can't be fixed.

GINA: What's the matter with you? No. I'm not gonna let you do that.

SANDRA: It's okay.

GINA: It's not okay. I'm not doing this. You're not doing this. Everything will be fine. You'll take some medicine and you'll be here forever. That's it. That's how it's gonna—.

SANDRA: It's too late. He's here.

(BENNY stands.)

BENNY: I'm running late.

GINA: We're back at my bar.

SANDRA: I shouldn't have come here.

GINA: It hurts. I'm helpless.

BENNY: It's our ten-year anniversary.

SANDRA: And we should see where it all began.

GINA: I bring you two drinks.

BENNY: Maker's on the rocks.

SANDRA: White wine.

GINA: Coming right up.

BENNY: She looks sad. Did I do something wrong?

SANDRA: You didn't do anything wrong. I did.

BENNY: I sit down.

SANDRA: You're wearing your crisp black suit.

BENNY: I want to tell you that I got a promotion.

SANDRA: I want to tell you that I've just come back from the doctor.

BENNY: I get down on my knee, and ask you if you remember what you said?

SANDRA: I do. Why does Permanent Patty decide that we're supposed to be forever? How does she know?

BENNY: She doesn't. It's just a ring. She's here to remind us of today. And if we ever do feel distant or lost, we can look down on our fingers and we'll remember this promise. And here we are ten years later. And.

SANDRA: You want to say the right thing. You want to say, "You see, we're still together. Our vows held up." But you didn't.

(Silence. Shift.)

RARE M(O)MENT

(All three look at each other.)

BENNY: Did she talk about me?

GINA: No.

BENNY: I can't believe she told you first.

GINA: I saw her first.

BENNY: I was her husband.

BACK TO THE (RING)

(Shift back.)

BENNY: And. When we got married, when I saw you walk down the aisle. All I could see was your smile. And I thought, you were smiling for me. And it was the most beautiful smile I'd ever seen and I told myself that there's no way on earth I'm going to take that away from you.

SANDRA: I was smiling for you. In that moment. It was all for you. *(Gets up and walks off.)*

BENNY: Does it ever stop hurting?

GINA: Why are you asking me?

BENNY: Because I know that she loved you.

GINA: It stops being real. After some time. And you miss it. So you create the memory to remind you of how much it hurt.

BENNY: Tell me about Jeff.

GINA: No. Why?

BENNY: Because I want to know what you were working with.

GINA: I call it. The last supper.

THE LAST (SUP)PER

(BENNY and GINA sit at the table. SANDRA sits across. Silence.)

BENNY: Mom, this was delicious.

SANDRA: I'm glad you enjoyed it.

(Silence.)

GINA: More wine?

BENNY: Sure.

SANDRA: Don't forget you're driving Jeff.

(Silence.)

BENNY: You know, Gina is a big fan of broccoli rabe.

SANDRA: You don't say?

GINA: Yes ma'am. It's very tasty.

SANDRA: You've eaten broccoli rabe before?

GINA: Well broccoli, I mean, I like broccoli.

SANDRA: My dear, it's not the same thing.

GINA: Either way I enjoyed it.

SANDRA: How did you two meet?

GINA: He picked me up at the bar I work at.

BENNY: I just got out of class and I needed a beer. And I saw her, bending over the table and I thought, "I got to get me some of that."

SANDRA: How romantic?

GINA: He's full of it. Normally, I don't pay the customers any mind. Bunch of drunks or hopped up college kids. But he was different. He sat in the corner. Staring into the froth, dreaming away. I knew he was...

SANDRA: He's very special.

BENNY: So is she.

SANDRA: So you work at a bar?

GINA: Yup.

SANDRA: Is that your life's ambition?

GINA: It's a job.

BENNY: And she's good at it.

SANDRA: And how long have you been dating her?

BENNY: Long enough to know.

SANDRA: That's up for debate.

GINA: Maybe we can do this another time.

SANDRA: No. I think this is the perfect time.

BENNY: I know this may feel a little rushed.

SANDRA: It's foolish.

BENNY: You and dad got married after only knowing each other for a couple of weeks.

SANDRA: And looked how that turned out.

BENNY: I'm just saying, I know she's the one.

SANDRA: How old are you?

GINA: Old enough not to let you speak to me in that tone.

SANDRA: You think he's your meal ticket? Your way out of whoreville.

GINA: Listen lady, I know he's your son but you—

SANDRA: This is your last shot isn't it?

GINA: Excuse me?

SANDRA: I know women like you. Desperate to make one last go of it. You're looks are fading, wrinkles make up the landscape. Womb is drying up, wasted away on eggs you've aborted so you trap whoever you can.

GINA: Who the fuck do you think you are?

SANDRA: He's just a kid.

BENNY: I love her.

SANDRA: You still love your Xbox.

BENNY: Mother.

GINA: You're gonna let her talk to me that way?

BENNY: Gina. Look let's all settle down. And talk about this. Mother, do you have any cheesecake?

GINA: Cheesecake? I'm going home. And I want you to come with me. We don't need her blessing.

BENNY: Sit down Gina.

GINA: Jeff. No.

SANDRA: You go. You go alone. You get no help from me.

BENNY: Can we just chill for a moment?

GINA: He looked at me.

And I looked at him.

I knew he was a boy. But I thought.

I've dated so many fucked up men, maybe he would be different. But he was a child.

And I couldn't be a wife and a mother.

BENNY: You left him?

GINA: I had to. Because she was right. He was my way out. And I loved that kid. I couldn't do that to him. Force him to choose. His life was still ahead of him. We had fun. He was clumsy in bed but he was honest. And I know he loved me. But it broke my heart. I got to pee.

(She goes to the bathroom. BENNY sits alone. He walks back into the back of the bar. Turns on a song.)

D(ance) B(reak)

BENNY: When I was a kid, the first album I owned was Neil Diamond. I was six years old. I have no idea how I got that album. But I would put it on and pretend that I was at a concert. A large stadium. A hundred thousand people. And it starts. *(He begins to sing Neil Diamond's "America.")*

SANDRA: You're an idiot.

BENNY: But I'm your idiot.

SANDRA: Yes you are.

(He continues the song. The song ends. They sing the last line together and stare at each other.)

BENNY: So?

SANDRA: So.

BENNY: I think we should try.

SANDRA: I hate that word. Try.

BENNY: I know. *(Pause.)* What do you think?

SANDRA: I never thought I'd get married much less become a mother.

BENNY: I always thought you...

SANDRA: You never asked.

BENNY: Who doesn't want kids?

SANDRA: I'm starting law school in the fall.

BENNY: So what do you want to do?

SANDRA: We can't afford to have a kid right now. It's bad timing.

BENNY: There is no good time to have a baby Sa.

SANDRA: I don't want to give up my life.

BENNY: We'll figure it out.

SANDRA: What's to figure out?

BENNY: I want to have kids. That's my vote.

SANDRA: But you don't have to give up everything you work for. It's not fair.

BENNY: You can go back next year.

SANDRA: And be one of those mothers. No.

BENNY: We'll work through it. Together. As a family.

SANDRA: A family? What are we gonna do? We can't live off of what you make. It's not like you want to make more money. You have no drive.

BENNY: I have—

SANDRA: No Benny. You're perfectly content.

BENNY: I'm doing what I love.

SANDRA: But having a child is a big responsibility. You have to man up. And I don't see that from you.

BENNY: What do you want me to do? Find a better job? Become a dog like all the other animals in the office. Fighting each other for scraps. Just so we can get a pat on the head.

SANDRA: It's called ambition.

BENNY: I'm not comfortable with that. Things will be what they will be.

SANDRA: I can't work like that.

BENNY: This is who I am. This is who you married.

SANDRA: And I accepted that. But this is different.

BENNY: I'm good enough to be a husband but not a father?

SANDRA: You don't get in the way. I manage things. If they go wrong, it's on me. I agreed to that. I don't mind carrying the load.

BENNY: You're always such the martyr.

SANDRA: I'm trying to have an adult conversation.

BENNY: Me me me me. I do things too. I carry things too.

SANDRA: You're the baby. You've always been the baby. And I don't need another one.

(This stings BENNY. Silence.)

BENNY: I want us to have one.

SANDRA: Why?

BENNY: We need it.

SANDRA: That's a bad place to be, Benny. To need a child. I don't like putting Band-Aids over deep cuts.

BENNY: It's a part of life. When we're old and our kids have grown up, and all we have left is our memories, decisions like this will have seemed trivial.

SANDRA: I hate being dragged into corners where I can't get out of.

BENNY: Having a baby is not a trap.

SANDRA: For me it is.

BENNY: Let's look at it from another perspective.

SANDRA: Don't try to sell me.

BENNY: I'm not. I'm just giving you different copy.

SANDRA: Pitch me.

BENNY: Let's think about this as freedom. An evolution of the self. Because you no longer have to be self-centric. And. AND. You will create something that will always love you. And you will always love it. No matter what. "Babies, unconditional for those who live by conditions."

(They stare at each other.)

SANDRA: I can't.

(She walks out.)

BENNY: Then I don't want this.

(A fractured shift.)

BAC(k) AT (THE) BAR

(GINA enters carrying a bus tub. BENNY shifts back to the candles.)

GINA: Want what?

BENNY: What?

(BENNY takes the bus tub from her and places glasses in it. He starts to set up the tables.)

GINA: What don't you want?

BENNY: I didn't say anything.

GINA: I heard you.

BENNY: Must be someone else's memory you heard.

GINA: Are you fucking with me?

BENNY: Wait. I know you.

GINA: Yeah. I know you too.

BENNY: You used to work here.

GINA: Huh?

BENNY: You don't remember me? I had a blind date. And you traded places. Funny. Now I'm working here. What was her name? Sarah?

GINA: Sandra.

BENNY: Right. Sandra.

GINA: She's your wife.

BENNY: What? I'm not married.

GINA: Stop it.

BENNY: Stop what? We didn't work out. We only had that one date.

GINA: I don't understand.

BENNY: Tell me about it. She was weird. Not for me. You alright?

GINA: I'm fine.

BENNY: You look confused.

GINA: I am.

BENNY: Must be trippy seeing me where you were. What are you up to these days?

GINA: I don't know.

(SANDRA walks up from behind. She covers GINA's eyes.)

SANDRA: Guess who?

GINA: Don't do that. *(Pulls away violently.)*

SANDRA: What's the matter with you?

GINA: I don't like when you do that.

BENNY: Oh man. It's you!

SANDRA: Shit. Hey. You're working here?

BENNY: Yeah. Lost my job. You know, the recession. Companies pulled back on the advertising dollar.

SANDRA: *(To GINA.)* Looks like I picked right. *(To BENNY.)* That's too bad.

GINA: You need to stop.

SANDRA: Stop what?

GINA: This isn't funny.

BENNY: Is she alright?

GINA: I'm fine.

BENNY: So. You guys are...

SANDRA: Ten years.

BENNY: Well, I'm glad one of us found love.

GINA: STOP IT!

(They stop.)

SANDRA: Isn't this what you wanted?

GINA: It didn't happen this way.

BENNY: Who's to say it didn't?

GINA: I'm not going to lie to myself.

BENNY: It makes it easier.

GINA: It's not that simple.

BENNY: I don't care. This is what I want. And that's how I'm gonna remember it. Period.

(He walks off. The continuation of the fractured shift.)

RE(DRESSING) WHAT'S K(NOW)N

(Finally, they can share a moment together.)

SANDRA: How come you never said "Te amo?"

GINA: In Spanish. No one really says "Te amo."

They say "te quiero mucho" which can mean "I need you a lot." That's kind of fucked up when you think about it.

Instead of it being about loving them, it's more about you needing them so badly you'll do anything

To keep them.

(Looks at SANDRA.) Close your eyes.

SANDRA: I hate the dark.

GINA: Come on. Close them. I got something for you.

(SANDRA does. GINA pulls out a gift.)

GINA: Open them.

SANDRA: What did you do?

GINA: Open it.

(SANDRA does. It's a special gift [up for you to decide].)

SANDRA: Oh man. Why? What is this?

GINA: Guess.

SANDRA: I don't know.

GINA: What's today?

SANDRA: Sunday.

GINA: And? Come on, take a wild guess.

SANDRA: It's all you can eat pancakes day down at IHOP?

GINA: Sa. Guess.

SANDRA: I don't really know.

GINA: It's the day you freed me.

SANDRA: Freed you from what?

GINA: You came into my bar, switched my life around and freed my soul.

SANDRA: It's been that long?

GINA: Yeah.

SANDRA: It's gone by fast.

GINA: That's a good thing.

SANDRA: Yeah. It is.

GINA: Promise me something.

SANDRA: You look so serious.

GINA: I am serious.

SANDRA: Okay.

GINA: Don't ever leave me.

SANDRA: That's not in my immediate plans.

GINA: I'm serious. Listen to me. Promise me that you're never gonna leave me.

SANDRA: It's a big promise to ask.

GINA: I know. But. I don't think I can make it without you.

SANDRA: You're being dramatic.

GINA: No. I'm done. This is my last chance.

SANDRA: Don't give me that four loves nonsense.

GINA: I'm not. I don't want to go through this again. You're it. This time I don't want you to leave. Never. In fact, I'm gonna make sure I die before you just so you don't leave me.

SANDRA: Gina. That's not funny.

GINA: I'm not joking.

SANDRA: You're not dying. No one's dying.

GINA: Promise me.

SANDRA: You know, you're asking the impossible.

GINA: Why?

SANDRA: Because how can I guarantee that? Who knows what's gonna happen or where we're gonna be ten years from now.

GINA: Well, if you promise, you'll be with me.

SANDRA: I'm not built that way.

GINA: Then just say it. Make me feel better. Say that you'll want me forever.

SANDRA: I don't want to say something and then it comes up and bites me in the ass later.

GINA: I won't hold it against you if it doesn't work out.

SANDRA: That's a lie.

GINA: I won't.

SANDRA: Yes you will. Every night, you'll be imagining a train running over me, shredding me to pieces, mangling my body, slices and ripping every part of me apart so I can feel the pain you're feeling.

GINA: That's terrible. Do you think I'm like that?

SANDRA: No. Bad joke.

GINA: Please. I'll never ask anything of you that's this serious again.

SANDRA: Okay. I'll never leave you.

GINA: Thank you.

SANDRA: You're welcome.

GINA: Te quiero mucho.

SANDRA: Te amo.

(They rise up slowly together. "Old Road" plays off in the distance. They lock hands. And dance gracefully. Raising each other up past themselves, out of their bodies. Two souls linked together. They sway, play chase, drifting back and forth, fitting in each gap of each others' bodies. GINA turns for a moment. When she looks again, SANDRA's gone.)

GINA: I needed her when I should have loved her. *(Exits.)*

BE(NN)Y

(BENNY moves into the bar slowly. He walks over to the table. He stares at the empty space on the other side of the table.)

BENNY: You wake up, the mind goes into automatic.

You do everything you programmed yourself to do.

Your eyes open.

You turn off the alarm clock.

You do a cat stretch.

You get up.

Sit on the edge of the bed. Feeling the hardwood floor on the ground.

You stumble to the bathroom.

Piss.

Miss the toilet.

Woops.

Wipe it clean. Put the seat down. Flush. Slide over to the mirror.

See how the day before has aged you.

Drink some water.

Go over to the coffee pot.

Turn it on.

Sit.

Wait for a cup.

Routine.

(He is dressed in his suit. He stares at the coffee cup. SANDRA enters. A new shift.)

THE (IN)EVITABILI(TY)

(She spots BENNY sitting at the table. She recognizes him.)

SANDRA: Hi. Sorry to bother you. Are you Benny?

BENNY: *(Looks up. A bit shocked.)* Yes?

SANDRA: It's me Sandra.

BENNY: *(Covers his head.)* No.

SANDRA: Our firm handled the Duane Reade fiasco with you guys. Remember?

BENNY: *(Doesn't want to look up.)* I don't want to.

(Awkward moment.)

SANDRA: You can't control it.

It's inevitable.

BENNY: What am I supposed to do?

SANDRA: This is where you should ask me to sit down.

BENNY: Would you like to sit down?

(They sit. Shifting back into new path.)

BENNY: Yeah, it's funny. What you remember. I normally have a horrible memory. You know, people will tell me things I said or moments that happened and I don't have any memory of it. Sometimes I feel like I'm an idiot. Or I wasn't present. In that moment with the person. Don't know where I was but I wasn't there. But what you told me, somehow it stayed with me. I hate change. I'm a control freak. But the idea that it's all random. And the only certainty is uncertainty. And if you want stability live in the instability. That it's a good thing. I've been trying to fuse it into my life philosophy.

SANDRA: Wow.

BENNY: Was that too much? I do that.

SANDRA: No. I just didn't realize that waiting for the bathroom with you had such an impact.

BENNY: It did.

SANDRA: Cool.

(Another awkward pause.)

BENNY: You come here often? Shit. Sorry. That's horrible.

SANDRA: No. It's fine. Actually, this is my first time. I was supposed to meet a friend of mine but she bailed on me. So. I was gonna go but then I saw you.

BENNY: Talk about randomness.

SANDRA: Yeah about that. I don't really subscribe to that anymore.

BENNY: What?

SANDRA: Nothing's random.

BENNY: Are you kidding?

SANDRA: I do that. Spout out whatever self-help bullshit I'm reading at the time.

BENNY: Really?

SANDRA: Yeah. It's a trait. I'm working on it.

BENNY: Wow.

SANDRA: I'm sorry.

BENNY: No. It was good. Makes me feel a little better. So what you reading now?

SANDRA: *Blink.* Following my gut intuition.

BENNY: Listening to the little man inside you.

SANDRA: One, who said it was a man, and two, she told me to come over and say hi.

BENNY: I'm glad *she* did.

SANDRA: Me too.

(They smile at each other. It starts up again.)

IN(EVI)TAB(L)E

BENNY: Year one.

SANDRA: He asks me to move in.

GINA: She comes to my bar.

BENNY: Year two.

SANDRA: I say yes.

GINA: We're friends.

SANDRA: Best friends.

BENNY: Year three.

SANDRA: Marriage.

GINA: I'm not invited.

BENNY: Year four.

SANDRA: Itchy.

GINA: Me too.

BENNY: Year five.

SANDRA: Work a lot.

BENNY: I don't see you.

SANDRA: I only notice her.

GINA: I walk the line.

SANDRA: Year six. I gave you that year.

GINA: Year six. I took that year.

BENNY: Year six. I lost that year. I get drunk at a bar. Meet someone else. Someone I work with. I was away. On a business trip. She smiled at me.

(In the monologue, GINA moves in. But, she's not GINA. She takes a scarf and wraps it around her neck. She's now COURTNEY. She smiles. This grabs his attention.)

C(HEAT)

BENNY: You want to know why men are compared to dogs. And it's not because they run around. Sniffing whatever ass they can find. It's deeper than that. It's attention. We crave attention. You see, a dog just wants to love unconditionally. And they want recognition for that dedication. They want a pat on the head. A belly rub. They want to know that you care about them. Neglect a dog. And he'll go looking for that attention somewhere else. Men are no different.

(As he continues the monologue they lock in arms, gliding to the ground. He rolls over next to her. Falls asleep. Morning after. BENNY has just had a one night stand with a woman at work. She wakes him up. BENNY reaches over. Touches her hand. He wakes up. Looks around. Realizes it's not SANDRA.)

BENNY: Hi.

GINA: *(As COURTNEY.)* Hi.

(A pause.)

BENNY: What time is it?

GINA: Almost eight.

(Awkward laugh.)

BENNY: Shit.

GINA: You going in today? I have work. You have work.

BENNY: Yeah. Right.

GINA: *(As COURTNEY.)* We could call in. Hang out. No pressure.

BENNY: Do you know where my shirt is?

GINA: Um... Over there?

BENNY: *(Looks around. Checks under the chair. Finds his shirt. Puts it on. He looks at her.)* I should go.

GINA: Okay.

BENNY: What kind of phone do you have?

GINA: What?

BENNY: My phone's dead.

GINA: You need a charger? I got an iPhone.

BENNY: That doesn't work.

GINA: You can use my phone if you want.

BENNY: No. That's not a good idea. Do you have any coffee?

GINA: I don't drink coffee.

BENNY: Okay. Listen Courtney—

(The room's getting smaller.)

GINA: Let's not... it doesn't have to be weird.

BENNY: Okay.

GINA: It was nice.

BENNY: Yeah. Can you sit down? I got to tell you something.

GINA: What?

BENNY: Please. I should have said something before.

GINA: I don't want to hear it.

BENNY: I'm married. I've been married for six years. I was drinking. You came up to me!

GINA: You're blaming me.

BENNY: No. I was drunk. You're gorgeous. You're so out of my league.

GINA: Ah don't give me that.

BENNY: Really. I never in a million years would ever've thought that a woman like you would wanna hook up with me.

GINA: You're full of shit. So full of shit.

BENNY: Sorry.

GINA: Doesn't matter. It was just sex. I'm good—you do this a lot?

BENNY: No. I've never—I never thought I'd be one of those guys—you're so gorgeous—

GINA: Stop.

BENNY: And you smiled.

GINA: Grow up.

BENNY: It was nice to feel wanted.

GINA: Get your shit and go.

BENNY: Okay. I just need to ask you something. Can we pretend that this didn't happen?

GINA: You're a real dick.

BENNY: I don't want to hurt my wife.

GINA: Oh now you're worried about your wife. Now you have a conscience. Your wife must be a lucky woman. You're such a stand-up guy. She picked a real good one.

BENNY: I'll take that as a yes.

GINA: Get the fuck out. Wait. I want to see you again.

(BENNY leaves. Christmas music comes on.)

GINA: I need to stop playing the lover.

(BENNY enters. He spots GINA. She raises a glass. He does a shy wave back. In this moment, she is his lover.)

CHRISTMAS P(ART)Y

(SANDRA walks in. She sees GINA. GINA smiles. In this moment, GINA is her lover. SANDRA ignores her. Walks up to BENNY. He's acting nervous.)

BENNY: Hi sweetie.

(He pulls her to the other side of the bar. Shifts. He looks around.)

SANDRA: What's the matter with you?

BENNY: Nervous. Boss. Cut backs.

(GINA sits at the table. She looks over at BENNY and SANDRA.)

SANDRA: Benny is thinking, "Please don't ask me about that girl?" Who's that girl? She keeps staring at you.

BENNY: I think her name is Courtney. She works in sales.

SANDRA: Mmmmm.

BENNY: Sandra is thinking, "Please don't ask me about that girl?" Hey, who's that girl? She keeps staring at you.

SANDRA: I don't know. I think her name is Gina. She works here.

BENNY: You want a drink?

SANDRA: Yeah. Sure.

(BENNY goes over to the bar to get a drink. SANDRA watches him leave. Then she quickly goes over to GINA.)

SANDRA: What are you doing here?

GINA: I miss you.

SANDRA: Oh god.

GINA: I do.

SANDRA: This is no good.

GINA: I don't care.

SANDRA: I'm married.

GINA: Tell him about me.

SANDRA: No.

(BENNY returns. He stops. He wants to run away. GINA waves him over. He makes his way.)

GINA: You want to join us?

(Awkward moment.)

BENNY: Sure.

(He sits. Another awkward moment.)

GINA: I love these kinds of parties. You never know who you are going to meet.

BENNY: Right.

SANDRA: That's true.

BENNY: You doing anything for the holidays?

GINA: I was hoping to spend it with someone I love but they keep letting me down.

SANDRA: I'm sure they have their reasons.

GINA: I think they're just being selfish.

BENNY: It's not easy. The holidays are tough.

GINA: Not when you know what you want.

BENNY: (Looks at his glass.) Sandra sweetie, will you get me a Coke. For my whiskey.

SANDRA: Sure. (Goes.)

BENNY: I thought everything was cool?

GINA: It is.

BENNY: What is this?

GINA: Fun.

BENNY: I'm not having fun.

GINA: Oh cheer up Tiny Tim, it's Christmas?

(SANDRA comes back.)

BENNY: Yeah, Merry Christmas!

SANDRA: Happy Hanukkah.

BENNY: What are we talking about?

SANDRA: Nothing.

GINA: Oh, that's that necklace you told me about.

(GINA reaches up and touches it. Softly.)

BENNY: Yes. She got it for me.

SANDRA: For our six-year anniversary.

GINA: It's nice. You guys must have a great marriage.

(She touches SANDRA's knee.)

SANDRA: I have to go to the bathroom. Wanna come with me?

GINA: Sure.

BENNY: Wait!

(BENNY grabs GINA.)

SANDRA: What are you doing?

BENNY: Who's gonna keep me company?

SANDRA: Be right... Be right back.

BENNY: What's the matter with you?

GINA: Nothing.

BENNY: Why are you doing this?

GINA: Because it's better than the alternative.

BENNY: Don't do this.

GINA: Tell her about me.

BENNY: Stop.

(SANDRA walks up. She sees them huddled together.)

SANDRA: What's going on?

BENNY: We should go home. I forgot about the dogs. I didn't leave out their food.

SANDRA: I'm not ready to go home.

GINA: *(Looks at SANDRA.)* I'll give her a lift.

BENNY: What?

SANDRA: Yeah, she can take me home.

BENNY: No!

(Awkward. GINA confronts BENNY.)

GINA: I want you to tell her about us.

BENNY: There is no us.

SANDRA: What's she talking about?

GINA: *(Confronts SANDRA.)* Tell him about me.

BENNY: What's she talking about?

SANDRA: You should have some water. You need some water.

GINA: You're lying. You're both fucking lying.

SANDRA: I don't know what you're talking about.

BENNY: I think she's drunk.

GINA: YOU ARE LYING TO EACH OTHER!

SANDRA and BENNY: We should go home.

(They leave. The Christmas music fades away. GINA gets up.)

GINA: That went well.

(Walks out. BENNY walks in.)

(MOVING) PAST THE FEE(LING)

(Kitchen table.)

BENNY: What time is it? God, what am I doing?

(SANDRA comes in. She's sick.)

SANDRA: Who are you talking to?

BENNY: Just thinking out loud.

SANDRA: Is that something new?

BENNY: I guess it is. I didn't mean to wake you.

SANDRA: You didn't.

BENNY: You should get some rest.

SANDRA: I'll sleep when I die.

BENNY: That's not funny.

SANDRA: I'm not being funny. I only have a few more months of awake time so I got to take advantage of it.

BENNY: Sa. *(Pause.)* You want something to eat?

SANDRA: I'll just throw it up.

BENNY: Can I get you anything?

SANDRA: I'm fine. Just let me sit here with you.

BENNY: I have to—

SANDRA: Sit. We haven't done this in a long time.

BENNY: What?

SANDRA: Hold hands. Sit next to each other.

BENNY: It's been a while.

SANDRA: Tell me a story.

BENNY: I don't know any stories.

SANDRA: Come on, you're a writer.

BENNY: Not that kind of writer.

SANDRA: Tell me a story.

BENNY: Like what.

SANDRA: Tell me something about you. Something you've never told me before.

BENNY: You know everything about me.

SANDRA: There has to be something. Tell me.

BENNY: I cheated. When I was eighteen, I cheated on my girlfriend. I was stupid.

And I'm not proud of it. But I locked it away. I pretended that it didn't happen. Took that memory and pushed way back. Where it couldn't be found.

SANDRA: You like to do that.

BENNY: I know. So that year, the same year, her father got real sick. We grew tight. I had lost my dad five years earlier so I knew what she was going through. Last week, I ran into her. At the grocery store and she gave me this smile. I hadn't seen her in a long time. And she gave me this great hug. It was... made me uncomfortable. She thanked me for standing by her. During her father's death. That if it wasn't for me, she doesn't think that she would've gotten through it. And the truth is, I only stood by her because I felt guilty. I was gonna be the best boyfriend ever because I had sinned. And this was a way to find some forgiveness. And when I saw her, the memory of that year flooded back in, for her, she saw support, for me, guilt. And I didn't tell her because I didn't want to demean that memory—

SANDRA: Doesn't matter. You were there for her.

(They sit in silence.)

SANDRA: I have never stopped loving you.

BENNY: I know.

SANDRA: All my life I was so afraid of being loved. It was easy for me to give. But for someone to love me back. I couldn't handle it. I didn't want the responsibility. But then I met you. And you took a part of my soul. And I wanted you to take it all but I couldn't—

BENNY: Maybe it's getting late. We should—

SANDRA: Listen, I'm trying to tell you something.

BENNY: Okay what?

SANDRA: I thought that I could go through my life only sharing that one part. The part you had. But I was wrong. Someone took the other part.

BENNY: What?

SANDRA: I had another love.

BENNY: When?

SANDRA: Doesn't matter.

BENNY: Who was it? Do I know him?

SANDRA: It doesn't matter.

BENNY: Why are you telling me this?

SANDRA: Because. I want you to understand.

(Silence between them.)

SANDRA: What are you thinking?

(BENNY doesn't say anything.)

SANDRA: Don't shut me out. Say something.

BENNY: You shouldn't have told me.

SANDRA: I didn't want to end it this way.

BENNY: I was perfectly fine not knowing. Jesus Sa, you shouldn't have told me.

SANDRA: I didn't mean to hurt you.

BENNY: It didn't happen.

SANDRA: What?

BENNY: This, what you told me. It didn't happen. This moment didn't happen.

SANDRA: You can't keep locking away memories.

BENNY: Yes I can. I choose what I want to remember and I remember you and I. Happy Marriage. Sure we had some rough spots. But we got through them. That's it. Nothing more. Nothing less.

SANDRA: Listen to me. I need you to forgive me.

BENNY: I love you with all my heart.

SANDRA: But do you forgive me?

BENNY: It didn't happen.

(He walks out. SANDRA's left alone. She drops a newspaper on the floor and then she leaves.)

(OBITUARY)

(GINA enters, she picks up the paper.)

GINA: It's cold.

I'm wearing my red scarf. A gift.

My jacket. A gift.

My snow boots. A gift.

My whole life feels like it's been a gift.

I start fresh.

Heading to who knows where.

I stop to pick up the paper.

Skim through the pages and there.

Center of the page.

There she was. Who she was. Who she left.

And I want to cry.

But I can't.

I don't know why I can't.

I'm angry. I'm frustrated. I'm silly. I'm tired. I'm feeling groovy. I'm ecstatic. I'm shocked. I'm still. I'm jaded. I'm hopeful. I'm hopeless. I'm tickled pink. I'm turning the corner. I'm jacked. I'm wired. I'm dancing. I'm light. I'm heavy. I'm moving like the wind. I'm mocking those who walk by. I'm twitching. I'm hunched over. I'm on my knees. I'm yanking off my boots. I'm kicking off the chill. I'm standing in the middle of the street. I'm yelling. I'm hearing my voice echo back. I'm flying high. I'm underground.

I'm alone.

I close the paper and I head to work.

Because that's the only place I know.

The only place that I can rely on right now.

(GINA comes into the bar. Standing there are BENNY and SANDRA.)

F(A)CING EACH OTHER

BENNY: I lost my wife.

GINA: I lost my lover.

SANDRA: I lost my soul mate.

BENNY: I lost my bearing.

GINA: I lost feeling.

SANDRA: I lost the past.

GINA: I lost your smell.

BENNY: I lost your smile.

SANDRA: I lost your hands.

BENNY: I lost my mind.

SANDRA: I lost some sleep.

GINA: I lost my food.

BENNY: I lost my CD's.

GINA: I lost my books.

BENNY: I lost my socks.

GINA: I lost the truth.

SANDRA: I lost the lies.

BENNY: I lost my courage.

SANDRA: I lost the nerve.

GINA: I lost my faith.

BENNY: I lost my disappointments.

SANDRA: I lost my fear of commitment.

GINA: I lost my fear of abandonment.

(Breath.)

ALL: I lost myself.

(They all look at each other. SANDRA walks off.)

CONC(LUSION)

(GINA grabs a bus tub. She puts out candles on the tables. She picks up some dirty glasses.)

GINA: Routine.

When all else fails, that's what you got.

What you can come home to.

You sign in.

Go over your section. Over the drink specials. How many kegs. Wood. Mirrors. The deer head.

Don't have to think.

Empty. *(Goes into the back of the bar.)*

(BENNY walks in. He wears a black suit and carries a rolling suitcase. He looks around. A small shiver shoots up his spine. He's been here before. GINA comes out of the back. She sees him. They lock eyes. Shift.)

BENNY: When it happens,

When you sit back and think about what you saw,

What you felt,

When you close your eyes and you try to recall the memory,

There are only two things that you can rely on.

What you remember and what really happened.

And they're not the same thing.

GINA: Can I help you?

BENNY: Huh?

(Shift to Present.)

GINA: You need something?

BENNY: Hi.

GINA: Hello.

BENNY: Do you remember me?

GINA: I do.

BENNY: I'm sorry.

GINA: Me too.

BENNY: Did you love her?

GINA: More than anything.

BENNY: Good.

GINA: You?

BENNY: I did.

GINA: Did you do your best?

BENNY: I tried.

GINA: Me too.

BENNY: I don't know what's real and what's a memory.

GINA: Does it matter?

BENNY: I need to know that it was worth it.

GINA: It was.

BENNY: It hurts.

GINA: I know.

BENNY: Does it ever stop?

GINA: I hope not.

BENNY: I should have been better.

GINA: Me too.

BENNY: What now?

GINA: We say goodbye.

BENNY: Goodbye. *(Heads out the door. Stops. Turns.)*

BENNY: Gina.

GINA: Yes.

BENNY: On the blind date, when you traded places...

GINA: Right.

BENNY: *(Smiling.)* It could have been you.

GINA: *(Thinks.)* Nahhhh.

BENNY: *(Small chuckle.)* Thanks.

(She nods. Lights fade as he walks out and she goes back to putting the bar in order. They fade till there's nothing left but darkness.)

(End.)

HERE I LIE

Courtney Baron

COURTNEY BARON's play *A Very Common Procedure* premiered at the Magic Theater (director Loretta Greco) and then at MCC in New York (director Michael Greif). Her play *Consumption* was commissioned and produced by the Guthrie Theater in partnership with the University of Minnesota. Other productions include: *Not Our Last Hurrah* at the Kraine Theatre, NYC; *These Three Here* at the Actors Theater of Louisville; *Earlstreetman* and *Confidence Man* as a part of Christine Jones's Theatre for One; *John Brown's Body* with the Keen Company; *In the Widow's Garden* and *Dear Anton* for the ChekhovNOW! Festival, NYC; and *To Know Know Know Me* as part of the KeenTeens, NYC. Her play with music composed by Juliana Nash was workshopped at Primary Stages. She has had plays read or workshopped at the Cherry Lane Theatre (mentored by David Auburn), The Atlantic Theater, MTC, MCC, the New Group, Famous Door Theater in Chicago, the Guthrie, EST, as part of the New Works Now series at the Public Theater, the Royal Court in London, and Theatre for the New City, among others. Courtney was nominated for the American Theater Critics' Osborne Award and was a winner of a Heideman at ATL. She is currently developing screenplays with Templehill Productions and Yarn Films. She is currently under commission by P2 Creations. Her play *Eat Your Heart Out* is part of the 36th Annual Humana Festival of New American Plays. She is a part of the Dorothy Streslin New American Writers Group. Courtney holds an MFA in playwriting from Columbia University.

VISIBLE SOUL INTERVIEW WITH COURTNEY BARON
Conducted by Zack Calhoon, November 6, 2010

How did you get started in theater? What made you start writing plays?

My mom put me in classes at the Dallas Theater Center when I was pretty young, so that was the beginning. When I was a junior in high school, I transferred to the public arts magnet. I wanted to be an actor, but it seemed to me that the acting teachers didn't like me so much. So, when the playwriting teacher showed me some kindness I bit. You know, in high school, you go where people like you. I wanted to be liked, so I started writing plays.

Tell me about your play, *Here I Lie*. What was the process like? How do you think the play is going?

Here I Lie is something I've been writing forever. It's about two people with Factitious disorder. It's a kind of psychological disorder that compels people to go to great lengths to feign illnesses. I mean great lengths. Injecting yourself with corn starch to create subcutaneous nodules; bleeding yourself to become anemic… you get the picture. I so totally understand it. It is the most surefire way to get attention, to feel cared for. The level of care is beside the point. The catalyst for the play was a story of someone I once knew who had faked cancer. I mean really faked it, people thought she was dying, her whole family. And it isn't like the people who fake things to raise money, Factitious disorder is about, it seems to me from my research, a need to be connected and to be important. And I think that it's going pretty well. Daniel is directing and he's great and Sam Soule and Denis Butkus are awesome. I'm feeling lucky.

What kind of writing inspires you?

This is a tough question, because writing I like inspires me and I have such varied taste. But essentially, I'm inspired by smart writing that takes you on an emotional journey. My husband is a writer too, and I have to say, his discipline and ability to write beautiful plays that are widely accessible inspires me.

Who or what has been the biggest influence on your work as a playwright thus far?

I used to do these workshops with the playwright Leslie Ayvazian that made a huge difference in how I approach the page. I think about Strindberg's *Dream Play* a lot, but that probably just makes me sound pretentious. Mostly, I just read a lot of articles about people with fucked-up medical/psychological problems and then write about them. And the Primary Stages writers' group that I was a part of for a lot of years, that's been huge for my writing. Oh goodness, and I think I dream about a production of Wallace Shawn's *The Designated Mourner* I saw years ago, directed by Andre Gregory. It was awesome. I think Wallace Shawn is a genius, if I could write something like *The Fever*, I could lay down my pen and feel complete.

Here I Lie, directed by Daniel Talbott, premiered on November 7, 2010, at the Seventh Street Small Stage at Jimmy's No. 43.

CAST LIST

Joseph .... Denis Butkus
Maris .... Samantha Soule

CHARACTERS

JOSEPH
MARIS

(JOSEPH scratches his head. He puts on a knit ski cap. MARIS takes off her jacket.)

JOSEPH: There is a small white patch in my mouth. I can show it to you. *(He does.)*

MARIS: I'm exhausted. Tired. All-of-the-time. *(She smiles, a big, syrupy smile.)*

JOSEPH: If you are my doctor, or maybe a nurse practitioner, you may ask me a series of questions. Like, the obvious: What are your symptoms?

MARIS: *(She answers.)* My periods are too heavy. Too short. I can't get a handle on what it is. My back aches. I feel like I'm getting fatter. But my stomach feels firm. Then my periods, they just, you know, stop. Every time I have sex, there's blood. I feel off. I have headaches.

JOSEPH: You. If you're doctor or nurse, you may ask: has it changed since you first noticed? Take a history. Examine the small white patch in my mouth.

(He goes to MARIS, she puts her hand in his mouth.)

JOSEPH: It feels firm, right?

MARIS: Do I look well to you?

JOSEPH: You may give me a prescription ointment.

MARIS: Do I look healthy?

JOSEPH: But it always comes back. It's a problem. This white, raw patch in my mouth is a problem.

MARIS: The way I feel, it's really—

JOSEPH: A real problem. It's serious.

MARIS: —serious.

JOSEPH: That's what the doctors will say, "It's serious." I'm freezing, it's freezing, right?

MARIS: Me, I work in publishing. You can tell by my shoes, right? Publishing girls have great shoes. No walking involved. English major at a Southern Ivy. Straight to one of the giants. Nonfiction/Memoir. A budding Nan Talese. But after five years something changed. I was working just as hard, you know, slugging through manuscripts. I read more than anyone. And you know, the truth is that there are a bunch of really bad writers out there. That's not my fault. Then one day, I read this memoir written by a young man struggling with cancer. He was going to die a horrible, terrible, painful death. It really touched me. But the writing was awful. A fantastic story, but he could barely put a sentence together. But people aren't always looking for the next Jonathan Franzen, are they? People want inspiration. They want the gory details of chemo and radiation, they want to know that this cancer guy had dreams. They want Chicken Soup for the Soul. So, I passed it on to my editor. She called me into her office and she sat me down and tossed the cancer memoir across her desk. She was going to downsize me. I didn't deserve it, but I know she was— She tossed it like it didn't mean anything. And I broke down. Tears from frustration, I guess. And I had to say something, so I just said, "That manuscript really touched me." And she just rolled her eyes. So I said, "It touched me because I know what the writer is going through." Total silence. She got this look, this look like, you know— And the tears well up in her eyes. Then we're both sobbing like babies, because we know I'm going to die.

(MARIS looks at JOSEPH.)

MARIS: What else could I do?

JOSEPH: Nothing.

MARIS: Nothing. I couldn't do anything else. In the office with my editor. I make my bed. But I don't have a choice, what else could I do?

JOSEPH: I'm a nurse. People always say, "Male nurse." Like nurse is automatically female. When a guy becomes a nurse, people figure it's because you couldn't hack medical school. But it's a job, not a calling, it just happened. I like the hands-on. I like taking care of people.

I specialized in geriatrics. Worked in nursing homes for years. I did it because no one wants to. No one wants to be around for the end. I have a real fondness for older people. But there's no money in it. Now, I work in the neonatal ICU at a private hospital. Money's better—good. And if you think male nurses are rare, shit. Once you get around babies, not a single guy nurse in the whole department. Like men wouldn't know how to take care of a baby, it's fucking ridiculous. Nursing is nursing.

MARIS: Most people think people who go into publishing are frustrated writers. Not me. I'm no writer. But I know how a good story can be told.

JOSEPH: If you go to school, get the degree, you can be a nurse.

MARIS: I'm young. All that "before her time" stuff applies to me. And then there's George, handsome, entry level at Morgan Stanley George. Makes good money, but I couldn't get him to commit. The second George found out about—he got down on his knee and proposed. Funny how people who failed you before suddenly clad themselves in armor and come riding to your window on a big white horse. It isn't that I don't appreciate it. I do. I'm lucky. My family's been I'm lucky. Some people never get to feel the love that I do. I'm lucky.

JOSEPH: In the NICU, like in the nursing homes— Babies die just like old people. The real difference is the families—families of the old folks don't have hope. Shit, they're mostly waiting for them to die. Hell, the old folks themselves are just waiting to die. But with babies, there's all of this hope. And the ones who make it, the babies who survive, even if they're just there because they're just a little premature, well, when the parents take them home they become miracles. The babies are like these fucking miracles. And the parents send you pictures from their first birthdays and you look at those little miracles with their little faces covered in chocolate cake. That's the difference. Hope. I was diagnosed with leukoplakia, these lesions in my mouth, when I found out they weren't cancerous: hope.

MARIS: There's this story I heard years ago about a woman who thought she was pregnant, her stomach grew for seven months and when she finally went to the o.b. she had a sonogram and found it was a tumor, not a baby. The thing had grown to almost volleyball proportions. Of course, they removed it. Like that woman I'm giving birth to a tumor.

JOSEPH: And I was diagnosed with aplastic anemia, and I started having all of these transfusions, every time I leave the hospital and survive: hope.

MARIS: Did you know there are at least three shelves at the Barnes and Noble at 66th dedicated to books about cancer. It makes sense, you know: in the U.S., something like 1,500 people die every day from cancer. I read that one out of every four deaths are from cancer. If I bring three of you over here with me—you three, I've saved you, you know, because I'm the one.

JOSEPH: The symptoms are there. Real symptoms. I live with them.

(JOSEPH passes out little baskets of snow. He shows the audience how to sprinkle the snow on the ground as she speaks.)

MARIS: I'm hot. It's hot, right?

JOSEPH: Really? It's cold. I'm freezing.

MARIS: *(Sweeps the snow aside with her feet.)* Follow this: the South Pole is a desert. The South Pole is the driest desert in the world. It's the lack of humidity. The South Pole is a desert. A desert is hot. You know? A desert is

hot. The South Pole is the driest desert in the world. Therefore the South Pole is hot.

JOSEPH: It's snowing.

MARIS: My mother sends these remarkable care packages and articles from health magazines and homeopathic remedies and self-help books and pamphlets. Two years ago she forgot my birthday. Now I'm special.

JOSEPH: Do you want my coat?

MARIS: No I'm hot. I'm special.

JOSEPH: It's snowing. See this?

MARIS: You aren't following: it doesn't snow in the desert.

JOSEPH: I did have a real canker sore in my mouth. I reach into the medicine cabinet. I open what I think is gly-oxide, a treatment for canker sores—and rub it on the inside of my cheek. But it burns. I almost pass out. I go to the emergency room. They examine my mouth. They ask me what's happened. I tell them I don't know. They call in a specialist and take a tissue sample and can't figure out what's caused the lesion. They can't figure it out. Because they don't know that the salicylic acid that is the active ingredient in Dr. Scholl's Corn and Wart Remover. They guess it's leukoplakia. They run tests. They send me home with antibiotics and painkillers. They tell me to get a oral surgeon, get a biopsy. I do, and I'm fine. But a week later, I'm in another doctor's office with an identical lesion on the other side of my mouth.

MARIS: My once upon a time is: I have ovarian cancer. A cancer patient is a hero. Those who help her are heroes too. We're a special segment on *Oprah*, you know? My best friend, Sammy, she sets up a national Sloan-Kettering blood donation network in my name. People are lined up, stuck, Band-Aided and given juice and cookies and a good feeling. I join a cancer support group. Wednesdays at seven in a church near our apartment. It's six women and one man. A psychologist runs it. We sit in plastic chairs in a circle. They seem wary of me at first until I tell them that when I asked my oncologist if the Taxol will make me vomit, he says that it won't. And after I vomit for days, he tells me it's not the Taxol it's the Cisplatin. They tell me to beat the Taxol to the chase, to go ahead and shave my head. I do. I shave my head and buy myself wigs. I buy wigs that I would never have thought of before, auburn numbers with bangs, I've never worn bangs.

JOSEPH: Just now, I remembered this one nursing class I took, the professor told us that being a nurse is like being a detective. Symptoms are clues. You piece them together and solve the mystery of the illness. I think being a nurse is really more like *reading* a detective novel, because really, you only know as much as the chapter you've read. And you may try to guess ahead, but really all you can do is go with the facts you've been given. Maybe in the end, the author will reveal that the butler had a secret love affair with the wife of the dead man, you could have never guessed it. So, a patient is like the author.

MARIS: I got into publishing because I love to read. A good story is entertaining, you know. You can't deny that. And I'll tell you what, I think that part of the reason I'm sad when a book ends is that I've become, you know, kind of friends with the characters. I don't read and say, this isn't true. While I'm reading, it *feels* true. The people, the characters, the people in the stories they *feel* real. You know? I'm so sick. I'm going to have to quit my job.

JOSEPH: I had been working in the NICU for about seven months. It's a private hospital. So, most of the babies we see, we have to dislodge a silver spoon when we intubate them. About seven months into my working there, this baby comes in. He's delivered at twenty-six weeks, he's about two pounds four ounces. Small. His hands are like the size of half of one of my thumbs. Twenty-four hours pass and there's no mother to see the baby. Sometimes the mothers die, sometimes they get sick, but usually *somebody* comes. He's called "Baby Moore." Which bugs me, it never had before, it's not strange for the babies to be called by their last names, it's what we call them even when they do have first names. But I'm not having it with Baby Moore, so I name him Joseph, after me. Joseph junior. Stupid. He's all hooked up: pulse ox, c.r. monitor, apnea monitor, temp probe, central line, endotracheal tube. The whole nine yards and then some. I call him Joe. His head is the size of a tennis ball. You never get used to seeing a baby this small. When he's brought in, he's septic, infection from the placenta. They're pumping him full of antibiotics. I start staying past my shift on the first night when they brought him in. It's impossible to explain, but we had a connection. Joe can't move on his own. But every now and then, I sort of, well, move him. Just a light touch to his foot or rock his arm to left or right. Babies this young are covered in lanugo, it's like fur. It's the softest thing you've ever felt. He's a skinny little fucker. Like a pencil or something. I start to talk to him, you have to be real quiet about it, premature babies' ears are real sensitive to noise. And you have to be careful not to stress them out, can cause them to have bleeds. So, I start to whisper to him. I tell him about the world.

MARIS: Every few weeks, my editor calls and pretends she wants to have lunch. Like it's the sick-employee protocol in the company handbook. I go once. She's uncomfortable. I'm thin and drawn, you know. And the Cytoxan has caused this unseemly rash on my arm. I scratch it and it gets worse and worse until there are little scabs on my forearms. I pick them just before the lunch, so there's little drops of blood just at the surface. I look terrible. I look sick. I look it and I am. She's chosen a fancy midtown place that she would have never taken me to before. Before at Burger Heaven, I wouldn't have cared, but at Le Bernadin, I'm sorry that I can't eat more. That if she saw me eat, she would be surprised. So, I take home, in a doggy bag, what I don't finish there. She tells me that everyone in the office misses me terribly. She tells me that they're actually considering the memoir of the cancer victim that I gave her at the beginning of all of this. Huh. She asks me if I would be interested in editing it. I excuse myself to the bathroom and shove my finger down my throat, bring up the taste of bile and head back out into the dining room. My eyes are all watery and my face is flush. She tries not to look at me. I tell her I'd like to give the manuscript a go. She smiles and when I start coughing she gets the check. She says she's sorry but she has to get back to work. I don't want to go. So, I tell her that my sister has been in a car accident. I cry, real tears, the story I tell makes me cry: my sister is two years older than I am and she lives in Dallas with her husband and two kids. About a two months ago, she found out that she was pregnant again. She's driving home from the o.b.'s office. She's just had a sonogram, it turns out that she's going to have a girl. She pulls out into the flow of traffic on the highway, a semi is trying to exit. They collide. The car is totaled. She's rushed to the hospital and there she miscarries. She's devastated. Before the wreck she had decided to name that little girl Maris, after me. So, I'm dead twice. That's the story I tell my editor and she

listens, she doesn't leave even though she said she had to get back to work. I tell her my sister is going to be fine. My editor is relieved. I am relieved. The lunch ends. We've shared something.

JOSEPH: I tell Joe about the world. I start with facts, tell him about evolution. I tell him where he's come from. He's not even two days old and I tell him the fucking birds and bees. I tell him about the Pilgrims coming to America, the parts I remember. Hell, it only takes me about an hour to go through the last two hundred years. I check his monitors, I try not to neglect the other babies, but every time I pass his incubator, I have to stop and tell him some more. Tell him the story of the world.

MARIS: After the lunch with my editor, she sent me a copy of the cancer memoir. I compared his experiences to my own story. He was from a normal family, grew up in comfort, but struggled in school. Just wasn't motivated. Had to spend a year in community college before transferring to state university. He majored in English. Said he had a real love for language. You wouldn't know it from the way he'd written his own story. I started in with edits. I cut his two-hundred-some-page manuscript down to like one fifty. I rearranged some of the parts, I began with the beginning. He had begun with the end. The part where he was going in for his fifth surgery. My mom keeps asking me about my own surgery, wants to know when. I told her that it wasn't time, that they were trying to resolve this with chemo. She said that everything she read said that I ought to have my uterus, fallopian tubes, ovaries removed. I want kids. She said I could adopt. She's never understood me. She's never given a shit about what I wanted.

JOSEPH: I tell Joe about the world. I tell him all of the good things I can think of, it's hard to think of them at first, but then the list sort of flows. I say, baseball, football, hockey, especially hockey. Then at about five in the morning, I realize that my entire list of good things have nothing to do with other people. I mean, I haven't said anything like "falling in love for the first time" or "having kids of your own." The list is really just things. Not people. Then I start to think about it, I look at him, and I say, "If you live, I'll be your friend. I can be a great friend." It's fucking ridiculous. This kid, if he lives, he's not going to be my fucking friend.

MARIS: I have a memoir. I have a life. It's ending now. But I have a life. And if I tell you my story. If I tell it to you, it becomes important. An important life told so that you can learn something about yourself through me. Isn't that why we read? Why we watch movies? To learn about ourselves, through other people?

JOSEPH: I think it's important to tell Joe about people. So, I tell him about Francie. Francie has great hair. Really thick great hair. And a great face. I mean great. Seriously. I tell Joe how I met her in line at the grocery store. She reached around me to grab a magazine, *People*, I think. Her hair is so great, thick. And when I got to the parking lot and suddenly she's there. Running over to my car while I'm loading groceries. And she says, "You a doctor?" I have scrubs on, that's why she asks. And I say, "No. I'm a nurse." And she smiles again. And gives me her phone number. Of course, I call her. Shit, it's not like this kind of thing happens to me all of the time. I call her and I'm good on the phone. And we make a date. And when I get to the bar and walk in and see her sitting there—I'm surprised. Shocked she's actually there. But she is. And we have this date, and I like her. Like her because she's a little

crazy. Changes directions midsentence and it's hard to follow her. She's crass. Uses "fuck" as an adjective to describe everything: "Give me a fucking glass of wine, please." "Excuse me I'm going to the fucking ladies' room." "So, you're really a fucking nurse?" She has me smiling. We're both smiling, a lot. I offer to take her to dinner, but she just pulls the cherry from her whiskey sour, pops it in her mouth, and says she's full. It's great. She's great. She gets a little drunk, I know she is when she says, "I'm not fucking you tonight." I say that I wasn't expecting her to—secretly, I'm just so glad she qualified it with "tonight." Like maybe tomorrow she would, or even next year, I didn't care, as long as it wasn't out of the realm of possibility.

(MARIS takes off her top, revealing a bikini. She puts a towel on the ground and lays out.)

JOSEPH: Then she says, as if she's been thinking it over, as if she's worried I didn't understand her, she says, "I'm not fucking you tonight. I usually fuck guys on the first date. I'm not a slut, but I don't usually see the point in beating around the bush." Then she's laughing, laughing so hard that there's tears running down her cheeks and she looks at me and says, "Beat around the fucking bush, get it?" Two weeks later, five dates, she takes me to her apartment. She sits me down on the edge of her bed. She stands in front of me and she undresses. Takes off everything but her shoes. She's got a great body. Hourglass, smallish waist, big breasts. I start to go towards her, she puts her hand up to stop me. The girls I've been with, they're the kind that take off their clothes in the dark and jump under the covers. So, there with Francie, when she stopped me from touching her, I thought, okay, this is some kind of game. She stands there for a while. We're silent. She grabs my hand, pulls me up from the bed. She tells me to undress. I do. She leads me to the full-length mirror. We're looking at our reflections. Finally, she says, "Do you like what you see?" Yes, yes, I like what I see. "Yeah?" she says. And then, slowly, with her eyes on me the whole time, she bends down and takes off her shoes. She stays bent down for a second. Then she stands. She stands perfectly straight. Her right foot doesn't touch the ground, just hovers there two inches above it. She says, "Look at yourself." Then she says, "Look at me." And she says, "Do you feel lucky?" And I say, "Yes." Then she says, "You are, you are lucky." In her system, I'm sub-par, looking in the mirror, she's showing me that I'm the kind of guy she thinks would be lucky to be with her even if her right leg is two inches shorter than her left. And she's right, I do feel lucky.

MARIS: I'm thinner than I've ever been. Not eating is the hardest part. But I'm thin now. So, sickness gives me something good. You have to look for the positive in these kinds of things. I will die with a good figure. Ha, ha, ha. My sister, when we were growing up, she was too thin. My mom was always making her drink these shakes, these protein sugar fat shakes, and she was feeding me slim fast or whatever was popular at the time. I know she meant well. Knew how hard it is to struggle with your weight. Now I have this incredible new discipline, because it isn't just about me anymore, it's about the people who see me. Because people need to see what's going on with you, need to see the manifestation of the illness to deal with it. I mean, to know what they're dealing with. It's all part of the story of being sick.

JOSEPH: Three days in, Joe develops a grade two intracranial bleed. This isn't so uncommon, but they have to give him steroids, which really knock

him out. The other nurses are starting to look at me funny for sitting with him when I'm not on shift. His eyes open on that third day, and I swear to god he's really looking at me. I fall asleep by his side and wake up when the apnea monitor alarm goes off. I try tapping his foot. Sometimes you can remind them to breathe properly. But it doesn't work, he goes from this perfect fucking pink rose to blue. We get his breathing going and add theophylline. I have to get out of there for a while, I jump in my car and go home to shower before my next shift. I'm sitting in my car. I look at myself in the rearview mirror and I think, "My son Joe." Fuck. I want to drive back to the hospital at that very fucking second, get in there and be with him. I try to shake it off. It doesn't work. I go into my apartment to shower and there's a message on my answering machine. The message says, "Joseph, it's Francie, I think that it's best if we don't see each other anymore." Just like that. A fucking message. It ought to bother me, but I'm just thinking about Joe. Francie says I'm too needy. Her limp is more than a little noticeable. It's sad. But here she is telling me that I'm the defective one. She's not lucky like me. I'm lucky, I have Joe. She has a short fucking leg. I'm lucky.

MARIS: I realize cancer boy writer has no conflict, just a lot of, you know, flowery sentiment about living his best life. It's touching, but it lacks substance.

JOSEPH: I'm lucky.

MARIS: But I have conflict, substance.

JOSEPH: When I get back to the hospital, there's this girl: Joe's mom. She's got her hand on Joe. I run over and warn her that if she touches him, she risks scarring him permanently. Babies this young are born with not even half of the layers of skin that we have. I scare the fucking shit out of her. I want her to go away. She looks up at me with her big stupid eyes and she says she's sorry. She doesn't want to hurt him. No one ever says they want to hurt anyone. Not really. But they do, people want to hurt people all of the time. But, shit, I feel bad. So, I ask her if she's named him. She hasn't. If she loved him, she would have named him. I ask her where the father is, there isn't one. So, suddenly, I change my tune. I think, okay, get in there Joseph. You can date this woman and marry her and little Joe will be your boy, really. She looks about twenty or so. I could get her. And she just says, "This is really my baby?" She asks it. Like it couldn't be true.

MARIS: The cancer boy writer doesn't know that his story is too predictable, that's my guess. Maybe he would change it if he knew.

JOSEPH: "This is my baby?" I tell her, yes, this is your son.

MARIS: Unlike the cancer boy writer, whose story is just the plot. Mine, it isn't just a story: It's the truth. The young editor diagnosed with stage 3B ovarian cancer. She's read everything there is to know about this cancer. She knows everything about it, so she can tell the story. She can live it. I can make it true.

JOSEPH: When she asked me if he was her son and I said yes, you know what she said? She said, "No. I don't think so, there must be some mistake."

MARIS: I never set out to be a story. I never wanted it to get this far. It's a mistake. But I'm not sorry. I know what I have to do.

JOSEPH: Joe is her mistake. But he's my miracle. I hate the mother. One day her father comes to visit. Joe has chicken pox, it happens every now and then, an outbreak on the ward. And so this girl's father isn't allowed to see

Joe. I go out to talk to him. He tells me that, "Sonia's been in and out of rehabs for years, and four months ago she showed up at his doorstep strung out and pregnant. No one knows who the father is." I want to say, "I know." Shit, I know. I'm the fucking father. I'm the fucking father.

MARIS: My symptoms are progressing. Blockage of the intestines. Nausea. Vomiting. Pain. Weight loss. I can't have sex anymore. I'm anemic. The headaches. You know. I can't do this much longer.

JOSEPH: It's all so fucking stupid. Sonia's father never came back. Sonia stayed the same. She'd be sitting in the fucking waiting room, all fucking strung out, and there'd be milk stains on her shirt. Like she didn't even notice. She should have at least been pumping. The other nurses felt bad for her. I didn't. I thought she's been given a precious gift and she doesn't know how to deal with it. Thank god he was sick, because then he was taken care of. At least, sickness made somebody look after him. At least. Shit.

MARIS: My best friend Sammy called, said she was going to get married. She called to ask me to be a bridesmaid. I don't want to do it. I tell her that I'm too sick. She insists. It will do me good. But, you know, the truth is that it will do her good. I tell her about the chemo, tell her it's made me sicker than I thought. She says it will be a quick service. I finally agree, send my measurements for my dress. When I fly home for the wedding, my mom has rented me a wheelchair. I go to pick up the dress, my mother makes a scene in the bridal shop. The dress is huge on me. One of those ridiculous pink ruffled things, people lose all sense of taste when they get married, it's odd. Anyway, I've lost so much weight. My mother cries. Sammy, the bride, tells me that she's decided that I should be her maid of honor. You know, I look sick, but good. Thinner than I've ever been in my life. I have to wheel myself down the aisle at the wedding. It's a bit of a spectacle, I can feel my wig shift slightly on my head and I know the others see it. And I know they pity me. I know it. I know that they see me rolling ahead of this wedding-cake-beautiful bride and I know they think, "Poor, poor Maris." They have sympathy for me, genuine heartfelt sympathy. You may think that makes me a horrible person, but they want to feel for me. It gives them something. It really does.

JOSEPH: One of the doctors asked me to go over to the cardiology department to return an EKG machine that we had borrowed when one of ours was on the fritz. So, I wheel the machine there. And on my way, I pass the hospital chapel. So, I park the machine outside and go in. I notice that there is a font filled with holy water. I get a Dixie cup and fill the cup with holy water. When I return to Joe, I sprinkle a few drops on his forehead. I baptize him. And when the water hits Joe's forehead, he wiggles, just a little bit, but the movement is like a sign. It's grace. It's impossible to describe.

MARIS: My thoughts are weird, morbid. Like at one point, I thought, "Drink a bunch of grain alcohol." You know, not to get drunk but to kind of embalm myself. So, that when I die my body will be sort of preserved. I know it's a stupid thought.

JOSEPH: My anemia. It's made me weak. The doctors keep pumping me full of iron and then they can't understand when it doesn't do any good.

MARIS: You can't be thinking: "Quit now. You're crazy." You know what I have to do. If I didn't, you would hate me.

JOSEPH: They test me for leukemia. I'm clean. After a while, the anemia goes away. But I'm diagnosed with a clotting disorder. There are these little nodules just under the surface of the skin. They don't know what's causing them. They try a blood thinner, but the nodules keep popping up. There's no explanation for it. I'm a medical anomaly.

MARIS: I won't let me down.

JOSEPH: I whisper, "There is no end." And maybe you think I'm being dramatic, but I'm right. I'm just saying that the way things kind of just go on and on, it's impossible to know whether or not the you you were yesterday is who you are today. Or if you who you are today is who you are tomorrow. Everything you believe has to be true, even if for just a second. And you get to be whoever you say you are. Joe was my son. I am sick. It's all endless. There is no end to this.

MARIS: I throw up. I throw up all of the time.

JOSEPH: After twenty-seven days, Joe develops meningitis. The MRIs show that the swelling hadn't been stopped in time. A rupture. It was pretty likely that he'd be brain damaged. I swear to god I don't care. I could take care of him. I knew I could. No matter what. All of the complications had stunted his growth process, I could pretty much hold him with one hand. And he fit, fuck, he fit just right. Another MRI showed advanced hydrocephalus. And that fucking bitch, god damn her, Sonia, she had a DNR order. And so. On a Monday afternoon, it was fucking Memorial Day, he arrested. Do not resuscitate. That's what his mother, his not-mother, she was just the receptacle that he had come to the world in.

I was all he had. And I had to watch him.

He died. Joe died. She had left the hospital before he was even totally gone. That was it. She had wanted it to be over and it was.

MARIS: I know what I have to do.

JOSEPH: And I still can hold Joe, here. Like a white patch in my mouth. Like these nodules on my arm.

MARIS: I call my mother, I call all of my friends, I say, this is it. If you want to say goodbye, come now. My mother comes with my sister. It's barely a week after Sammy's wedding, she's on her honeymoon, but she cuts it short to come to New York.

JOSEPH: I get sick. I take Joe's place. I open myself up to be loved, just like I loved Joe.

MARIS: George moves out. My mother and sister move in. I tell them I have just weeks, maybe days. I stop eating. I tell them that I'll know when it's time for hospice. I tell them that I've made all of the arrangements. I show them the pamphlets and everything. My mom gives me a copy of Elizabeth Kübler-Ross's *On Death and Dying*. And friends do come. They hold vigil at my bedside.

JOSEPH: Maybe I take a hypodermic needle and inject cornstarch just under the surface of my skin, it creates these nodules. Doctors can't figure them out.

MARIS: I'd been stockpiling painkiller for months. I had gone to five or six gynecologists and complained about really serious menstrual cramps. And I said I had a history of endometriosis. They give you the painkillers to shut you up.

JOSEPH: Maybe I had been bleeding myself to make the symptoms of anemia. Maybe I had been ingesting small amounts of rat poison because I know that brodifacoum in d-CON II rat poison thins your blood. Maybe if you were my doctor or nurse you wouldn't be able to solve this mystery, not without the facts, just what the author is giving you.

MARIS: And then my mom begins to insist on hospice, wants to call a nurse, she wants to call my doctor, my sister is pushing me too. So I know it's time.

JOSEPH: I know that at some point, at some fucking point, if you are a doctor or nurse who is like me. You will start taking care of me out of professional obligation, but then—

MARIS: The day I decide to do it, it's a few days before Memorial Day and I got an email from the cancer guy's parents. He's died. Dead. He's dead.

JOSEPH: I look in the mirror all of the time now. It's a disaster. I'm so sick of myself, I'm sick. It isn't about pity. It isn't. I never pitied little Joe. I didn't. When I call home and talk to my mom, she asks me if I'm taking care of myself.

MARIS: My cabinet is filled with prescription drugs. I know that it is all coming to something, even if the something is the end. There are no false expectations. I'm dying and it erases any record of where I've been. History is meaningless. The future is gone. I understand something pure. Dying is as pure as it gets.

JOSEPH: Take my coat. Take my mittens. Take care. My scarf.

(She does.)

MARIS: They all gather in my apartment. While they're in the kitchen making tea, I take the painkillers. I count out fifteen of each, I make sure to swallow them with just enough water to cushion them, but not so much as to make myself throw up. It's late at night, so when they come in and see me sleeping, they won't bother me. I'll be dead by morning. All these lies washed away. Perfection.

JOSEPH: I have this newfound clarity, shit, it's so clear I can practically see through myself. I know exactly what's happening to me, because I make it happen. It's religious. I want to be like the babies who go home. I want to be a miracle.

MARIS: It's so simple. You know. I'm dying and suddenly all of the things that were killing me disappear. I'm dying and it gives me purpose. Grace.

JOSEPH: Take my boots.

MARIS: Won't you be cold?

JOSEPH: Here? In the desert? I don't think so.

MARIS: (Smiling.) No?

JOSEPH: Go ahead.

MARIS: You want me to take your boots?

JOSEPH: Yes.

MARIS: I'll take them. I'm cold.

(She sits down and puts on his boots. She'll end up in her bikini, his muffler, mittens, and boots. He'll be barefoot.)

MARIS: I am having this dream, I haven't totally passed out or fallen asleep yet.

I'm having this half-conscious dream. In the dream, I find someone who is just like me and we love each other despite our faults. And we don't have to be sick. But you can never find anyone to take care of you the way you want to be taken care of. That's impossible.

JOSEPH: In my professional opinion: you're really dying.

(JOSEPH looks at MARIS.)

MARIS: I think it's snowing.

JOSEPH: In the desert?

MARIS: Here. I believe it's snowing here.

JOSEPH: I want to be a miracle.

MARIS: Okay.

JOSEPH: Next week I'm scheduled for a nasal cauterization. To stop what they think is causing these uncontrollable nosebleeds.

MARIS: I die. I'm perfect.

(Snow falls. They sing.)

(Blackout.)

(End play.)

THE STRAY DOG

Kristen Palmer

KRISTEN PALMER is a member of the 2010-12 Women's Project Theatre Lab and a 2010-11 Dramatists Guild Fellow. She received the 2008-09 Jerome Fellowship at the Playwrights' Center. Her plays include *The Melting Point*, *Local Story*, *The Heart in Your Chest*, *Departures*, and *Gloucester Point*. They have been produced and/or developed with New Georges, Blue Coyote, The Playwrights' Center, P73, Soho Rep, Circle X, The Orlando Shakespeare Festival, and others. She is an associate artist of New Georges, a Soho Rep Writer/Director Lab Alumni, associate playwright of P73 Productions, and a former company member of Printer's Devil Theatre in Seattle. She is a graduate of Bretton Hall College in Yorkshire, England, and NYU's Gallatin School (MA) where she focused on Writing and Drama-in-Education.

VISIBLE SOUL INTERVIEW WITH KRISTEN PALMER
Conducted by Zack Calhoon, January 21, 2011

How did you get started in theater? What made you start writing plays?

There were mysterious teenagers up the street, the rumor was they were drama freaks—no one you wanted to mess with. I totally wanted to mess with them. This led to community theater and then doing plays in high school. My teacher was big on '30s comedies and Shakespeare, typically two Shakespeare plays a year. He also got us out of class a lot and took us to see theater and movies in the big city of Washington, D.C.

Writing plays came a lot later for me. I was a member of a theater company in Seattle, Printer's Devil Theater. We produced new work. After a few years of secretly writing in my notebooks I started to share some bits and pieces and worked on my first play as a part of our New Play Bonanza (twelve plays in twelve weeks—a glorious three months of the year). In 2002 I moved to NYC and it was here that I really found my footing, learning loads in Pataphysics workshops at the Flea—these are master classes with fantastic playwrights and finding multiple fantastic communities of artists here—New Georges, Blue Coyote Theater Group, Flux Theatre Ensemble, Women's Project, and Soho Rep—to name a few. Writing plays fits both sides of my working head—the solitary writing time and the collaborative process of making theater.

Tell me about your play, *The Stray Dog*. What has the process like? How do you think the play is going?

The Stray Dog comes out of my long-time obsession with the great Russian poet Anna Akhmatova. Thinking about writing a site-specific play for the back room at Jimmy's led me to thinking about the Stray Dog cabaret where she and other artists of the time gathered to share work and drink and be together. This led to thinking about why we make theater, what we sacrifice to do it, the thin magic that is a theatrical event and what happens when the belief goes out the door.

Having a deadline, a space, actors and a production to work for lit a fire under the writing. I think I wrote the first draft in August and have done four rewrites since then. I think it's going awesome. We have an amazing cast, I get to work with a fantastic director in Julie Kline, and Rising Phoenix rocks hard.

What's it like being married to another playwright? How do you feel you compliment and influence each other as writers?

It's great being married to Adam (Szymkowicz). Sometimes it's hard to be married to a playwright. Talking shop starts to take over at times. It's a pursuit with lots of rejection and frustration, so we have to be vigilant and not let it drag us down. It probably helps that we both have to deal with that, so we're adept at cheer-leading, redirecting, and sometimes just saying—"GO DO YOUR WORK!" Which is sometimes all you need to do to shift your outlook on the world.

What kind writing inspires you?

Writing that connects my reading brain, my imagination and my experience to something beyond my self. Writing that broadens my experience of living and the potential of existence. I read a lot of fiction and poetry, listen to a lot of music and read a lot of plays. The more I read, the more excited I am to find work that makes the synapses fire, that draws me in and does that thing where when you shut the book or leave the theater or turn up the volume everything seems to shimmer for a while.

Who or what has been the biggest influence on your work as a playwright thus far?

Everyone and everything I've loved for any amount of time are my biggest influences.

The Stray Dog, directed by Julie Kline, premiered on January 23, 2011, at the Seventh Street Small Stage at Jimmy's No. 43.

CAST LIST

Jasper...Chad Goodridge
Elsie...Jelena Stupljanin
Martin...Haynes Thigpen
Girl...Laura Ramadei
Initiate 1...Brian Miskell
Initiate 2...Stephen Brown

CHARACTERS

JASPER (male, 20-40s)
ELSIE (female, 30-40s)
MARTIN (male, 30-40s)
GIRL (female, 20s)
INITIATE 1
INITIATE 2

SETTING

A small space, not a theater. Where the audience has to pack in and probably sit on the floor. There should be a door to the outside and a second, possibly a third entrance/exit. The action takes place in and around the audience.

A central altar, with candles. A framed picture of Anna Akhmatova. A photo of The Stray Dog from 1912 in St. Petersburg. A bowl of water. Radishes. A book of poems.

Other smaller altars can be located around the space dedicated to other poets of the era—Marina Tsvetaeva, Velimir Khlebnikov, Osip Mandelstam, are some ideas.

TIME

This moment.

POEMS

In the production, recitations of poems by Anna Akhmatova, Velimir Khlebnikov, Osip Mandelstam, and Marina Tsvetaeva were incorporated into the event. Each poem was followed by speaking the poet's name and the date the poem was written. Due to copyright restrictions, these are not included in the printed edition.

In the spirit of the poetry cult, readers and potential producers of this play should accompany their reading with their own engagement with the poetry of the time. Start with *The Stray Dog Cabaret: A Book of Russian Poems* translated by Paul Schmidt, and insert your own choices for the recitations. Further inquiries, or requests for more specific suggestions, can be directed to the playwright.

The AUDIENCE arriving.

JASPER, a young man, extraordinarily tall and boisterous, greets people as they enter. Gets them situated. Suggests that they could put their coats behind their seats. That they may want to get a drink at the bar. That they may want to order food. He is casual and delightful. There are two others (1 and 2), possibly more, in long cloaks who are seating and ushering folks more ceremoniously. Purifying them with smoke. They are bestowing each audience member with a hat made of folded newspaper.

JASPER: Welcome! Sit! Sit! Grab a seat.

Please. No recording devices—a one time only event. Imagine that—no replication.

No—don't worry—you won't be compromised. 'Specially if there's no record. Hah!

Turn off your sound and light boxes. Especially if they have GPS. Make sure that is shut down.

Here—there's enough room for everyone. Move in.

Don't be shy—we're packing you in like sardines tonight. The only fish you should be eating anymore. That and anchovies really. There—hang from the rafters if there's no room left because—tonight—

We are so glad you are here. So glad.

We are summoning a moment...We are escaping our times...We are honoring those gone...

(The INITIATES proceed to string fairy lights, light candles. Burn incense. Dip their fingers in ash and draw baroque landscapes on the walls. Sing a folk song. Does one play an instrument? Pluck a guitar? Something like this. Create some magic.)

JASPER: To begin, years before this year. On a night—cold. A hundred years before. On this night The Stray Dog opened in St. Petersburg.

Imagine. St. Petersburg. Before the wars. Before Stalin. Before the collapse. A moment between the old and the new and there was such faith in the new. Such a dream for a new world built on the hopes of each beating heart—the end of the Czar, the end of oppressive hierarchies—they could taste it—with vodka on their tongues and fingers wrapped in cloth against the frozen St. Petersburg night—

I am guessing. I was never there. But tonight—we are gathered to raise the memory. Tonight, shoved between a new old and a new new, we'll make a space for the time in between. The time where anything could happen.

Raise what you're drinking—here—take your eyes and roll them back in your head—your hand—place it on your heart. Feel it beat. Don your paper hats. You received them when you entered? Yes? Good.

Now. Whisper your most treasured line of poetry, the one you committed to heart and swallow it. Now. Wash it down with drink. Now grasp the hand of your neighbor—now Breathe. Just breathe for a moment.

(JASPER recites a poem. "All I Want to Do Is Escape the Madness Here..." by Osip Mandelstam is suggested. ELSIE enters. She is grand.)

ELSIE: Thank you Jasper. That was lovely. A beginning. Sometimes that is all you have. A beginning. It is nothing to sneeze at.

JASPER: Thank you.

ELSIE: Of course. Now, let us begin.

Our patron poet, Anna Akhmatova, spent many nights at the Stray Dog Café, reciting the poems that would create her legacy as one of the most beloved poets of Russia and later of any who dare endure in the folly and the imperative that is art.

JASPER: For that we thank her.

1: For that we are grateful.

2: For that we continue.

ELSIE: We continue as she did.

Anna put the words down. Anna committed them to memory. Anna whispered them to her friend's open ear and they migrated out of Russia. They oozed onto the printed page—they became part of the world—while Anna—faded. Aged. Declined. Departed. As we all Age. Decline. Depart...

(ELSIE surveys AUDIENCE. Gazes for a moment into everyone's eyes. Pause.)

ELSIE: *(To JASPER.)* He's not here.

JASPER: Not yet.

ELSIE: You promised me.

JASPER: I said I'd try. Elsie—we are all here.

ELSIE: NO. What's the point—what's the point? *(To AUDIENCE.)* I'm sorry. I'm sure you're all lovely. Obviously you are all lovely—just—just—you know what it's like when you imagine performing for a particular heart, or maybe—cooking for a particular mouth, doing for the one who matters the way that only one can matter and—ach—they are not there?

1: I know about that.

2: Shhh.

ELSIE: Without him—it's just—Going through the motions.

JASPER: Elsie, I did try. He—he didn't have it in him. Barely registered the invitation.

ELSIE: His eyes were glazed.

JASPER: Like a donut.

ELSIE: Then it's hopeless.

1: We could try the candle thing.

JASPER: The what?

1: The candle thing?

ELSIE: You didn't do it?

JASPER: We swallowed our poems.

ELSIE: Not enough. Do it. Do the candle thing.

JASPER: Fine. The candle. It may not make a difference.

ELSIE: Perhaps, but the maybe—the maybe is why we drag ourselves out of bed on these dark cold mornings, is it not?

(A paper, a pen, a bowl of water are brought by 1 and 2. ELSIE proceeds to quickly copy a poem from a book.)

ELSIE: *(Whispered.)*

"As the future ripens in the past,
So the past rots in the future—
A terrible festival of dead leaves."

(ELSIE whispers the lines to JASPER who solemnly whispers them to a member of the audience, who should be encouraged to whisper them to their neighbor. 1 and 2 whisper it to different groups/rows as well. ELSIE takes the paper and burns it in the flame.)

ELSIE: Now. A moment for those we have lost. Those we always hope will return—eyes bright and hearts shining.

(A pause. MARTIN enters from outside. 1 and 2 subtly make their way to block the door.)

MARTIN: Oh—sorry. Excuse me—

ELSIE: *(To AUDIENCE.)* Wonderful. Oh—you are all wonderful. Thank you.

MARTIN: Oh—I'm sorry, I didn't meant to—

ELSIE: It's fine. You're exactly where you're supposed to be.

MARTIN: No—I'm sorry. I was cold? The light was on? I—I think I was lost?

ELSIE: Of course. Beckoned here. Something pulling. Ah—I'm so glad you're here.

(She takes his hands in hers to warm them. He lets her for a moment, and then pulls them away.)

MARTIN: Do I know you?

ELSIE: You do.

MARTIN: I don't remember—this seems unfamiliar. *(Takes an inhaler from his pocket and breathes through it.)*

ELSIE: Take a breath. Remember Better. You must—you must remember—

JASPER: Leave him be. Let him settle in—take your time.

ELSIE: No! I'm tired of my friends disappearing. Their brains squashed. Their hearts wrapped in cellophane.

JASPER: Oh come on.

ELSIE: What? You think it's not true? Fool you.

MARTIN: I—I think I ought to be going.

(1 and 2 block his path. ELSIE slaps him.)

MARTIN: Ouch! What the hell?! Get out of my way!

ELSIE: Tell me something.

MARTIN: No. I'm sorry—I didn't mean to come here—this—this is clearly an aberration. I am used to doing the most simple things. Really. I'm sorry I interrupted your service—your whatever this is.

(MARTIN scrambles to leave. 1 and 2 grab him.)

ELSIE: STOP!

JASPER: Let him go.

(1 and 2 look to ELSIE for direction. She indicates that they should retain their grasp on him.)

ELSIE: Martin!

MARTIN: How do you know my name?

ELSIE: I know much more than your name.

MARTIN: I've never met you.

ELSIE: Fine. But you're here and I'm so glad. Stay, just stay

MARTIN: *(Overlapping.)* I can't—I have—I was running an errand—

ELSIE: And then?

MARTIN: I saw the light on—

(ELSIE indicates they should loosen their grip, as MARTIN stops fighting…)

ELSIE: And you came down the crumbling stone stairs—

MARTIN: I heard a voice—I heard—something, it echoed off my head—

ELSIE: Good. Sit with me.

(MARTIN does. Tentatively.)

ELSIE: Continue, please. The History.

(ELSIE attempts to attend to the service—but is fixed on MARTIN.)

JASPER: The History.

(The History is presented with photographs of the people and historical time.)

1: In 1911 Anna was young. Newly married. Still awkward on the stage.

2: Her husband overshadowed her, but not for long. Soon she would be known as the greater talent.

1: And he would go to Africa. To Afghanistan. To any place to escape her.

2: Or for adventure. Because he was a poet. Before the poets got pasty. And he wanted to impress her.

1: By leaving her alone.

2: By wandering the unknown.

1: Places she could not go

2: To prison. To the firing squad. Leaving a black mark on her and her son.

1: Making them fair game for the police.

2: Leaving them haunted.

ELSIE: *(Leans over to MARTIN.)* This place is nicer now. See? There are no longer rats in the kitchen. There are no longer cockroaches— you remember the cockroaches?

MARTIN: I—don't. I've never lived somewhere there were cockroaches.

JASPER: Shhhh.

ELSIE: Let me just talk to him. Can't I just have a conversation?

JASPER: We're in the middle of—

ELSIE: I know that. You think I don't know that?

Here—everyone. Here.

Another history, not as grand. Two decades ago. We were so young. He was sleeping—in the corner on a pile of curtains he'd folded up and called a futon. He woke up with a tickle in his nose? A tickle that got worse and worse, he rubbed it and rubbed it. In the morning, when he blew his nose, a cockroach fell out.

MARTIN: That never happened.

ELSIE: Oh, you were so worried. For days—you imagined you'd be out with friends, or speaking to a crowd and a swarm of baby cockroaches would emerge from your nose. Hatched and free after their nasal incubation.

MARTIN: That sounds horrible.

ELSIE: Many things are horrible.

JASPER: *(Trying to get things back on track.)* We come here to remember. To recall. That as horrible as things are, there are those who continue as Anna continued—

ELSIE: There was the year we didn't turn anyone away. The time when we had to say yes as a spiritual practice. You were so good at that.

MARTIN: Being agreeable?

ELSIE: Not simply agreeable, All-Accepting. There were challenges though. We took in so many, some were inevitably disappointments. I put a stop to it when those kids with the piercings and the tattoos arrived.

MARTIN: Body Art.

ELSIE: Whatever. That's another rule that we did finally agree on. None of that flesh desecration. Holes and ink and what not. We're fine the way we are. We are beautiful the way we are.

MARTIN: I have a tattoo.

ELSIE: No.

MARTIN: I do.

ELSIE: Who told you to do that?

MARTIN: Nobody. It's something I wanted.

ELSIE: No. No. Someone encroached on you—someone must have come in the night and whispered the idea for it in your ear.

2: Some cockroach.

1: Something creepy.

ELSIE: That is why you mustn't sleep alone. That is why you must always make sure you are covered. We are covered.

(The others express variations of religious experience—sign of the cross, kneeling, an "Ommm.")

MARTIN: Well. It was something I wanted. I'm sure of it.

ELSIE: They haven't sucked out your brain have they?

MARTIN: Who?

ELSIE: Oh, Martin. You were—oh—it's terrible. I pleaded for leniency—for some other intervention but they—they are merciless. They took all your—Memories. You don't even recall this—

(She touches him—wonderfully.)

MARTIN: But I—do—that's vaguely—

ELSIE: Yes?

MARTIN: Familiar.

ELSIE: It should be. I should be. But far more than vaguely.

MARTIN: Your name is Elsie.

ELSIE: Yes.

MARTIN: You have been the leader of this cult for years.

ELSIE: Hah! They tell you these things.

MARTIN: They don't tell me anything—

ELSIE: You believe everything don't you? You always did. Here. We've prepared an event, a public re-calling—perhaps we'll figure out a wedding? Some gentle consummation—

Jasper. Sometimes life is just magic, isn't it?

(MARTIN is hustled to a central spot, standing and visible to the audience.)

MARTIN: I'd feel more comfortable where I was before

ELSIE: (Overlapping.) Trust me. Jasper? You may start.

(JASPER gives MARTIN a shot of vodka.)

JASPER: (To MARTIN.) Take a drink. Do it! Now. Wait. Take another! Do it!

(JASPER provides MARTIN with another shot. Everyone stares at MARTIN. MARTIN grows increasingly uncomfortable. Pause.)

MARTIN: (Whispered to 2.) What do I do?

2: Here—read this—

(2 hands him a poem.)

MARTIN: Where the winking wax-wings whistle

JASPER: Louder.

MARTIN: Where the winking wax-wings whistle
in the shadows of the cedars,

JASPER: Clearer.

(MARTIN recites a poem. "Where the Winking Wax-Wings Whistle…" by Velimir Khlebnikov is suggested.)

ELSIE: Beautiful.

1: Thank you. Really that was very good.

(Applause, AUDIENCE is encouraged to applaud as well.)

MARTIN: Thank you—but—I didn't practice.

JASPER: You did fine. Really. We couldn't have asked for better.

2: Well, we could have.

ELSIE: Stop it. You all, he was lovely. Lovely. Thank you Martin.

MARTIN: Oh—well. You're welcome. I've um, never done that before—or did I?

ELSIE: Ahh—you did. You used to. Listen to poems by the light of a candle—your little red oil lamp.

JASPER: Should we go on?

ELSIE (To MARTIN.) Here. Have you noticed the back room?

JASPER: Elsie? The next section—we're not finished.

MARTIN: The back room?

ELSIE: Where you and I used to—remember? I have tried to keep it—somewhat familiar. Come.

(ELSIE leads MARTIN towards the back room.)

MARTIN: Oh—

JASPER: There are all these people—Elsie?

ELSIE: You see—the moldings? The wood floor. There's a texture to the parquet that

MARTIN: (Overlapping.) It's lovely. What—what should I remember?

ELSIE: Hmm. Up to you isn't it?

(A door shuts.)

JASPER: Shit. I'm sorry. Everyone. Please. Forgive our discombobulation.

1: They may be in there for a while.

JASPER: Drinks? Who needs drinks?

1: Everyone's glass is filled.

JASPER: Well—

2: I could read a poem.

1: Don't.

2: It's my own.

JASPER: New?

2: Yes.

JASPER: Go ahead.

2: Above the clouds, the ozone keeping
   the oxygen in.
Keeping us connected to the earth
And what if there was no gravity?
What if we stopped believing?
What if we stopped believing?
And were released from the ground—
Left to float un-tethered into space.
Above the clouds, the ozone keeping
   the oxygen in.

1: That's terrible.

2: You're terrible.

JASPER: It's not bad. Really. The repeti-
tion and the sentiment—it's not bad.

1: Quiet.

2: What?

1: Listen.

*(Sounds of lovemaking. Distant music.
A charming laugh.)*

2: That sounds nice. That sounds like
progress. She must be so happy.

JASPER: Good for her.

1: Suck. Why does he get to waltz in
here and get all the attention?

JASPER: Quiet.

1: What if he stays?

JASPER: Then he stays. He'll probably
leave though.

2: She'll be sad.

1: She's always sad these days.

2: I wish she wasn't.

JASPER: And I wish for environmental
restoration and world peace.

(2 sighs.)

JASPER: C'mon. There are preparations.

1: There are always preparations. I'm
sick of it. And nothing changes. Not
for years.

2: Maybe we do need him— She seems
to.

1: That guy? Seriously? I'm better than
that guy.

2: Dream on. Fortification?

JASPER: Indeed.

1: I can't stand it.

2: Deal.

(2 pours three vodka shots.)

1: A toast?

2: Make it good.

JASPER: Let me. *(To AUDIENCE.)* Raise
whatever you have.

Over time, you realize, this will fade
away into the forgetfulness of man. The
crisis will overtake us or not. Some will
live. Some won't. In either case there
are losses. But there are always losses.

1: Hear, hear.

*(They drink and exit. The lights go
down on the audience. Time passes.
MARTIN reenters. Disheveled. The door
opens from the outside and a young
woman enters with the cold and the
snow. Ideally there will be snow. The
young woman is bundled up in coats.
Gasping for air.)*

MARTIN: Oh dear—are you okay?

GIRL: *(Horrible gasp.)*

MARTIN: Are you asthmatic? An inhaler? Do you have an inhaler?

(GIRL nods—yes she is asthmatic—no she does not have an inhaler. MARTIN finds his in a pocket.)

MARTIN: Here. Use mine.

GIRL: *(Takes a long breath on it.)* Thank you.

MARTIN: You should rest. Water? Do you need water?

GIRL: Do you have something stronger? *(Looks around. Spies a bottle.)*

MARTIN: Vodka?

(She nods. MARTIN locates a glass. Pours her drink. Is distracted by her…)

GIRL: *(Drinks.)* Thanks. *(Takes another hit from the inhaler. Another drink.)* The air is horrible today. In the winter it's often better but they've started burning paper, coal, wood—wet wood—the smoke is terrible. It's just hanging out there, a layer under the clouds—if there even are clouds. It may just be the smoke.

MARTIN: It was snowing earlier.

GIRL: That was just ash.

MARTIN: Oh.

GIRL: *(Takes another hit from inhaler.)* My glass seems to be empty.

MARTIN: Oh, sorry. Here.

GIRL: Thank you. If there's nothing you can do—at least you can drink. Cheers. *(She downs it.)*

MARTIN: I'm sorry—but—um—do you know where you are?

GIRL: I always know where I am. Aren't you going to offer me something to eat?

MARTIN: Like what?

GIRL: Pomegranate. I am partial to pomegranate.

(An unseen hand tosses a pomegranate to MARTIN.)

MARTIN: Oh—Uh—here?

GIRL: Perfect. *(Grabs it and bites into it, red juice spilling down her arms and face. She devours it as if she is devouring a heart.)* I know you. You are that man with the hangdog face. Surprised you're back. After what they did to you.

MARTIN: I'm sure nobody did anything to me.

GIRL: Oh. It's like that. Okay then.

MARTIN: Like what?

GIRL: They did it quiet. That's good—less disruptive. You don't even know there's a difference. You enjoy things now don't you? The shows? Going to work? Things are just nice?

MARTIN: What? Well—yes—

GIRL: Good. Well. Not good. Clearly it didn't take. I mean here you are.

MARTIN: I didn't mean to come.

GIRL: Oh. Of course. Okay. Whatever you say guy. You want some of this?

(GIRL approaches him with the pomegranate.)

MARTIN: I don't really care for—

GIRL: Just a few seeds.

MARTIN: Really. I don't like the way it dries my mouth out—

GIRL: Oh this one won't. It's juicy. See? *(Juice is running down her face.)*

(GIRL shifts gears. She slowly, erotically feeds Martin, seed by seed. ELSIE has reentered. She watches closely. Like a leopard.)

GIRL: There you see

ELSIE: Perfect.

GIRL: There's no going back now

ELSIE: Each by each

GIRL: Something about the kernel.

ELSIE: I think it's the red.

GIRL: The jewel-like pop in your mouth.

ELSIE: The dissection required to access each—

MARTIN: What—

GIRL: He's awfully kind.

ELSIE: Everybody is

GIRL: It seems a shame to deprive them

MARTIN: Deprive them of what?

ELSIE: They don't appreciate what they have.

GIRL: Oh—they do—they just get so sad sometimes, they forget.

ELSIE: Bah! Jasper? Jasper!

(JASPER enters with the INITIATES.)

MARTIN: Wait a minute.

ELSIE: Darling. There is no waiting. There is only now and what we can do now. You arrived. You ate. You drank. You made love. Now you can stay. You can stay with us. You'll like it, don't worry. Get going Jasper. Girl! The flowers!

(GIRL procures a basket of flowers, pulls off the petals and strews them.)

JASPER: Are you sure?

ELSIE: Do it!

JASPER: Fine.

As with all things there are beginnings and there are endings. As we fall into our own endings we are seeking here a new beginning. Elsie, when you look into the eyes of Martin, do you see the beginning that you seek?

ELSIE: I do.

JASPER: Martin when you look into the eyes of Elsie, do you see the beginning that you seek?

MARTIN: I wasn't seeking a beginning.

ELSIE: Look at me.

MARTIN: I wasn't looking for anything.

1: What'd I tell you?

2: Shh.

ELSIE: Look!

MARTIN: I'm—I'm sorry—I don't see anything—I just—Look, I need to get home.

ELSIE: No. Home? There's no such thing.

MARTIN: I don't think that's true—is that true?

GIRL: Um. Whatever she says goes. That's just the way it is down here.

ELSIE: If you'd just look—you'd see—

MARTIN: I—really ought to be heading out.

GIRL: It's unpleasant out there.

MARTIN: Thank you for—everything— you all have been—you've been more than kind and I look forward to—to seeing you again—um. But I—I think I left a pot on the stove. The iron on. A baby in the bath water. (Exits.)

ELSIE: Noooooo!

1: Shit.

JASPER: Not this again

2: Get the vodka.

GIRL: Elsie?

ELSIE: What?

GIRL: You okay?

ELSIE: That word means nothing. Okay. Okay. Stupidest word in the fucking language.

GIRL: Can I get you something?

ELSIE: Jasper! Can you try?

JASPER: Not again. No.

ELSIE: Please. Please—he was so close—

JASPER: Fine. I'll go—you two—do the thing in the place.

1 and 2: Yes. Done.

(JASPER, 1, and 2 kiss ELSIE as they go. ELSIE collects herself at the altar. Draws a circle in chalk on the floor. ELSIE recites a poem quietly. "I ask you to pray for my poor, my perplexed/For my living soul..." by Anna Akhmatova is suggested.)

GIRL: Elsie?

ELSIE: Not now.

GIRL: Would you—

ELSIE: What?

GIRL: I just thought maybe—instead of this—

ELSIE: Agh—out with it.

GIRL: I just—well. I wondered if you would—if you wouldn't rather like to go out on a date with me?

ELSIE: Oh. Dear.

GIRL: I thought—maybe—since Martin's gone and really—he's pasty, he's—dim? I mean, what can you care about him? Maybe we—we could go out. I do know some places. I could show you a good time. I just think—you, you should have a good time.

ELSIE: Sweetie. I don't leave. Sorry, but I haven't left—you know—for years. It's, it's just not something I would do.

GIRL: I just thought. Maybe you'd like to get some ice cream. I've noticed you don't have a freezer here and maybe it's something that you like—or that you liked?

ELSIE: Hmm, I did. I do—you could bring me some?

GIRL: Sure. I could. What flavor?

ELSIE: Peanut brickle.

GIRL: Okay. You sure you wouldn't like to come with me? Just to see—

ELSIE: No. It's not what I do. And he'll be back any minute. I can feel it. Imagine—to be lonesome no more. To always have the desired audience of the mind, here. In the flesh. With that I think I could go anywhere.

GIRL: You'd go?

ELSIE: Maybe—If I needed to—or if I had to.

GIRL: But how would I find you?

ELSIE: Sweetheart, you'll always be able to find me, or someone—or—something—you'll be sitting on a dock one day, pitching rocks into the river maybe? Watching the oil sheen make trippy rainbows across the once-clear waters, and a convoy will rumble past—they'll ignore you. And you'll giggle—maybe it surprises you—but the thing is you know what they don't, and you've just stumbled across something in your own dear head that they can't see. You'll find some place, don't worry. You'll find me there, me or not me, but someone.

GIRL: That's not what I want.

ELSIE: Many things are not up to you. Stick a radish in your lapel and move on.

GIRL: I want you.

ELSIE: Come here.

(GIRL goes to her. ELSIE kisses her head.)

ELSIE: Now stop. You deal with what you have. Okay?

GIRL: Okay.

ELSIE: You have a lot.

GIRL: I don't.

ELSIE: You do and you better figure out what it is or you're not going to be okay. Not at all. There are things you can only learn from being alone and listening to yourself—

GIRL: I'm not good at that.

ELSIE: Practice.

GIRL: It's hard. It hurts.

ELSIE: Hah! Of course it does dearest.

GIRL: Is it worth it?

ELSIE: Worth? There is no worth. It's just necessary.

GIRL: Should I stay?

ELSIE: No—go on. Get the ice cream. But when you come back—could you? Would you—wear something special? A dress? Something that he would like—I have a notion...

GIRL: What?

ELSIE: Here—wait a moment.

(ELSIE disappears to procure a dress. GIRL waits patiently looking off after her.)

GIRL: There are the people who never notice. But the love that you give them is the thing that they are living off of. There are people who never absorb it. But the care that you float their direction is what they are nourished by. There are people

(ELSIE returns with a party dress and heels.)

ELSIE: *(Overlapping.)* Here it is—could you? I think you'd look charming in this—not now. You'd be too cold out there. But, when you get back. Put it on. Something to occupy his eye while I do what I need to do. Yes?

GIRL: Okay. I will.

(GIRL takes the dress, kisses ELSIE on the cheek, and exits out into the cold. ELSIE considers the space.)

ELSIE: You won't believe it now but there used to be such parties here. Things weren't so expensive. People would just bring a bottle, leave a bottle—bring food from the Chinese restaurant down the street—maybe a casserole. Sure there were people who never brought anything—but nobody minded. They would at least be good company. Now—well. So many things are over. Ice cream will be a treat. I wonder where that girl gets her money?

Jasper? Jasper? Are you there? Is he with you? Did you find him.

(JASPER enters. Stomping the snow off his boots.)

JASPER: I—yes. I found him. He's not interested.

ELSIE: He will be. We simply need to remain dedicated. Maintain our current practices.

Do you remember that year we only ate carrots?

JASPER: That didn't happen.

ELSIE: The time I etched messages in restaurant windows all over town, for my love—whoever they may be?

JASPER: Elsie.

ELSIE: Or the year we spent throwing our hearts out, telling each other everything, until the place was a sodden mess of blood and tears.

JASPER: That I remember.

ELSIE: The era of secret loves—sneaking off for kisses while wearing a straight face and the sober grin of the chaste.

JASPER: Yes.

ELSIE: What of it? Now I mean. What of it now? You remember when I didn't speak for a year? When I moved as little as possible, eating only rice and seaweed?

JASPER: I worried about you then.

ELSIE: You got me such wonderful seaweed—how did you ever manage it?

JASPER: Commitment. We were in the midst of a transition.

ELSIE: Where has everyone gone?

JASPER: The girl left to get you ice cream—the initiates are—studying. Preparing their performance. But we— we're waiting.

ELSIE: Oh Good. The shawl!

JASPER: Are you sure?

You will call her?

ELSIE: All we can do is maintain our practices. Harbor wishes. And do what we can.

JASPER: Excellent. *(Exits to retrieve the shawl.)*

(ELSIE stands in the charcoal circle to take in the spirit of ANNA.)

ELSIE: In Anna Akhmatova's life—each story, each legend, the starving—sharing a boiled carrot, giving all her food to the sick child next door, the TB, the heartsickness—in bed for weeks. The cold and controlling lovers, dependent always. The husband executed, the son in prison, her poems forbidden—all the horrors of the siege of St. Petersburg, of Stalin, of the victim of a police state, and still you wrote, throughout it all, you wrote. Anna. Thank you.

(JASPER returns with the INITIATES. They settle her shawl around her shoulders and step carefully out of the circle. Melt into the audience as ELSIE takes in the spirit of ANNA, transforming into a second self. Partially

obscuring her face with the shawl. A pause for the Muse's voice... MARTIN enters.)

MARTIN: Elsie?

(No answer.)

MARTIN: Elsie, look. I'm sorry I left—

ELSIE: NO! Anna. Anna of all the Russias.

MARTIN: Oh—um. I was here earlier? I left abruptly, unfairly, I think—and there was a girl? She has my inhaler.

ELSIE: Ahhh—she stole your breath.

MARTIN: Oh no. It's for my asthma. You know about asthma?

ELSIE: No. I know about poetry. About the inconsolable nature of existence. About vacant cruelty and love. Too much about love.

MARTIN: Wait, what are you—

ELSIE: I lived a ridiculously long life. I tried to end it so many times, I—was always too strong to depart. Too vital. And still my spirit wanders. Some of us never do really end after all.

MARTIN: Maybe you're still looking for something?

ELSIE: Aw. That is a dear explanation. Spoken like a truly modern man. You must enjoy the whole vogue of psychoanalysis? Of pleasantly palatable explanations for the impossible souls we're born with?

MARTIN: I—I know it's helped me. That and the medication.

ELSIE: Hmmm. Hold on to what you can young man. Hold on to whatever you can. Your modern world is such a sad thing. But it's been brewing for so long. We saw it coming—the groundwork was laid on the blood of my contemporaries.

MARTIN: It's um, it's not that bad. Day to day—it can be very pleasant.

ELSIE: With drink and delusion all can be very pleasant. Even the hangover. I love a good hangover.

It is so good to be in a body! This one—your Elsie's? Not what I was—but, you know. Who could be? She's a bit short. I was five eleven—very tall. There's an unbelievable angle to my nose—Modigliani painted me. Tried to capture it—barely could. Who could really capture another? We keep so much hidden.

MARTIN: Not all of us.

ELSIE: This one does. Dreams of dying. She doesn't have the strength you know—when things collapse—she's not the one who's going to be standing. She can't weather things alone. So few can. No matter. This world will take all we give it. Gobble it up. Spit it back out. Do it again.

MARTIN: Wait—Elsie—Elsie—are you there?

(The lights go out. A single candle remains. ANNA/ELSIE wanes. 1 goes to help her. 2 takes the shawl, slowly recites a poem to comfort ELSIE. An excerpt from "A Poem Without a Hero" by Anna Akhmatova, which begins, "There is no death—everyone knows that," is suggested.)

(Lights return to normal. ELSIE has collapsed, is diminished. 1 and 2 are attending her, bringing vodka, a bit of bread, an apple. MARTIN stands, uncertain about what to do.)

MARTIN: Elsie?

(ELSIE sighs.)

MARTIN: Are you—okay?

ELSIE: Huh?

MARTIN: You're pale. You're—stressed. Your heart can't endure—

ELSIE: Oh. My heart can endure many things.

MARTIN: You were possessed.

ELSIE: Anna. She's brought you back.

MARTIN: No. I was looking for you, not her.

ELSIE: That would be nice.

MARTIN: I was.

ELSIE: Thank you.

MARTIN: I don't think you should do this, thing—whatever you're putting yourself through.

ELSIE: Maybe.

MARTIN: And—you shouldn't help her.

1: Shhh.

2: Quiet.

MARTIN: There are other ways to live—even now—especially now.

1: You can't breathe outside.

2: The sky is glowing red half the time

1: The other half it's black.

2: Thick with some kind of toxic smoke.

1: I don't think calm is what's demanded.

2: Panic's no good either.

1: So—we are vigilant.

2: Call attention to things.

1: Remain porous to experience.

2: To the dreams that flicker by.

MARTIN: Still—Elsie? I'm, I'm worried for you.

ELSIE: Oh, Martin, that's so sweet.

(GIRL enters with ice cream, wearing the dress ELSIE gave her. She has done up her hair and makeup with elaborate care. *She's wearing high heels that give her some trouble, but she's bravely trying.)*

ELSIE: Well, look at you.

GIRL: I found it—here, peanut brickle—it's not the best brand—but it's a very good brand—they didn't have much—just this scoop—I'm sorry. I didn't know everyone would still be here.

ELSIE: Don't worry—a spoon?

GIRL: Oh no, I didn't—I forgot. I can get one—I can—find one.

ELSIE: No no, it's not necessary. *(Takes a scoop of ice cream with her tongue. It is delicious. It revives her.)*

GIRL: Is it okay?

ELSIE: Divine. Thank you.

MARTIN: That dress—

GIRL: It's Elsie's.

ELSIE: Used to be. Yours now dear. It looks lovely on you.

MARTIN: Elsie—you're not, considering—somehow—harming yourself?

ELSIE: Would it disturb you if I was?

MARTIN: Of course it would.

ELSIE: I thought you didn't remember me.

MARTIN: Elsie. It would disturb me. Harm coming to you.

ELSIE: Well I've thought of it. But thinking is different.

GIRL: Less threatening.

ELSIE: Exactly. Like daydreaming—like here are all the possibilities—and this is one. It can seem like a relief—if it all gets too bad, like if I can no longer breathe outside—or if I am walking and there are no bird songs—no crickets at night. If the oceans rise and they're filled with stinging nettles.

GIRL: No fireflies blinking. No bees buzzing.

ELSIE: If there was only silence—

GIRL: You are lovely

ELSIE: Thank you. But that's not exactly what I meant to share—it's a different type of imagining that you have to worry for—when pictures start forming in your head. When you know if your oven is gas and you know how to seal off the kitchen. When you've done inventory on the knives in the house and you keep one sharp enough. When you hoard pills, the good kind, or have a map of accessible bridges and cliffs etched on your brain—so that the route, if necessary, becomes involuntary.

GIRL: When you test ropes

ELSIE: Sure.

GIRL: When you buy a gun.

ELSIE: That too.

MARTIN: I—I am worried.

ELSIE: Don't be. Dear, can you arrange for a reading?

GIRL: Of course.

(GIRL kisses her and exits.)

MARTIN: Before—when we were younger—we were in love.

ELSIE: As best we knew how.

MARTIN: And now?

ELSIE: Now there are other things we try for. Listen, here he is. He's been practicing so long for this.

(1 appears. 2 and JASPER accompany him. 1 recites a poem. Something by Marina Tsvetaeva is suggested.)

ELSIE: Thank you.

1: It's from the other translation.

ELSIE: It's fine.

1: Fine?

ELSIE: Exactly right.

1: Thank you.

ELSIE: You're welcome.

(1 and 2 exit. JASPER lingers, inconspicuous.)

MARTIN: Why do they keep doing that?

ELSIE: Just take it in. It's worth it.

MARTIN: When did it start?

ELSIE: The poems? After the period of silence. We tried to write our own, but—there's something necessary? Something to be gained, a DNA that needs replicating in these poems. So, we find them. We resurrect them.

MARTIN: Oh.

ELSIE: It's a small gift.

MARTIN: I had to leave.

ELSIE: You remember?

MARTIN: It was messy.

ELSIE: Hah! Yes. It was.

MARTIN: My stories make sense now.

ELSIE: Are you sure?

MARTIN: Yes. I found some other sort of life out there, a sustainable life.

ELSIE: But really. You don't know that—if it's sustainable. You're guessing. Really—there's no way to be sure.

MARTIN: You need to come out of here.

ELSIE: Why?

JASPER: Yes, why?

MARTIN: Because—because it's—it's—it's crumbling around you—this air can't be good.

JASPER: Better than out there.

MARTIN: But there's no point in this. It's not like you're—doing anything.

ELSIE: Is that all you see?

MARTIN: Nobody even knows you're here.

ELSIE: You do. That girl does.

JASPER: We do. People find us. We don't need to advertise.

ELSIE: Anyways. I don't want just anybody coming round. What fun would that be? We'd have to hire a manager or something.

JASPER: I do not want to be a manager.

ELSIE: Nobody does.

MARTIN: Um—I do. I mean. That's my job. I'm a manager. It's—helpful.

ELSIE: Oh. Well.

JASPER: Good for you.

ELSIE: Yes. Good for you. We'll just avoid having that sort of thing down here.

JASPER: Exactly.

ELSIE: And really, I don't want to be a part of that world. I don't want to "join in." There's so much you have to give up.

JASPER: And, honestly, we're not too hopeful about your chances up there.

ELSIE: You need to be careful about what you believe.

JASPER: I'm guessing that you have nightmares. That you're overcome. That there are mornings you can't get out of bed, that you imagine your legs no longer work—that they collapse under you. I imagine that you're overcome from time to time with a regret? A nostalgia? For something you can't quite remember—it's like the opposite of déjà vu.

MARTIN: I was wrong to come back. I won't bother you anymore. I'll forget this place ever existed.

ELSIE: As if you could. You tried—or—they tried—but, I'm sorry, you can't. Anymore than you can cut off your arm.

JASPER: People cut off their arm. If they have to save themselves.

ELSIE: That's horrible.

JASPER: It's true. This guy—trapped under a water heater—he did it. Another guy—in the desert, trapped under a rock. He did it. In matters of survival we are ruthless. And really—all he has to shed is a memory. What's that? People shed them all the time—they have to—and they'll keep doing it—no other way. Forgetting is the only way forward.

ELSIE: No.

JASPER: It would be merciful.

ELSIE: Hah! That's the last thing I want. Fine. Go—Go! Don't come back. Enjoy the life you made for yourself. Enjoy your Management. I can't imagine you there. That's fine. You can't imagine me anymore.

MARTIN: It's the best thing. (To JASPER.) You'll—um—look out for her?

ELSIE: Just go.

(MARTIN turns to go, tries the door.)

MARTIN: The door's locked.

ELSIE: Well isn't that strange.

MARTIN: Unlock it.

ELSIE: There's no key.

MARTIN: No key?

ELSIE: It's too bad. I guess you'll have to stay for the party after all. Jasper!

JASPER: Because the moon is full. Because the day is done. Because time

has done its thing and passed. Tonight—tonight we will celebrate. We will tip our glasses back in our throats—(Claps hands.) Drinks! Everyone. Drinks.

(1 and 2 enter with trays of vodka shots that they pass out to everyone. Lights back up on entire space.)

1 and 2: (Ad lib.) Here, here you are—don't drink yet—all at once. All at once. You're smelling it first? Smart cookie. You never know about clear liquids.

1: Martin—for you?

MARTIN: No. Not for me.

2: You're still here.

MARTIN: The door's locked.

1: It is?

2: Interesting.

1: The door's been locked on us for years.

2: You'll come to like it.

1: Or at least to find some joy.

2: It's not so different than your life before.

1: There's always some door isn't there?

2: Why not be happy?

1: Why not make something gorgeous.

2: You're beautiful.

1: So are you.

(1 and 2 toast and drink and kiss. The kiss slowly escalates.)

JASPER: A toast? Elsie—a toast?

(ELSIE recites a short poem, no more than four lines. "Marble crumbles, steel rots like a leaf…" by Anna Akhmatova is suggested.)

JASPER: Oh.

ELSIE: What?

JASPER: That's—beautiful.

ELSIE: It's Anna.

JASPER: Exquisite.

ELSIE: Why? Why exquisite?

JASPER: The—the sentiment—the ineffable something.

ELSIE: So what?

JASPER: So what? So—it is. It just—is.

ELSIE: What if it's not? What if he's right? What if it's nothing at all?

MARTIN: I didn't say that.

ELSIE: You didn't have to.

JASPER: Elsie, you're not yourself. Here—listen—we have others prepared—

(JASPER rifles through pages for a suitable poem.)

ELSIE: You're simple. How do you stay so simple? You think listening to me, doing what I say, is the way to create something—what? What do you want?

JASPER: You don't mean this.

ELSIE: Don't. I mean I'm tired of you. Tired of this—go. Go! Take them with you—what are they doing?

(1 and 2 are making out.)

ELSIE: Oh my god. That is it. GET OUT! There's nothing you can do. Nothing we can do—that doesn't go. Poof. Gone.

JASPER: Elsie—

(ELSIE throws something at him.)

ELSIE: Go!

(JASPER, 1, and 2 scurry out.)

ELSIE: It's all a crock of lies. Don't you see? The knock on the door. The place to be allowed in. This is nothing but our own invention. This is nothing but the outcome of our presence. Our will, our habits, our customs. Nothing but that. You were right, after all.

MARTIN: I didn't say that—

ELSIE: Pah. You did. Gloat. I don't care.

MARTIN: Elsie—I just—I don't know what you want.

ELSIE: Fine. Here—the first time we were alone. The backseat of your sister's car. Driving overnight to go skiing. I used to love skiing—flying down hills, the snow. Remember the snow—

MARTIN: A bit.

ELSIE: We were young. You'd asked me and my parents said yes—they were preoccupied. My father was dying. Anyways. I remember your sister was playing the Grateful Dead and maybe she was smoking—

MARTIN: Her name was Jenny.

ELSIE: Right. Jenny. She was so pretty.

MARTIN: She's joined some sort of libertarian Christian enclave.

ELSIE: Her boyfriend was with us. In the car. The skateboarder.

MARTIN: Dave.

ELSIE: He died of a heroin overdose.

MARTIN: I remember.

ELSIE: We went to the funeral together.

MARTIN: His mom couldn't stop weeping—she couldn't look at Jenny. Jenny was with him when he—

ELSIE: But that night, we were in the backseat.

MARTIN: Sitting like this.

(ELSIE sits next to MARTIN, a palpable space between them.)

ELSIE: The snow was falling, Jenny threw her cigarette out the window—we turned to watch the sparks skitter across the roadway. You said they were like fabulous yellow roman candles exploding like spiders across the night.

MARTIN: Kerouac.

ELSIE: You loved the Beats.

MARTIN: I wanted to write like him. Words flooding in a continuous stream. Never ceasing except to live with my wild friends.

ELSIE: You wanted many things.

(MARTIN starts singing/humming the Grateful Dead's "Casey Jones," uncertainly. ELSIE joins him. Remembering something from long ago.)

ELSIE: You saw me then

MARTIN: You touched my arm.

ELSIE: Like, this.

MARTIN: And then—

ELSIE: Then I leaned against you.

MARTIN: My face buried in your hair.

ELSIE: Our breath steaming the window.

MARTIN: When Jenny stopped for cigarettes.

ELSIE: You kissed me.

(They kiss. MARTIN pulls away.)

ELSIE: What?

MARTIN: It didn't happen.

ELSIE: It did.

MARTIN: Not like that.

ELSIE: You're wrong.

MARTIN: No. I'm not—we—we just sat there. And you barely spoke. You were sulking—and I barely knew you then. I tried to hold your hand but you pulled it away.

ELSIE: It was sweaty.

MARTIN: And when we were alone you—you told me about some poet you discovered, about Anna Akhmatova? St. Petersburg? I don't know—I just wanted to kiss you.

ELSIE: No.

MARTIN: Elsie—

ELSIE: No. I'm not wrong. I remember it. I know it. That night we were so new—

MARTIN: Okay.

ELSIE: Even our tongues. Brand new—your breath—my stomach trilled when your hand brushed against it, down to my hip bone.

MARTIN: Like this?

(MARTIN touches her stomach.)

ELSIE: It doesn't anymore.

MARTIN: Oh

ELSIE: It's just—skin. It's just—what is it?

MARTIN: What we make it—right? That's what you were saying. Right?

ELSIE: Yeah. What we make it—till—till we just can't anymore. (Gets up to leave.)

MARTIN: Are you okay?

ELSIE: I'm fine. Good night. The door should open for you now. (Exits.)

MARTIN: What if I don't want to go? Elsie? What if I want to stay? I think I should stay.

(JASPER and the INITIATES enter and take down candles and lights, block his way from the back room. Collect the hats. Remove the magic. Exit.)

MARTIN: Elsie? Elsie?

Oh.

Oh.

Oh no.

(He gasps. An asthma attack. He pats his pockets for an inhaler. He finds a poem. Tries to breathe through it.)

(Blackout.)

(END OF PLAY.)

THE UPSTART

Emily DeVoti

EMILY DeVOTI's plays have been developed and presented in NYC by New Georges, Rattlestick Theater, New York Theater Workshop, Ars Nova, Abingdon Theatre Company, HotINK/NYU, Cherry Lane Theatre, Six Figures Theatre Company, Judith Shakespeare Company and Perry Street Theater, and supported by residencies with The Orchard Project and The MacDowell Colony. Her play *Milk* was produced Off-Broadway by New Georges in Spring 2010 and is published by Samuel French. Her play *Dirt* was recently workshopped by the National Theatre Studio, London, in collaboration with Max Stafford-Clark. She is currently working on a commission for Shakespeare & Co. and Colorado Shakespeare Festival, for their American History play cycle (2013-14). She is a member of New Georges's Kitchen Cabinet and is a founder and the current Theater Editor of the *Brooklyn Rail*. She holds an MFA in dramatic writing from NYU/Tisch and an AB from Princeton University.

VISIBLE SOUL INTERVIEW WITH EMILY DeVOTI

Conducted by Zack Calhoon, February 12, 2011

How did you get started in theater? What made you start writing plays?

When I was five, I saw *A Midsummer Night's Dream* outside. The fairies disappeared into the woods, and I was riveted. It was the very first performance by Shakespeare & Company, up in the Berkshires, where I was born and grew up. I think I'll always have a love of outdoor theater because of this, and by extension site-specific theater.

My dad is a poet, as well as a teacher and photographer, and he brought Shakespeare & Co. into his high school. He also started a visiting artist circuit for poets—it was the '70s, and he brought people through the schools and into my young life, people who were at the beginning of their careers, like Galway Kinnell, Shirley Kaufman, John Haines. So, my first writing was poetry. As a teenager, I got into journalism, and was lucky to get a job as a reporter on a weekly newspaper. I feel like my path to theater is very much a fusion of these two interests. The more I met people and talked with them, the more I wanted to capture their stories and the complexities behind them in a way that I couldn't achieve through journalism.

In college, after a stint studying architecture (the final element to playwriting!), it finally all came together. My senior thesis was a modernist stage adaptation of *The Turn of the Screw* by Henry James. It was really well received and soon, it was produced—a tantalizing start… I was hooked. I started writing historical dramas—I loved finding the moments in history that have shaped our present, getting in there and finding the dark sides, the conflicts, the struggles that could have gone any direction—those that we take for granted today. I like to humanize them and show that nothing is fixed, almost everything is gray, and the decisions we make and passions we face in ourselves are what make history.

Tell me about your play, *The Upstart*. What has the process been like? How do you think the play is going?

The Upstart is about a young writer who is moving into an apartment above a butcher shop in old Italian Williamsburg. She totally romanticizes working class Brooklyn, and tries to be accepted into it, in part out of a desire to distinguish herself from the encroaching hipsters. In the process though, she needs to face the actual racism and anti-Semitism of that community. Simultaneously, she's writing a one-woman show about Brigid Hitler, Adolph's Irish sister-in-law (yes, true story) for an aging Irish diva. She delves into Brigid's story to help her find the answer to her own conflict, which is basically: What ethical compromises do we make to survive? And where do we draw those lines?

The *Cino Nights* process has been amazing. It's also really intense. This is a new play for me. Two months ago, there was no script. It's a play I've had in my mind for a while, but it really only started to come alive for me this fall when I visited Jimmy's with Daniel. I wrote it for that space.

Last week, we had a first read-through of the play. There was way too much Brigid Hitler. Over the weekend, I attacked the play. I had a series of great phone calls with Taibi Magar, our director, and that rewriting session is where I really found the play and discovered how the overlapping voyages worked. By our first rehearsal on Monday, I had shed sixteen pages from the script. In rehearsals, we've really grounded every moment in terms of the actions and intentions of the characters. This is of course the ultimate goal, but it rarely happens so quickly in the development process. Usually, there are so many readings before a play gets produced, and the feedback to those readings can be really hazardous—you end up walking away with general feedback, ungrounded in action, and no way to test it out immediately. Scripts can get very airy and poetic. The difficult part about developing and honing a play in such a short period of time is that there is not really much time to explore moments and give them time to work. A lot of changes and cuts have to be made on instinct. But I've found that for the most part, that kind of pressure is really for the better. The script has become lean and clear, and I'm really happy with it. And I respect Taibi, it's been a good, dynamic collaboration. We also have some wonderful actors to inhabit the roles, and explore with us, and that is HUGE.

What kind writing inspires you?

I'm inspired by writing that feels lived, that challenges my assumptions, that makes me face and feel things that I am scared to face and feel. I admire writing that sends me out of the theater thinking about the world in a different way than I did before I entered the theater. I like strong stories that are at once clear and richly layered. I like deep intelligence. And no matter what kind of drama, I need humor—the deeper the play, the more humor I want to get me there. I'm inspired by writers who challenge themselves to write outside of their comfort zones, and who challenge an audience to step outside of their own comfort zones, too. I also admire beautiful writing—not self-conscious writing, but writing that makes me believe absolutely in the voice of each autonomous character, and yet lets me come away from the play with an overall sense of the writer's own voice. That's actually really, really hard to do.

Who or what has been the biggest influence on your work as a playwright thus far?

The writers who have influenced me most are Shakespeare, Caryl Churchill, and George Bernard Shaw: In Shakespeare, I recognized humanity. In Churchill, a passionate, iconoclastic engagement with history. In Shaw, a battle with social contradictions and incongruities.

I'm also constantly influenced and inspired by my peers. I met a lot of these folks at NYU, where I went to grad school, at Tisch (Dramatic Writing), others through New Georges, a theater community which has become a real home to me, still others through The Good Writers (my writers' group) and now a new set of writers (many overlapping!) through Rising Phoenix Rep, which is an astonishing community.

The Upstart, directed by Taibi Magar, premiered on February 13, 2011, at the Seventh Street Small Stage at Jimmy's No. 43.

CAST LIST

Laura .... Julie Kline
Maureen/Brigid Hitler .... Anne O'Sullivan
Butchy .... Edward Carnevale
Waitress .... Jelena Stupljanin

CHARACTERS

MAUREEN—late 50s, an Irish actress, vulnerable, but with a strong front.

LAURA—mid- to late 20s, Italian, educated, tough, sweet, Dickey's wearing, and dare we say, just a little bit of a hipster.

BUTCHY—50s, gruff, quiet but prone to sudden impassioned outbreaks, looks like an axe murderer, but is really a butcher and a vigilante with a soft side.

BRIGID HITLER—Adolph's Irish sister-in-law, late 50s, dressed tidily in 1950s apparel, tough, manipulative, vulnerable. Pale skin, black hair. To be doubled with Maureen.

WAITRESS—Savvy bar gal, any age.

SETTING

A bar, Manhattan, present
The apartment behind a butcher shop, Brooklyn, present
The living room of Brigid Hitler's Long Island ranch home, 1950

AUTHOR'S NOTE

The character of Brigid Hitler is based on the real-life public figure by the same name who was indeed the Irish-American sister-in-law of Adolph Hitler.

> *"It is perfectly true, as philosophers say, that life must be understood backwards. But they forget the other proposition, that it must be lived forwards."*

—Søren Kierkegaard, *Journals*

(*MAUREEN sits alone in a bar. The WAITRESS brings her a shot. She knocks it back, tries to give the glass back to the WAITRESS, but she's gone. LAURA enters. She checks out the table, looks around. She shifts the book she holds so it's casually, yet prominently, displayed. It's black with yellow lettering: The Memoirs of... The rest is obscured. MAUREEN sees it, squints.*)

LAURA: Are you—?

MAUREEN: Looking for someone, Love?

LAURA: Maureen! I—recognized your voice.

MAUREEN: Ahh. (*With vain pleasure.*) From the Colgate commercial.

LAURA: No, from the *phone*.

MAUREEN: Oh, I thought— Never mind. Come. Have a seat, Love. What'll you have? (*Flags the WAITRESS down.*) Ah! That's one of the McCourts—Hello, Malachi! (*She waves and smiles fatuously as he walks by.*) We were youth together, he and I. The Irish community here in New York—very small. You don't want to... cross anyone. Do you?

(*Awkward pause.*)

LAURA: So. Dermot.

MAUREEN: Dermot and I go way back, to The Abbey Theatre.

LAURA: You were at The Abbey?

MAUREEN: Didn't he tell ye? We were actors together, he and I. I knew Dermot when he was the Playboy of the Western World!

LAURA: I thought he was the artistic director.

MAUREEN: (*Tossing her a look.*) Well, yes, he was, technically... for a bit. It's just... a turn of phrase, Love. Anyhow. He'll give us our first shot, in that little theater of his—

LAURA: A real production. That's what he says.

MAUREEN: Of course, there are productions and there are productions... You know what I mean, Love?

LAURA: ...of course. (*Smiles, uncomfortably. She would give her left nut for a production of ANY kind, but she's not gonna let MAUREEN know it.*)

MAUREEN: And your play—the reading—The Big Pageant play—I went with my friend John, John O'Hannihan, do you know him? Faaaamous Irish actor, old friend. He said: "That girl sure can write." "And how." Only...

(*MAUREEN looks out of the corner of her eye, tentatively, then opens the space between her hands like an accordion. The WAITRESS comes over.*)

MAUREEN: *Lemonade*, please.

LAURA: It's a little long, I know.

MAUREEN: It's just a—

(*MAUREEN lunges for the hidden shot glass, but the WAITRESS deftly scoops it up.*)

WAITRESS: Have another?

MAUREEN: (*To LAURA and the WAITRESS at once.*) Just a wee bit, Love.

WAITRESS: And you?

LAURA: Lemonade.

MAUREEN: (*Conspiratorially.*) And—? Come, now, my treat. Keep me company.

LAURA: Sure. Well, uh, no, actually. I've given it up...especially in the, well, in the morning. Just. Plain. Please.

WAITRESS: Lemonade. On the rocks.

LAURA: Thanks.

MAUREEN: It's my throat, you know— an actress *is* her voice. It's a muscle, you know, a machine. You're no younger than your voice—and *no older*, either. Especially in my line of work. I have an audition this afternoon. I'm a little nervous. And it's a little scratchy. And sometimes it just needs a little—

LAURA: Lubrication?

MAUREEN: *(Lands her gaze on The Book.)* Where did you get that? I have the only copy. It's mine, you see, I found it years ago, and I've never seen one since.

LAURA: Online. They have old copies, they—

MAUREEN: *(Conspiratorially.)* We have to be very quiet about this. It's a very rare story. No one knows about it.

LAURA: There was a *New Yorker* article.

MAUREEN: *(Makes a sour face.)* Besides that. It's Top Secret.

LAURA: Brigid Hitler. Adolph's Irish sister-in-law. Married his brother. It's quite a story.

MAUREEN: Irish-*American*. She moved to Long Island. World War II. Her whole family, her son, his sons. Blood heirs. They had to be secret *then*, you can imagine. What with... the climate.

LAURA: She was a Fascist.

MAUREEN: She was a *mother. (Pause.)* I have a son. Adores me. He lives on Long Island. Wayyyy out. On the very... tip. *(Naturally unfurls her hand and extends her finger out as she speaks.)* So. You can see why I'm meant to play the role.

LAURA: *(Scrutinizing her.)* Yes...

MAUREEN: I can't pay you, you know.

LAURA: Oh. *(Pause.)* Uh. It's okay, I have a day job.

MAUREEN: We all have to survive—

LAURA: It's not so bad.

MAUREEN: No, I mean the story. We all have to. To use what we have. At our disposal. To survive. As a single woman alone, you know...or do you? Are you married, Love?

LAURA: Yeah, actually I am.

MAUREEN: Funny, I couldn't tell.

LAURA: *(Looks at her. She looks down at her hands. She's not wearing her ring. She places them in her lap.)* Where did you say your son lives?

MAUREEN: On Long Island.

LAURA: But as you said it before, entirely, can you remember? As you said it with your body. "I have a son," you said, "he lives—"

(MAUREEN remembers, as LAURA scrutinizes her.)

MAUREEN: ...on Long Island. Wayyyy out. On the very...tip.

(Tentatively, as she says it, she extends her arm and finger to the side, in a very actorly, Shakespearean gesture, wrist up. LAURA scrutinizes her. MAUREEN freezes in profile, basks in the attention.)

LAURA: Good.

MAUREEN: What were we talking about?

LAURA: You can't pay me.

MAUREEN: Right.

LAURA: But—

MAUREEN: When I make it. When I get on that stage, and actually—well, you know, as great actors do, *BECOME* her! I knew, the second I read it, my Fate was mingled with hers. We can work out the royalties later. There will be enough to go around, of course. All *you* need to do, after all, is write it. It's all right there. I mean, really—how hard can that be?

(Shift to: LAURA on the phone.)

LAURA: It's great stuff. Yeah, true story. A Nazi sympathizer? I don't know. I mean, she was a *Hitler*. Does that really count if you're related? Hey, do you have my copy of *Mein Kampf*? Great. Can you put it on my pile? I don't' know, it's a job, I mean, *no*, but it'll get *produced*. It is so a big deal. Do you know how long I've been trying to get a production? Listen, I gotta go, I got another call. *(Carefully.)* Um... yeah. I am. This weekend. *(Breaking.)* Jesus Christ, we've gone over this fifty times. *(Recomposing.)* You can go to a movie or something while I'm moving out my stuff— He is NOT a psycho. Besides, the rent is incredible— And the location! I mean, it's still close, it's just...my space. Besides, I'm really gonna need to focus on this play. Listen, I really have to—right— *(Feeling a little sick.)* Bye. *(Hits call waiting button.)* Hello. Hello?

(Nothing, but dead air, like someone's there, but...not.)

LAURA: Hello?

(Shift to: LAURA sits at a café, with her books and computer. She begins to write, reads as she does, trying for a warbly Irish accent.)

LAURA: "It all started at the Dooblin Horse Show..." *(Shakes her head, that's not it.)* "The year was 1909. And I was a wee seventeen..." *(No.)* "He was the most exquisite thing I had ever—" Fuck. *(No.)* "I was meant for the stage..." *(She hits on something here, goes with it.)*

BRIGID and LAURA: "I was always meant for the stage. I used to be one, you know, an actress. Oh, not *real* drama..."

(Lights up on a little stage: BRIGID [MAUREEN], dressed as a middle-class suburban woman, circa 1950, is seated on a nice couch with two flowered throw cushions.)

BRIGID: ...Harry Lauder's company, England. Chorus girl. We traveled round the—well, *across Europe*, across the... Western World! When I wasn't being a secretary.

LAURA: "Sec-re-tary..."

(LAURA quietly sounds it out; as she focuses on her writing, BRIGID takes over.)

BRIGID: You do what you must when you're a mum, you know... *(Placing it.)* Not to mention a Hitler.

(Beat.)

Oh, I used to love the look that brought to their faces: "A Hitler." "Brigid Hitler, how do you do? And have you met my son Pat? William Patrick Hitler? Nephew to Adolph, blood heir to...*Der Führer?*"

(Beat.)

But that look, the faces, they changed, over the years. From nothing, of course, in the beginning—Oh, we Hitlers were nobody, I married into a family of nobodies!—to a faint spark of recognition, to astonishment, to envy, to horror, to... And that's when I stopped. Saying it, you see.

(Beat.)

I came to Long Island to forget.

LAURA and BRIGID: Bury my past. Start anew.

BRIGID: "Long Island"...It had such a ring to it. A long stretch of land, pointing, like... like a finger, out to a future.

(LAURA and BRIGID both outstretch one arm, in the actorly gesture. Then fold back their first three fingers, so only the pointer and thumb are extending, to form Long Island.)

BRIGID: And what was it made of? Miles and miles of...not fields, no, no more fields, but...little identical cottages. So tidy. So neat. You can get lost in that, disappear, that's what I thought, when we first came here, it was so... appealing. We settled in— Not the tip. Too exposed. But the fist. *(She makes a strong fist.)*

BRIGID and LAURA: It looked...safer.

(Shift: Loud scratchy radio from a paint-spattered, beat-up boom box. Falling down, wire-exposed, half-plasterboarded apartment space. On the wall behind it are hand-printed prices for meats, as if painted on a shop window: MEAT, Chicken: $1.39/lb. Pork chops, $2.19/lb. Frozen shrimp, Jumbo, 24 ct., $5.99, etc. But they're all written backwards, because we're inside the shop looking out. LAURA pokes her head in. She carries a little suitcase, a computer bag, a plant.)

LAURA: Hello? Hey...Butchy?

(An axe chops through a plasterboard wall. LAURA jumps back, shrieks. BUTCHY, wearing ripped overalls, pokes his head out.)

BUTCHY: Hey. I didn't hear ya.

LAURA: I was just down in the shop... getting some, you know, bacon. And Jimmy said you were up here *working*.

BUTCHY: Uh, yeah.

LAURA: And so I thought since I'm moving in this *weekend* and all...

BUTCHY: I didn't have as much time—

LAURA: I might as well...

BUTCHY: —As I thought I would to...

LAURA: *(Simultaneous.)* Stop by—

BUTCHY: *(Simultaneous.)* Work on it.

LAURA: *(Her expectations deflated.)* Take some...measurements.

BUTCHY: I thought I'd knock this wall down. Make it more... airy.

(They look around. Thoughtful. It's clearly a wreck.)

LAURA: I... guess it won't be done by this weekend.

BUTCHY: Yeeeah...

LAURA: Right. So, uh, when, do you think? Just, you know... ballpark.

BUTCHY: What, you in a hurry?

LAURA: Well. I kind of have my stuff all packed up—

BUTCHY: I dunno. Coupla months.

LAURA: Months?!! But you told me— Three months ago, you told me: three months. April 1st! Oh my god. April Fool's.

BUTCHY: What?

LAURA: April— *(She looks at him in a panic.)* It's...still mine, isn't it?

BUTCHY: I said so, didn't I? *(Beat.)* Gimme your number. I'll call you when it's ready.

(He takes some brown butcher paper from his pocket. He takes a Sharpie pen from behind his ear. She writes her number down. Hands it to him.)

BUTCHY: I'll put it on the hook.

LAURA: Okay. *(Awkward.)* Two months! *(Recalculating.)* June 1st! Right?

BUTCHY: *(Unconvinced.)* Yeah, sure.

LAURA: Great. I'll see if I can... I mean, I did tell him—*her,* I mean... *(Pause.)* Can I leave this here?

(She holds up the houseplant. He shrugs. She positions it somewhere, carefully.)

BUTCHY: I don't water.

LAURA: It's okay, I'll...swing by once in a while. It'll be fine. *(Turns to leave.)*

BUTCHY: Hey.

(She turns around hopefully.)

LAURA: Yeah?

BUTCHY: You live in the neighborhood, right?

LAURA: Nine years.

BUTCHY: What, are you being evicted?

LAURA: *(Avoiding.)* I love this neighborhood, y'know? It's a *real neighborhood*, with *real* people, who really *live* here, not all these bullshit—

BUTCHY: Where do you live?

LAURA: But you know, everyone's selling. And the condos! It's like living in a construction site.

BUTCHY: WHERE?

LAURA: Other side of the BQE.

(He stares her down.)

LAURA: *(Reluctantly.)* Mary Petruzzi's.

BUTCHY: Petruzzi. She selling?

LAURA: I... uh, think she might be.

BUTCHY: I didn't hear that.

LAURA: I...suspect.

BUTCHY: Oh.

LAURA: I don't know for sure, I just... need to move.

(LAURA slips into her chair. She picks up the books. Reads. Types. BRIGID is holding a manuscript. She reads the first line, then puts it down.)

BRIGID: "It all began in 1909 at the Dublin Horse Show. I was seventeen years old."

(LAURA puts down the book and just types.)

BRIGID: Father was talking with Mr. Jameson, from the bank. Beside them was a man, a good ten years older than me, *worldly*, I could tell that at a glance—three piece suit, gold-handled cane, *spats*. Oh, he spared no expense. His moustaches were waxed and curled

up right *a la Kaiser*. He introduced himself as Alois Hitler, from Austria.

The way he looked at me, it was as if he was sizing up a mare—a country bred Irish mare, ready for the races. We eloped to London—fled really—at a full gallop. You can imagine the racket. Father kept yelling he'd *have that Austrian foreigner arrested*! Oh, he wasn't clairvoyant—he was just a country man, he thought *every* foreigner was a criminal.

Those first few weeks... The champagne. The finery. Petticoats, dresses, hotels! From London, we moved to Liverpool. That's where I started to get to know him. After the marriage, after the romance, after the sheets... wore thin.

(LAURA's cell phone rings.)

LAURA: Hey. How's it going? No, I haven't been by, I'm at a café. *Writing*. Sure, I'll be home for dinner. Wow. You're gonna—that's so nice. Yeah, you know I love duck. How'd you get the cash for— Oh, you need— Okay. I've got some money in the back of my desk drawer. I checked it last week. Oh, I see. No, that was it. Yeah...sure... I can pick up take-out. Yeah, I know what you like, listen, I really gotta— *(She clicks the line. She looks like she feels defeated. She returns to her writing.)*

LAURA and BRIGID: Alois was always just about to make a fortune. He told Father he was "in the restaurant business." He was a *waiter*.

BRIGID: He had some money when we met—from a *horse*—and we bought a little restaurant. Then a rooming house. But the big hotel, that's when our troubles really began. I told him it was *too big*, we *couldn't afford it*. But oh, no, Alois had dreams! "You think too small, Cece!" he said, "You think too—" He'd taken to calling me Cece by then. After St. Cecilia, or rather after a portrait of her he particularly admired. You know, Cecilia—patron saint of the blind? The *blind martyr*?

So maybe I did think small. I confess it. After all, there are worse things to think about than if your baby's going to have his milk for the night, aren't there? We'd had Pat by then, of course. Nine months—well, within the first *year* of marriage.

I remember that first time—*after* the bankruptcy—when Alois appeared, gay, smiling, beaming really. He flung this fat roll of bills on that kitchen table; he took it out of his top pocket and just tossed it there, like...dice, and shouted: "Cece, we're rich!"

LAURA and BRIGID: Do you know, I really believed him? I still did, back then.

(LAURA stops typing, takes a breath— she's still getting over her phone call.)

BRIGID: If I'd only known *then* what I know *now* about all gambling money... But when he won—he was so... light-hearted and... beautiful and... light-handed. As opposed to...the other times, of course.

(Shift: The sound of butcher cleaver hitting bones on a butcher block. In shadows, BUTCHY repeatedly cleaves the meat. Above him hangs a big fat meat hook. The butcher paper with LAURA's phone number hangs on it. LAURA enters the apartment, carrying two paper coffee cups. BUTCHY joins her, wiping his hands on his bloody butcher apron. He carries keys.)

LAURA: I brought coffee.

BUTCHY: *(Gruffly.)* Thanks.

LAURA: I was just passing by, you know, I was just—

BUTCHY: —in the neighborhood?

(They look around, not much more has been done.)

LAURA: Wow. It looks...exactly like I remember it!

BUTCHY: I... been busy.

LAURA: It's only been a coupla weeks. I didn't expect it to be done. I just thought— *(Changing her approach.)* You painted!

BUTCHY: I gave that wall three coats, and still the shit keeps coming up from under it.

LAURA: ...what shit?

BUTCHY: Nicotine, tar, it's in the walls. Lady who used to live here? Smoked like a fuckin chimney. Then her son moved in—it was supposed to be for a week— *he* smoked crack. Mother and son, all cozy...couple of degenerates. Five years, he was here. It's in the walls now. Look at it. Yellow shit. You try to cover it, it bleeds right back out. I got this friend—he's a Puerto Rican, a super in the projects. He gave me this paint they use to cover crack stains, neutralizes it. I was trying it out.

(LAURA's never heard him talk more than a sentence at a time. She looks at him.)

LAURA: Wow.

BUTCHY: What?

LAURA: Nothing.

BUTCHY: *(Pause.)* What do you think?

LAURA: It's... bright!

(BUTCHY takes a sip of coffee.)

LAURA: Like it? I got it from the old place on Jackson.

BUTCHY: Near Carmine's?

(Slowly but surely, LAURA's accent begins to shift to more Brooklyn, her language gets looser, she pairs her phrasing with BUTCHY's.)

LAURA: Carm— Oh, the pizza place, yeah. NOT the new place up the block, with the chalk board on the street? ... I'm boycotting it. I won't go in there—you've gotta draw the line somewhere, you know? Buncha fucking hipsters. Literally, bunched up around the doorway. Like it's an island and if they step off, they'll...disappear.

But this place, they *serve coffee*, you know? People go in, they get their coffee, they read the *New York Times*... they have a direction, a focus. They're not just vamping around. It's a real place, you know? *(About the coffee.)* It's good, right?

BUTCHY: *(Looks at her, assessing.)* We make coffee in an old percolator, on a burner. In the shop. *(Takes a sip.)* It's all the same shit.

LAURA: *(Disappointed.)* Oh.

BUTCHY: *(Realizes he's disappointed her, takes another sip.)* It's not bad.

LAURA: Thanks.

BUTCHY: You shoulda seen this place.

LAURA: I did.

BUTCHY: Before that. That son was a piece a shit. See that alley? Knee deep in beer cans. Still smells like beer and piss out there. The minute they stopped paying their rent, I locked them out. Fucking dope fiend. *(Goes into the bathroom, demurely puts the seat down. Points to the ceiling.)* He left his stash up there—in the ceiling, above the john. Lurked around for months trying to break in. Psychopath. That's why I put the bars on the windows. He still doesn't know I found it.

(They stand there looking at the bars.)

LAURA: They don't look like they actually lock.

BUTCHY: Yeah, well. You can't tell that from the outside.

(LAURA looks uncomfortably back to the bathroom ceiling, home of the "stash.")

BUTCHY: You know, we're lucky. Not that long ago, the crapper? Used to be out in the yard. Then, they moved it into the hallway. All the apartments shared one, one per floor.

LAURA: I remember— My grandmother's apartment, there was still one in the hall. She lived on 9th Avenue, in the city. "Hell's Kitchen." It was so exotic, I threw up every time we were about to go.

BUTCHY: To the john?

LAURA: *No*, the City. We lived in the country. It was— Her apartment, it was so...exciting. New York City...with the john in the hall! I always kind of thought they kept bodies in there. I held my breath when I walked past.

BUTCHY: Yeah, there's probably a good reason for that.

LAURA: My mom grew up there. Hell's Kitchen. "Clinton." She always apologized for raising me in the country. Clean air! Green grass! A real neighborhood. I always wondered what that felt like.

BUTCHY: You Italian?

LAURA: Yeah.

BUTCHY: Me, too.

LAURA: I figured. What part?

BUTCHY: The North.

LAURA: Us, too.

BUTCHY: Way North.

LAURA: Well, my dad. My dad's dad's... dad.

BUTCHY: Austria, actually.

LAURA: Oh! Uh. Not... that far north.

BUTCHY: Or it was, before the war, before... Reparations.

LAURA: Right. World War I. The "Great War"...

BUTCHY: But my ma, they were from the south, so. Who the fuck knows. I'm a mutt.

LAURA: *(Relief.)* Me too!

BUTCHY: Maybe we're related.

LAURA: May...be. *(Pause.)* Hey—could I help?

BUTCHY: I'll get it done.

LAURA: No, I mean, I don't want to pressure you, I just... want to learn! How do you... do *this*?

(She picks up a sanding block on a long stick. Starts to work on a plaster spot high up on the wall.)

BUTCHY: No, not up and down. Just... do... little circles. Light, but— You want it flat, right? So... But not— Here...

(He guides her, then lets go. She tries. It's fine at first, then her arms ache.)

LAURA: It's harder than it looks. My arms... This is harder than yoga.

(Plaster has rained down on her, turning her white. He chuckles and take a rag, tries to clean her up a little. But it's too much contact. He hands it to her.)

BUTCHY: You've got some— *(He gestures to a part of her face.)*

LAURA: Oh, thanks... *(She wipes her face.)* That was fun.

(Shift to: LAURA writes, the Brigid Hitler book to her left, Mein Kampf to the right.)

BRIGID: "I first met Adolph in 1912, when he came to visit us in Liverpool."

(LAURA scans through Mein Kampf. She puts it aside.)

BRIGID: Oh, put away your *Mein Kampf*. You won't find any of this in there. Adolph always denied that visit. He denied... all of us. Historians call it his "lost year," the year between when he disappeared from Vienna and showed up in Munich where... it all began. "Lost year." I'll tell you where he was: in a very pleasant three-room flat. Sleeping on my very own sofa!

Adolph was twenty-four years old when came to us, and he'd never worked a day in his life. He'd blown through the *entire* family inheritance, had been living off the city of Vienna in a home for old men, and was evading military conscription. Mandatory, mind you. And that's how he came to us: a no-good draft dodger.

Adolph sat in my kitchen for hours, playing with Pat. He didn't say much at first. I was only twenty, myself. But when he had his black moods, oh! then he'd moon and storm about. You see, Adolph liked to consider himself an artist—he made watercolor copies of tourist postcards and sold them on the street. An "artist"! He was very disappointed not to have gotten into the Kunstakademie—that's the art school over in Vienna. Apparently, they told him he couldn't paint!

"But if I could paint, why should I go to the Academy?" he would counter. Or rant, really, it was really more of a rant.

But the times he'd really look alive is when he'd pull out Alois's maps of Europe. He had this idea, you see. He always came back to it. Usually, it was how Germany was going to take its rightful position in the world! First would come France, he would say, then England... Naturally, I didn't care for this kind of talk— I had a house to clean, mind you— nor did I take it very seriously—I was used to the Hitlers with their "big plans"—but whenever I tried to get away, Adolph would begin to shout. It would start softly, but the second I tried to move away, he would whip himself into such a fury! And he'd go on and on until—eventually, he'd go hoarse. But by then, of course, *Pat* would start screaming, and *he* wouldn't stop.

I can't help thinking sometimes... If they'd only admitted him to that Kunstakademie... he might have put his skills, his flair for the stage, for color, for BUILDING things... into something...quite...different. Or if we could have afforded to support him for a few years—to "develop himself," as he said. It's preposterous to even think, but... Would he have become an artist? Or would we have unwittingly funded the simmering years of a new, of a terrible... of an empire? Did we do that already?

(Beat.)

It was too much after a while. Adolph had been with us six months. He would not budge...without incentive, without a little..."development" money.

We sent Adolph off to Munich. Oh, we were going to send him off to *America*. Well, you can imagine that would've been a different story all together, now, wouldn't it have?

(Shift to: Whack. Whack. The axe is swinging, but this time it's LAURA who's swinging it. BUTCHY's hammering something. They're working in perfect unison.)

LAURA: I am not a violent person—but every time I pass that fuckin coffee shop? I want to smack someone. You ever feel that way?

(BUTCHY shrugs.)

LAURA: Today, there was this sign: "Come make a neighborhood!" With a bunch of chalk flowers drawn around it. Like there wasn't a neighborhood here

before they got here? Fucking hipsters. I went to this one place, before I came here? Craigslist. The place on the corner. Frost and Graham?

BUTCHY: This side of the street? Yeah, I know that place. Johnny Branzino put that up five years ago. Put it up, moved out to Jersey. Comes back once a year with the assessor.

LAURA: Six tiny rooms, one in a row, like a stable. Eight-fifty a pop. *(Wham.)* That's—

BUTCHY: Five thousand bucks and change for that place. Piece o'shit.

LAURA: I felt like a B-circuit race horse. So, this girl, she starts interviewing me, and then she says, get this: "So, let's talk shower schedule." Shower schedule! They had a fucking chart! *(Wham.)* *(Wham.)* If I see another fuckin hipster shop in this neighborhood, I swear I'm gonna—fucking hipsters! *(Wham.)* Fucking hipsters! *(Wham.)* And they're not even *artists*! *(Wham. She takes a final whack, then sits down, exhausted.)* Oh my God, that's good.

BUTCHY: That's a good axe. I got that axe...twenty, twenty-five years.

LAURA: *(Coming down.)* It's a good axe.

BUTCHY: That axe has been around. *(Starts giggling.)*

LAURA: What?

BUTCHY: There was this one time, Pinky—he lived right there at the corner of Graham and Frost—

LAURA: The stables?

BUTCHY: Other corner. Caddy corner.

LAURA: The one with the boy's club—?

BUTCHY: Veterans, yeah. Used to be. Now it's the architect. He left the sign up—likes the effect or some shit. Anyhow. He lived there. Pinky. This was back in the Eighties, before the sting. When they were just cracking down around here.

LAURA: Who?

BUTCHY: *(Raises an eyebrow at her.)* Anyhow. Pinky's nephew was dealing drugs. Now, Pinky, he could do whatever shit he likes, but he wanted his family to be on the up and up. So, Pinky's downstairs in the shop when he hears about the nephew, and no sooner than he does, right on cue, the nephew walks through the door. Pinky goes apeshit. I'm there, nice and quiet in the corner with my axe—

LAURA: What were you doing with your axe?

BUTCHY: *(Waves her off.)* —and he grabs it. Raises it at his nephew. Like he's gonna use it—and trust me, he would, I seen Pinky go ballistic on people he don't even give a shit about. So, the nephew takes off. And before I know it, Pinky's running down Graham Avenue with *my axe* raised over his head, chasing the nephew. So, then the FBI agents across the street—they'd been trailing him for months, they jump out of their car, completely blow their cover, and start chasing Pinky. To stop him. So now we have the nephew, Pinky with the axe over his head, and two FBI agents running down Graham Avenue and *me* at the end, because I want my axe back— *(Wheezing with laughter.)*

LAURA: What happened?

BUTCHY: Pinky got life in the trap.

(Shuddering, LAURA looks at the axe in her hands.)

LAURA: Did he kill the nephew?

BUTCHY: Naw... They had more on him than that. *(Cryptically.)* "Tax evasion." *(Pause.)* He had to go in a hurry. We took over his business for him.

LAURA: I thought the shop was your dad's.

BUTCHY: It was. And before that his dad's. You know what they say about being born with a silver spoon in your mouth? Well, for us, it was a cleaver.

LAURA: So then, what was Pinky's business?

BUTCHY: The Merry-Go-Round.

LAURA: He ran an amusement park?

BUTCHY: Titty bar. Jimmy and I took it over, ran it five years.

LAURA: Why'd you stop?

BUTCHY: Eh...Pinky ended up in the dryer. Family had to sell the business.

LAURA: He was like... all washed up.

BUTCHY: No, the DRYER. Inside job. In the PEN. Found him one morning stuffed in the dryer, in the laundry room, rolling around and around on fluff an' fold. You got enough enemies, nowhere's safe. You got something someone wants, they find a way, know what I'm sayin? *(Nods to the bathroom ceiling. Pause.)* Besides, The Merry-Go-Round? That's where I met Jessie.

LAURA: Oh, she was a—

BUTCHY: *(Warning.)* Entertainer. *(Pause.)* Exotic dancer. *(Pause.)* Who am I kiddin, she was a stripper. Nice girl. We got two kids now.

LAURA: How long have you been married?

BUTCHY: I didn't say that.

LAURA: But you said—

BUTCHY: I never made that mistake.

LAURA: But—

BUTCHY: *I never married her.* That's where it all goes to crap.

LAURA: Oh.

BUTCHY: You gotta be careful who you marry.

LAURA: *(She gets quiet.)* Yeah.

BUTCHY: *(He senses this, pushes it.)* You gotta choose carefully, right?

LAURA: *(Evasively.)* I guess.

BUTCHY: Because everything could happen to them—? You share it, right?

LAURA: Sure...

BUTCHY: Even if you don't mean to. There was this one lady, from the neighborhood, nice, put together, Mary Donatto, she coulda married anyone—she married Anthony Pugliese, over on Skillman. This was fifteen, twenty years ago. Nice place, fancy gate, crystal chandeliers. Well, he gets in a mess with the wrong people. So, one day, the doorbell rings. She's not supposed to be home. She opens it. Someone blows her face off.

LAURA: Wow.

BUTCHY: Another one—Freddy the Nuts, lived down on Frost. Wife dies of cancer, he marries one twenty years younger, a real number. Not for nothing, but she bends over? You could see all the way up to her tonsils. Why the fuck not. They take off down to Miami. Whoop it up. No one hears from him again. P.S. Three years later, she sends his ashes back in a coffee can: *US Postal System.* I shit you not. You gotta choose carefully.

LAURA: I guess.

BUTCHY: *(Shaking his head.)* I never made that mistake. *(Carefully.)* Did you ever make that mistake?

LAURA: Yeah, I... That's why I... Yeah.

(Beat. A moment of understanding between them. BUTCHY points to the axe.)

BUTCHY: I'll let you keep that here awhile. In case that loser comes back.

(Shift to: LAURA is writing.)

BRIGID: Two years after Adolph left for Germany, Alois followed. For a little visit of his own, to "explore our prospects." Two months later, the war broke out, The Great War.

Pat and I made a new life for ourselves for the duration. And when the war was over, and we didn't hear from Alois... well. There were a lot of widows in England. Life went on.

And I...became an actress! Why not? I was still young, early twenties. I was already married—no reputation to tarnish with a theatrical life! My parents moved in to care for Pat. And I went on tour. Harry Lauder's company. Musicals, revues...

One of those tours took me to the Continent—Holland, Belgium, France: Lyons, Nice, Monte Carlo... *That's* where I saw my husband again. Oh, no—not some romantic ghost, some gauzy memory of youth, no—my husband, in the flesh—in the second row, in fact, a bit stage right—older, heavier, his moustache cropped *a little smaller*, but definitely...definitely Alois. He saw me at almost the same instant. He whispered to a woman next to him, and together...they left.

I didn't tell Pat. About his father. He stayed gone. No use confusing things.

A few years later, Pat showed me the article about an uprising that had taken place in Munich, it took the authorities twenty-four hours to suppress—the famous Munich *putsch!* organized by one Adolph Hitler. Pat was proud as punch of his sleuth work. "I'm sure Uncle Adolph will answer my letter," he said. A letter?! And I knew none of it?

Well, Pat didn't receive a letter, but I did. "Dear Madam, It has come to my attention that you have been making enquiries of me, and I beg for you to

state what it is that you want of me."
It was signed... Alois Hitler, of Hamburg!

If that wasn't enough to set my Irish temper ablaze! Oh, I wrote him— I wrote back that *I* wanted nothing from him, but I believed he owed his son an explanation! Alois had remarried and had a new son—a bastard. He claimed that he'd believed we'd been killed in the air raids. Actually, we'd only moved down the block. And now, due to "lack of research," he was being charged with bigamy!

(Beat.)

This... began a period of time I like to refer to as our "second courtship." Oh, the letters that poured in now, after years of silence, to his "dearest Cece," the "only one I ever loved"... florid, lengthy outpourings, *begging*... for a divorce.

(LAURA's cell is ringing.)

LAURA: Hello? *(Pause.)* Hello? Listen, whoever this is, you can't just keep calling and then hanging—

MAUREEN: Hello, Love.

LAURA: Oh, Maureen.

MAUREEN: *(Slurring.)* How'd you guess?

LAURA: Colgate commercial.

MAUREEN: Did ye see that one?

LAURA: No, I— It's pretty late, Maureen.

MAUREEN: *(Desperately.)* Are ye done yet, Love?

LAURA: It's only been a month.

MAUREEN: I'm not getting any younger. Ye've got my future there, you know.

LAURA: I work, you know, a day job, and I'm trying to—

MAUREEN: I haven't had it so easy, Love. Not in this life.

LAURA: —I'm trying to *move*.

MAUREEN: You only know Dermot now that he's an old geezer, but oh, we go back. He dated my best friend and married the other, not necessarily in that order, Love, if you know what I'm saying.

LAURA: I've met his wife.

MAUREEN: Oh, not *this one*. This one wasn't born yet, this one. He played Christy to my Pegeen, did ye know that? In *Playboy*. He always did have more bravado than skill, but oh, you should've seen me.

LAURA: I wish I could have.

MAUREEN: I was something to look at. I played them all. I played Mary—*Juno and the Paycock*, of course—and then later Juno herself! Mother and daughter. A career double. Oh! I worked. That's all we ever want, isn't it, Love?

(This strikes LAURA particularly.)

MAUREEN: Only. I don't know what happened. I sit and I try to figure it sometimes. And. Time. I suppose. Happened. The roles, they...disappeared. *(Beat.)* I haven't had it easy, Love. My husband's dead fifteen years now, bless his soul.

LAURA: I'm sorry, I didn't know—

MAUREEN: He was a bastard. Drank 'round the clock. Would come home at three in the morning, and lay his hands on me. I got to sleeping with my son. Protect each other. As my boy grew, I started to wonder who was protecting who.

LAURA: Do you really want to tell me this, Maureen?

MAUREEN: We're partners in crime, you and I. You have to KNOW me to write for me.

LAURA: Well, I suppose...

MAUREEN: He used to call me into the bathroom in the morning, and there he would be, his shirt hanging off, still in his cups—two, to be precise—shave cream to the right, whiskey to the left. And you know what that bastard had the nerve to make me do?

LAURA: *(Wincing.)* ...No?

MAUREEN: Shave him. With a straight razor. All up his neck. Can ye believe it? After laying into us the night before. Claimed his hands were too shaky, but I knew he was having me on. Devil testing the Lord's sheep is what he was doing. How I wished sometimes that my hand could slip, that *I* could get shaky—

(Crash on her end of the phone.)

LAURA: Maureen? Are you there, are you—

MAUREEN: It's all right, Love, it's alright. Just a little... slip. Oh, I'm so sleepy... I'll just have another.

LAURA: Maureen, can I... ask you something. Something...personal?

MAUREEN: Of course, Love.

LAURA: Why did you stay? Why didn't you divorce him?

MAUREEN: I'm a Catholic, Love. I waited 'til he died. *(Beat.)* Join me for a nightcap?

LAURA: I should really go.

MAUREEN: *(With sudden* good *dramatic delivery.)* "It's nearly time we had a little less respect for the dead, an' a little more regard for the living."

LAURA: I— Wow, that's really *good*, that's—

MAUREEN: That's from *Juno*, Love. Remember. You've got my *retirement* there. Hurry...

(LAURA hangs up, places down the phone carefully. She starts to write.)

BRIGID: A divorce. Which I would not do. I'm a Catholic.

But Alois wrote of Pat, too: "In England, he will be a young man like millions of others, but in Germany, he will be one of the only descendents of the man who bears the most prominent name of the present generation in Germany!"

I granted Alois a "separation" eventually—that seemed to be enough for the *Germans*. When Pat was eighteen, I sent him to Germany for his two weeks' holiday. A trial run.

Sure enough, Adolph became Chancellor of Germany in 1930.

(LAURA's phone rings.)

LAURA: Hey. I'm just writing. Yeah, Adolph just became Chancellor. No, not yet, but— Yeah, goombahs. Yeah, ginzos. Bottabingbotta— Yeah... you know what? Stop. Chris, those are... my people. Yeah, I know: "Ha! Ha!" *(Uncomfortable pause.)* He is not a freak. He works really hard, I...I don't know. I like him. He doesn't need to rent this place, you know? He's just. Doing it. For me. Yeah. I'll be home late. You'll probably still be out.

(Shift to: LAURA walks into the room. BUTCHY's working on a light fixture.)

LAURA: Hey, Butchy. How's it goin'?

BUTCHY: Same shit, different day. *(To the wall.)* Piece o'shit.

LAURA: What's wrong?

BUTCHY: Eh,...I cut the hole wrong.

LAURA: Anything I can—

BUTCHY: I'll make it fit.

LAURA: Wow—fixtures!

(There's some yelling/laughing, loud music from the street. Teenagers.)

BUTCHY: Hear that?

LAURA: What, those kids?

BUTCHY: Puerto Ricans. You know how you clear them out? You take that two by four, go out in the middle of the bunch and start swinging. Take a couple out. That'll do it.

LAURA: Do what?

BUTCHY: Clear out the PRs.

LAURA: Jesus, Butchy—

BUTCHY: What?

LAURA: *(Catches herself.)* Bad day?

BUTCHY: Naw, I just got behind.

LAURA: Deliveries?

BUTCHY: Naw, I... had to go to this thing.

LAURA: What thing?

BUTCHY: Ceremony, some shit. They gave me that.

(He nods to it. She picks it up.)

LAURA: Local Citizenship Award? What did you do, start an after-school program?

BUTCHY: Last spring. There was a woman got mugged, corner of Graham and Devoe. I was there with my cart, you know, delivering to Cono's. Well, I see it, I drop the cart, grab the guy by the scruff of his neck.

LAURA: And you handed him in? That's so great. It makes sense that you get a—

BUTCHY: Yeah, I handed him in. I beat the shit out of him. Broke both his arms. You shoulda seen him. Couldn't even wipe himself by the time I was done with him, piece-a shit. He got what he deserved.

LAURA: Wow. And you...got a plaque!

BUTCHY: *(He catches the irony in her voice.)* You think I shoulda handled it differently?

LAURA: No—I mean, maybe, I mean... I don't know. Did you have to break *both* arms?

(He shrugs. Lets it go. More street noise.)

BUTCHY: Fucking PRs.

LAURA: What about your friend with the paint?

BUTCHY: He's different. He's my friend. What, you like them?

LAURA: Sure. I...like everybody.

(He raises his eyes at her.)

BUTCHY: It don't work that way. You can't like everybody. You gotta choose. Most people? Are pieces of shit. You like everybody, you end up fucked. You know what I'm saying?

LAURA: I guess.

BUTCHY: Unlike those people, I work twenty fucking hours a day.

LAURA: You do?

BUTCHY: Ten at night, I start my deliveries. Manhattan, Brooklyn, the Bronx. Eight in the morning, I get to the shop. Seven at night I go home again. Ten o'clock, depending on the night, midnight, 3 a.m., I start all over. Six days a week.

LAURA: Don't you sleep?

BUTCHY: I don't need sleep. I'm okay as long as I keep movin. As long as I don't *stop. (Chuckles.)* Give me one of those, will ya? *(He points to a box on the table.)*

LAURA: Granola bars. What, are you on a health kick?

BUTCHY: Have one. They got caramel inside.

LAURA: No that's okay—

BUTCHY: Don't be shy. We got fifty thousand of them. Trailer jack-knifed on the Turnpike.

LAURA: ...Thanks.

(They bite into their granola bars together.)

BUTCHY: I should sell this shit place.

LAURA: *(Panic.)* The building?

BUTCHY: Naw. The shop. Guy came along last week, offered me 5k rent a month to turn it into a barber shop. Salon. *For men.* What the fuck. I could sit on my ass and just rake it in.

LAURA: Would you do it?

BUTCHY: Wholesale, that's where the money is. I keep this place open for my brother Jimmy. *(Pause. BUTCHY glances over at her, sets out to prove a point.)* You know McCarren Pool?

LAURA: I love that place. Classic. They don't make them like that anymore...

BUTCHY: You better believe it they don't. You ever swim in it?

LAURA: It's been closed since *way* before I got here.

BUTCHY: Exactly.

LAURA: When I first got here, it was all factories around the pool. I mean, they were vacant, but they were like—these beautiful skeletons, you know?

BUTCHY: Yeah, and *twenty* years ago, they were still working. Mattresses, lighting, steel manufacturing. You name it. Whole fuckin neighborhood worked there. Families bought these houses around here off those factories.

LAURA: And now, three years, start to finish—I watched it happen. Gutted, transformed. Condos. Each and every one of them. And now the pool. They want to make it a "community center." Like...an indoor park for white people and...condo investors with hands in the right pockets.

BUTCHY: Fuckin Pincher.

LAURA: Huh?

BUTCHY: John Pincher. Community Board fuck. The developers got their hands in *his* pocket. Jerkin' him off.

LAURA: *(Uncomfortably.)* Uh. Yeah.

BUTCHY: I hope they never reopen it.

LAURA: I hope they make it a real pool again, you know? They say they can't afford it, but— One of those real old community pools, a neighborhood place where everyone can swim. Real people. Working people, you know? Like in *Raging Bull*. Classic old civic utopia.

BUTCHY: *That pool* is what drew those PRs here in the first place. What? They're from Puerto Rico. What am I supposed to call them? Puerto Ricans. Blacks. They all came to that pool. This was the Seventies. It was a shitfest. One day, they threw a car in. Fucking animals. The neighborhood, it was... outta control. So one night, Johnny Caccione, he pours *four bags of concrete* into the pool in the middle of the night. That did it.

LAURA: What?

BUTCHY: Fucked up the filtering system—it was made of sand. That did it.

LAURA: Shut the pool.

BUTCHY: Shut out the PRs.

LAURA: Wow.

BUTCHY: Johnny was a cop. Always had his head on a little loose. He just drove up there in his cop car. But you want something done, you gotta take care of it yourself. You know what I'm saying? That worked for about twenty years at least. I hope they don't reopen that pool. Johnny's not around anymore to fix it. There. *(Referring to the light fixture.)* I bent the screws. I made it fit.

(He flicks on the light. It works.)

Listen, I been in business a long time. And there's one thing I learned, it's this. You're in something, it's making money, you're happy, great. But then something starts to turn. And when it does, you got to get out. Make the call. Cash in. Get what you can for it.

It's the same with people. They screw you once, okay. They screw you twice, cut it. Just like that. If you don't, it's your own fault. I don't pity you. You're an asshole. *(Pointedly.)* You still in your old place?

LAURA: *(Hesitantly, embarrassed.)* Yeah.

(He looks through her, nods.)

(Shift to: LAURA sits and types.)

BRIGID: Oh, Adolph had a plan. How can I explain it? *(She reaches under the cushions and takes out an original edition of* Mein Kampf.*)*

He is family, after all, but I can't exactly leave it on the coffee table, can I?

Mein Kampf. His Kampf. He doesn't even mention us in that tome of his! Almost a thousand pages, and not a mention of his family. Don't you see the danger in that? Excising details for the sake of a clean story? A neater truth?

(Beat.)

We moved to London. Oh, all eyes turned to us then. We sold our story to the *Evening Standard* and the *Evening News*—the biggest papers, the best opportunity to...to disseminate the TRUTH. Why, who else was going to do it? Pat, you see, why, he was the only legal heir to the Hitler name. The only heir!

That's when we got the telegram. Or, rather, Pat did:

"FATHER DYING STOP COME BERLIN AT ONCE STOP AUNT ANGELA"

Pat left for Berlin. Six days later, he returned. He could barely speak.

When he arrived in Berlin, there was a black Mercedes waiting at the train station. Angela, Adolph's sister, was inside. And Alois—fit as a fiddle. They brought him directly to Adolph.

(As Adolph, BRIGID gives a nice dramatic pause. Softly.) "To me, exactly to me, this has to happen."

(Building.) "I am surrounded by idiots. Yes, you, you are idiots. You are tearing everything I have built up with my own two hands!"

(Holding her hands around her face, a silent film gesture.) "They put personal questions to me, to me! My personal affairs are being discussed. Anyone can say who I am, where I was born, what my family does for a living. They mustn't learn about this stupid bigamy. I can't have it. I have never said one word they can use, and now *this* happens."

Pat tried to *reason* with a Hitler—coughed out something about "the truth." Well, that was enough for Adolph: "The truth! The truth! I am being attacked by every side. I have to stand before them without the slightest stain, the slightest blemish. And now you want to tell the *TRUTH*? Can't you understand? Or are you too stupid? I am surrounded by fools. My own family is destroying me!"

Then suddenly, he collapsed in a heap: started sobbing, helplessly, then started muttering something about killing himself, putting a gun to his head, etc., and—

(She starts clapping.) Bravo! Bravo! Encore!

Adolph left the room. His *rôle* was over. It was Angela who really took care of things. She asked Pat the name of the article he'd authorized.

"My Uncle Adolph."

"Well, it's not true," she said. "Your father isn't related to Adolph, and so neither are you. Now go home." And he did. And that might have been the end of it.

LAURA and BRIGID: If he didn't have his mother to set him straight.

(BRIGID raises her eye at this challenge.)

BRIGID: Well, of course Angela'd lied to Pat. But, we proved it. We gathered the evidence, we wouldn't be denied, we wrote to the Viennese embassy and got copies of their birth certificates, Adolph's and Alois's, and they were blood alright—

(Beat.)

So maybe I did encourage Pat. To appeal to his uncle. To present himself. To take advantage of ...the cards his genes had dealt him. Alois taught me that. To make the best of a rather miserable little hand. Wouldn't you? If your brother-in-law, say he worked for a company, a very prosperous company, with politics that your pretty head wasn't made to fit around... But if you saw him rising there, cashing in more profits than he knew what to do with, making millions for other people's sons, why... Wouldn't you do the same? A little... phone call?

(LAURA's phone starts ringing... She starts, and just looks at it.)

BRIGID: I didn't do any more than any good mother would do. And no *LESS*, either.

LAURA: *(Picks up the phone.)* Hey. I can't talk about this right now—I'm writing. He's fine. Listen, I'm not coming home tonight, I— Why do you always have to— No, it's not like that. I mean, he could be an uncle or something. Listen. Meg and Len need a cat-sitter? And I thought. You know, we're gonna try this anyhow, so I might as well... A

couple of weeks. I actually, have my bag with me. I. Yeah. I... *(Cringes.)* Me too.

(Shift to: The apartment.)

LAURA: Hey. How's it going?

BUTCHY: Same shit, different day.

LAURA: Amazing how fast they go, isn't it? One after the next.

BUTCHY: What?

LAURA: The days? They just, add up into months. I'm just sayin.

BUTCHY: Yeah. Whatever.

LAURA: The place looks good.

BUTCHY: I gotta put down floors. You like those tiles—you know, the ones they put in school cafeterias?

LAURA: Why?

BUTCHY: I got a friend... So I figured—

LAURA: I don't need a floor, Butchy.

BUTCHY: What are you talking about?

LAURA: Floors are overrated. Besides, it's getting a little close, isn't it?

(He gives her a blank stare.)

LAURA: It's not gonna be done by next weekend, is it.

(He shuffles. Goes back to what he's doing.)

LAURA: You don't have to finish. I mean, this is fine!

BUTCHY: I'm gonna finish. Aaaa...nother coupla months.

LAURA: I can just move in as is. Kind of work on it from the inside.

BUTCHY: It's gonna be nice.

LAURA: I don't need it to be nice. I just need a place.

BUTCHY: It's gonna be nice, and *YOU'RE NOT GONNA MOVE IN UNTIL IT IS.*

(He gets really fucking scary when he gets irate. She shrinks.)

LAURA: Okay! *(Beat.)* Tough day?

BUTCHY: Know that back lot, just behind us?

LAURA: Yeah, it's full of stray cats.

BUTCHY: Crazy old lady used to live there. There were fifty cats in that place. She dies, and they knocked the whole thing down. It's a fuckin health hazard. Smells like shit. Now? A Jew owns it.

LAURA: How do you know he's a—

BUTCHY: He's got the curls. And one of those big black coats. And talks like—

LAURA: Oh, he's Hasidic—

BUTCHY: He's a *Jew.*

LAURA: Right. Okay, so.

BUTCHY: He comes over to the shop last month. Offers me two hundred and fifty grand for this place.

LAURA: Wow. *(Nervously.)* You...gonna sell?

BUTCHY: Two hundred fifty grand. What does he think I am, a retard? He owns the lot, and he's got a bid on the laundromat, on the corner. He gets this place, he can level half the block. So I look him in the face, and I tell him— "You want this place? You give me two mil. *Cash.*" He looks at me in disgust. Like *I'm* a crazy person. "You're gonna put up a twenty-unit condo. That's how much you're gonna get profit within *two years.* Right? Piece o'shit. You come back when you want to give me that." He looks at me and spits. Like I don't know my ass from my elbow. Like I don't know what things are *WORTH.* What kind of asshole does he think I

am? Does he live here? Does he care what happens to the neighborhood? That the people who live here all their lives get evicted? Family homes get torn down? The lady around the corner with the big eagles and angels and shit on the roof? Is charging *twice* this rent for an illegal basement apartment with a bathroom in the closet— I could get *twice* as much for this apartment—

LAURA: *(Nervously.)* I know you could...

BUTCHY: You know that piece of shit condo over on Humboldt? The one with the big glass walls where you see every shit they do? Guess what one of them goes for? One unit? One-point-five mil. *ONE APARTMENT.* You know what the heat on that cost last January? Three thousand for *HEAT.* Just heat. No insulation. People move in, people move out. Whole fucking town is gonna be a ghost land before they're done with it. Does he live here? No. *He* goes home.

LAURA: It's true. I mean, who owns those places? They just sit there and... suck up space.

BUTCHY: Yeah, while they're over in their fuckin ghetto. "Chosen people."

LAURA: Hipsters paying three grand a month to lounge in front of their glass walls looking hip.

BUTCHY: So fucking special...

LAURA: So fucking special.

(Beat.)

BUTCHY: P.S. Two days later, the health inspector pays us a visit. Never steps foot on the fucking sawdust, until that Jew. He's in bed with Pincher, our esteemed Community Board member. So, I go over to Pincher, and I tell him— "Hey, not for nothing, but I know your Jew is paying you off. And if another health inspector sets foot in there, I'm gonna come back and beat your *FUCKING* head in." Next week, we're denied a loading permit. You know how many tickets I gotta pay each month, just to get my orders, just to run my fuckin business? Pincher is a piece. Of. Shit. So, this morning, the Jew comes back. Asks if I've *changed my mind.*

LAURA: No fucking way.

BUTCHY: Yeah. So I tell him: "You know where you can put your two hundred and fifty grand." He spits and goes to walk away.

LAURA: Good for you. Fucking slumlords.

BUTCHY: And then I says to him: "*I know what to do with your people.*"

LAURA: You— What?

BUTCHY: And he stops in his tracks, and he turns around and he looks at me. Waits. His little curls steady as a kosher fuckin pickle.

LAURA: Oh, Butchy, you didn't, you—

BUTCHY: I've seen his kind before. They tried to destroy Germany in World War I. They tried to *ruin* them. They will. If you let them. Who loans money, then screws you? Who thinks they can buy you with chump change, because they look at you, and they think: You dress a certain way, You're not educated, You're *stupid.* And I looked at him, and I told him: "There was a man in Germany. And he knew what to do with your people. *He* tried to take care of things. And *his name*, was Adolph Hitler. And he was *not wrong.*" (*To LAURA, his eyes strange and blazing.*) He was NOT WRONG.

(*LAURA's body recoils, but she holds his gaze.*)

BUTCHY: Do you not agree?

(*She looks at him, as if hit with a blow, a nervous smile plastered across her face to make it okay. Survival.*)

(*Shift to: LAURA sits, tries to write. Glassy-eyed. Phone rings. LAURA jolts.*)

LAURA: Hello?

MAUREEN: (*Wobbly.*) Hello, Love.

LAURA: It's... really late, Maureen.

MAUREEN: Have you finished yet, Love?

LAURA: This isn't helping.

MAUREEN: Laura, *Love*— It's my retirement you have in your hands. You realize that.

LAURA: I have a lot to juggle right now. It's getting...complicated. I'm doing my best.

MAUREEN: And then Dermot will do it at his little theater, right?

LAURA: That's what he says.

MAUREEN: It's not much, but—it's a start.

LAURA: It's really hard to get an opportunity.

MAUREEN: It really isn't much, you know.

LAURA: It's a start.

MAUREEN: Oh, when I was a girl, Love, I could have had the pick of the roles.

LAURA: I know, Maureen.

MAUREEN: Why, Beckett himself, he wrote *Happy Days* for me, you know. We were youth together, he and I. Or, almost...

LAURA: That was produced in New York. You weren't even here yet. You were— my god, you were way too young.

MAUREEN: "Oh, this is a happy day!" This is going to be another happy day...

LAURA: *Maureen—*

MAUREEN: Oh, Love, I'm old. I'm getting so old. You HAVE to make it. You

HAVE to make my role. It is *THE* role. It was made for me. You have to make it for me, Love...you... *(Pause.)* You're a *GOOD* listener, do you know that, Love? It's a gift, it is.

LAURA: Thanks, it—

MAUREEN: You *LISTEN*. It's a real... *(MAUREEN's voice fades out.)*

LAURA: Maureen?

MAUREEN: *(Light snore.)*

LAURA: *(Softly.)* It doesn't mean I agree.

(LAURA tosses back a shot of whisky, and starts to write.)

BRIGID: What were we supposed to do? We needed to eat. We certainly couldn't find work in Britain. The *newspapers* pay for what they want. So why couldn't Adolph?

I sent Pat back to Germany... Adolph got Pat a job at a bank. It wasn't a particularly good job, not what we'd hoped—I could tell that through the letters, self-censored as they were. And I? Waited a year—of cryptic letters, of solitude— I couldn't take it anymore. I booked a trip to Germany. I wired Pat, didn't wait for an answer, and I was off to him!

Pat met me at the station. That's when he told me everything. That I should never have come. That he was in constant peril. You see, while I was in England, the threat of *publicity* kept Pat alive. Adolph was in check. But now that I was inside? In Adolph's own...empire? Adolph had me right where he wanted me. He'd never let me leave again. We hatched a plan. I had to *pretend* I wanted to *move* there.

Oh, everyone greeted me then. Angela—She gave me these little pillowcases, see?

(She turns over her little throw pillows, to reveal swastikas on the other side. They remain there for the rest of BRIGID's scenes.)

There was Nazi bric-a-brac everywhere. Made by little devoted German girls, like... Heidi!

(LAURA back-space-deletes, retypes.)

LAURA and BRIGID: Made by little old Jewish women in prisons.

(They look at each other. Beat.)

BRIGID: I met Alois, too, of course. His horse finally came in: *Chez Alois.* A nice big restaurant, the fanciest in Munich, hundreds of Nazi flags fluttering all over the place. Everyone was there. In one corner was Goring, in the other corner Hess! The waiters greeted every new diner with a cheery "*Heil Hitler*"! Alois greeted me with a kiss. He wanted no trouble. Well, neither did I. I just wanted to escape this...lavish, beautiful, privileged world that I had been privy to, had a *right to*, really, I— *(Catches herself.)*

There are venal rumors that I *wanted* to repatriate, that I was a *Nazi lover*, that my son tried to get me away from him, so I wouldn't ruin his career— *I hated Adolph.* I knew what he was doing was wrong: my Pat had been in Germany for over a year, and still he was barely making a living wage. He was never invited to dinner. He was never given an advantage. His own flesh and blood, his own...*kin.*

Right at that table with Alois, I started the process, then and there—I had to. Only then could I ask Adolph permission to leave Germany. I'd tell him I just needed to leave for a few weeks, to— "collect my things" and then I'd be back. *Heil Hitler!* Only then could I *escape.*

A week later, Angela and I were in a black Mercedes, being driven...all the way up to the Eagle's very nest.

(Shift to: BUTCHY is in the apartment nailing up some molding. LAURA walks in, slowly. He doesn't look at her. A few weeks have passed this time. With no word from her. He tries not to show he's bothered.)

LAURA: Hey.

BUTCHY: Hey.

LAURA: How's it goin?

BUTCHY: Same shit, different day. *(Pause.)* Haven't seen you for a while.

LAURA: Yeah, I been...busy. *(Pause.)* You got a lot done.

BUTCHY: Yeah, I been busy.

LAURA: I moved...

BUTCHY: Where?

LAURA: Bushwick.

BUTCHY: *WHERE?*

LAURA: Morgan and Troutman.

BUTCHY: *(Nods.)* You know the corner of Troutman and Jefferson?

LAURA: Yeah, it's only a block away.

BUTCHY: More drug traffic on that corner last year than anywhere else in NYC.

LAURA: Great, I thought I was in the middle of nowhere. I'm near a real landmark. What, do you read the police blotter?

BUTCHY: Unofficial survey.

LAURA: It's just temporary.

BUTCHY: Why are you the one's gotta move?

LAURA: I'm the one that left.

BUTCHY: What kinda man lets a woman move to Troutman and Jefferson?

LAURA: Morgan. Troutman and Morgan. It's what I can afford. It's fine. I live across from a school.

BUTCHY: Yeah? Why do you think it's the drug capital? *(Shaking his head.)* Eh. What can you expect from a bunch of nigger kids.

LAURA: Jesus Christ, why do you always have to—

BUTCHY: What?

LAURA: Can you just stop— can you just stop— saying these things out loud?

BUTCHY: That makes it better?

LAURA: It's a start.

BUTCHY: You really think so?

LAURA: Yes. No, I—I don't know.

BUTCHY: You rather I say black kids?

LAURA: Sure.

BUTCHY: "African-American"?

LAURA: Better.

BUTCHY: It's all the same shit.

LAURA: No. No, actually, it's not. People need to be respected, people need to be, I don't know, not treated like a big group of scum, like—I mean, what do you think that *DOES* to people?

BUTCHY: Listen, I call 'em like I see 'em. Each person. One at a time. I treat people the way they *deserve*.

(Beat.)

LAURA: I don't know if I can do this.

BUTCHY: What are you talking about?

LAURA: It all seemed so simple when I started. A real butcher shop. No bullshit. "Shop local"!

BUTCHY: What the fuck are you talking about?

LAURA: People come here because it's local.

BUTCHY: People come here because it's cheap.

LAURA: Where does your meat *come from*, Butchy. Do you even know?

BUTCHY: Sure I do.

LAURA: Where?

BUTCHY: A truck pulls up at three in the morning. Right to the curb, outside your window. What could be more local than that?

(She gives him a look.)

BUTCHY: It comes from a nice little farm in Pennsylvania. With lotsa nice grass.

LAURA: You been there.

BUTCHY: Yeah, I visit the cows. Each one has a name, too... "Chuck" steak, "Rump" Roast, "T-Bone." "Filet" Mignon... I get it from a distributor. I get a deal. Meat is meat.

LAURA: (Impulsively.) I'd want to go there. I'd want to *see* it.

BUTCHY: What the fuck is wrong with you?

LAURA: Why not?

BUTCHY: It's a slaughterhouse. You don't want to see that shit.

LAURA: I feel like— If I'm gonna eat it—if I'm gonna consume it, I should... I don't know, know where it came from.

BUTCHY: I'll bring you to the freezer.

LAURA: Like— I mean *ideally*, I should be prepared to kill it with my own two hands, you know? Butcher it myself. Bite into its flesh. Like— I should be responsible like that. I should be prepared to...to... *FACE* that. For everything I do, for everything I *feel*—

BUTCHY: You're fucking crazy.

LAURA: ME? (She looks at him in disbelief.) Could you get me into one of those places?

BUTCHY: What, do you wanna write about it?

LAURA: *NO*. Well, maybe.

BUTCHY: *Investigative* journalism?

LAURA: *No*, I'm actually a playwright—

BUTCHY: Listen to me. *YOU DON'T COME OUT OF THOSE PLACES ALIVE.*

LAURA: Ha!

BUTCHY: You don't believe me? Those places are made to process meat. It don't matter what kind. They throw all the scraps in a big vat. All the body parts, they don't give a shit.

LAURA: Don't you think that's a *little*—

BUTCHY: They render the fat and send it off to the cosmetic industry. You listen to me. You stick your nose in that, next thing you know, someone's rubbing you on their ass trying to get out the sunspots. *YOU HEAR ME?*

LAURA: Oh!...K.

BUTCHY: *YOU PROMISE ME.*

LAURA: O-*kay*. Butchy. I...promise.

BUTCHY: I got enough to worry about without— /

LAURA: You don't have to worry about— / me.

(Shift to: LAURA swigs some whisky from a bottle as she walks to her computer.)

LAURA: (Typing.) I was ready for my confrontation.

LAURA and BRIGID: To prove my mettle.

BRIGID: To hold my chin up.

LAURA and BRIGID: To tell him *what I really thought.*

BRIGID: Adolph didn't join us for dinner. He fell asleep early. The next morning, he didn't join us for breakfast—he slept *late*. I finally met him before the noonday meal. I was summoned to the back garden. The view was glorious. You could see all of Austria behind him.

He looked at me then for a long time, right into my eyes, like he was reading me. Finally: "The years have passed over you without touching you, Brigid," he said.

That was our only allusion to Liverpool, to the past.

"So. Tell me. Is there anything you would like to ask me. Anything at all?"

My mind went blank. I hated him, I had so much I wanted to say, but I looked at him and— "Why have you never married?" I heard myself chirp. *Why have you never married???* I looked down. My hands were trembling. In, I don't know, anger—at myself, at my weakness, my stupidity—or...was it terror? I couldn't breathe. I blushed.

But Adolph, he was all sophistication. "Do not be embarrassed, Brigid." He smiled, a droll, shrewd little smile... that traveled up my spine. "You are not the first to ask me this question, and I shall tell you, if you are interested. It is a question of statistics. You see, there are approximately twenty million women in Germany, and all of them are more or less attached to me. Then in the Hitler-maid battalions, there are approximately twenty million girls being brought up as mine. Twenty million women plus twenty million girls equals forty million Germans. If I were to marry one of these women today, I'd lose the personal interest of thirty-nine million, nine hundred ninety-nine thousand, nine hundred and ninety-nine. *Nein, nein, nein!* I cannot afford to do it!"

He laughed this loud, boisterous, open laugh, more delighted than a child at his own cleverness. The only more terrifying thing to hear was the sound of my own laughter—where did it come from?—joining him.

"*Mein Gott*, Brigid," he said and I'm sure...oh, I'm sure I leaned in toward him to accept the confidence... "I myself cannot explain it, but the women are mad about me. They all love me, and I assure you I do nothing, absolutely nothing, to encourage that sort of thing. Can you believe there are women here in Germany who would not wash their hands for a whole week, after shaking hands with me? They say they cannot bear to wash off their Führer's handshake!"

"No," I said, "Really?"

"Yes," he insisted, "*Mein Gott*, yes, and...Goring tells me that when they do wash their hands, these women, they put the water in a bottle and keep it to show their friends!"

(As Adolph, throws up her arms.) "Yes! They are crazy!"

Yes...they are crazy, aren't...*they*.

(Beat.)

And that, *that*... was my moment in the spotlight with the Führer. I left Berchtesgaden. I left Germany. I left England. And I came...here.

(Shift to: The original café where MAUREEN and LAURA first met. LAURA is sitting, fidgeting with a letter. A glass of lemonade before her. MAUREEN enters, carrying a shot glass.)

MAUREEN: Well, you're the early bird, now, aren't ye, Love?

LAURA: Our old table.

MAUREEN: *(Confused.)* Was it, now?

LAURA: I guess it's been a while. It's just we've talked so much, I feel like I've just seen you.

(MAUREEN grips the side of it, woozy.)

LAURA: Maureen. Are you alright?

MAUREEN: Oh, just a bit unsteady, Love. You know, *nerves. (Woozy.)* I was a bit of an early bird m'self.

(She holds up her glass. The WAITRESS comes over with a bottle of whiskey.)

MAUREEN: Would ye be so kind?

(WAITRESS fills the glass. LAURA raises her lemonade glass.)

WAITRESS: Another lemonade?

LAURA: Oh, just... pour it in here.

(WAITRESS pours whiskey into the glass. MAUREEN puts her hand on the bottle. WAITRESS leaves it on the table.)

MAUREEN: I was up early, reading over my letter. *(She pulls it out of her purse.)*

LAURA: Me, too. *(Holds up hers.)*

MAUREEN: What did he tell you?

LAURA: That he can't do it—

MAUREEN: *Won't* do it—

LAURA: In that... "little theater of his." *(Pause.)* What else?

MAUREEN: That he likes the bit about her being an innocent country lass. Being—

LAURA and MAUREEN: —"swept away!"

LAURA: He says that here, too.

MAUREEN: But after that...

LAURA: I didn't finish the play. I still have to write the ending.

MAUREEN: *(Mimicking.)* "She's just not like any Irish woman I know." *(Beat.)* What does *he* know about women? Can ye tell me that, Love? *(Pause.)* What did he tell you?

LAURA: Oh, I'm not very good at the Irish. I can't—

MAUREEN: Go on. Try me.

LAURA: *(Reads, with an excellent Irish accent.)* "You're *such* a brilliant writer, Love. Only...Why do you always write about women? *They're so dull.*"

MAUREEN: Oh, I think you've got him quite good. That's Dermot, tip to toe. He thinks he's such a hotshot. He tells everyone that he was the Artistic Director of the great Abbey Theater!

LAURA: Yes, I know, he told me that too—

MAUREEN: Did he tell you how he left? Did he tell you how long he was there? *(She pours another shot. Tosses it back.)*

LAURA: No, I just assumed—

MAUREEN: Eight months. 'Til they fired him. Kicked him out. On his derriere. When I was looking to come to America, do you know what he did? He refused to write me a letter. To recommend me, for my green card. He was afraid that I'd blow his cover! Here in America, he's the Big Man. He moves here, and suddenly, "Oh, he was a theater *genius* back in Ireland"— *HE WAS AN ACTOR.* He was no better than me.

LAURA: Why didn't you tell me this before?

MAUREEN: *(Looks at her, is about to look away, but holds her chin up.)* I thought he was going to help us.

(Beat.)

LAURA: We don't need him. We don't need connections. There are lots of opportunities—

MAUREEN: We had *this* opportunity.

LAURA: You said yourself it wasn't much.

MAUREEN: It was everything, Love, it was our chance.

LAURA: Well, maybe if you didn't make me send it before it was done.

MAUREEN: Maybe if you were Irish, you would have gotten her *RIGHT*.

LAURA: You... said she was right.

MAUREEN: *(Faltering.)* I thought she was.

LAURA: You said yourself: he doesn't know any better than you.

MAUREEN: I know, Love.

LAURA: Who do you believe, Maureen, yourself or him?

MAUREEN: I don't know, I don't know, I don't know what to believe— *(Pause.)* Oh, Love. I'm finished.

LAURA: *Maureen.* It's just one theater, one tiny little theater— Listen. I have a submission list. I'll just finish the play, that's all, and then—

(She gets woozy, swoons, LAURA grabs her to support her.)

LAURA: Maureen?

(Pause. MAUREEN regains herself, marginally.)

MAUREEN: I need to go home, Love. *(Gets up, carefully, and, tracing her hand along the side of the wall to steady herself, exits.)*

(Shift to: LAURA sits at her computer, drinking. A solid bottle of whiskey beside her. The computer screen stares back at her. She attempts to write. Stops. Backspaces over it. Pause. Drinks. Starts to write again. Stops. Backspaces over it. Drinks. Pause. Starts to write again... BRIGID appears on her little stage. LAURA and she make eye contact.)

BRIGID: Have you ever looked at him? Adolph. Really taken a good look? Maybe it takes another actor to see it, but... he owes everything to the stage.

First, his stance—legs spread wide like a cowboy—oh, he loved American westerns. Westerns and detective novels. Now add the arms, across his chest, like a soldier at ease, but defiantly so, like he was daring you to make him do anything he didn't want to do. Add the dark tufts of hair against that white skin... those mooning eyes, a bit of the lost romantic, a silent film star, staring right at you, through the haze, right at *YOU*.

(LAURA gives up writing. She begins to explore the stage options, as BRIGID describes them.)

BRIGID: The whole thing was a classical stage stance, when you really look at it. Legs placed at an artful angle, to distribute the weight, chest held high, body facing the audience, broad but just a bit askance, and the chin—high, that's most complementary. It opens up your chest, too, so that the air, the breath, is free to rise, so that the voice is—

And that arm— Why, it's a modification of the age-old theatrical gesture, to "indicate"— *(She holds out her arm in a stagy, noble, generous gesture, its inside showing.)* —but with a difference.

(She and LAURA both turn their arms high, in the Heil position. BRIGID particularly looks just like Hitler now. Light shift. The sound of cheering at a Hitler speech.)

BRIGID and LAURA: *(With Hitleresque intensity.)* HEIL!

(The phone rings.)

LAURA: *Heil!* I mean, hello? *(She rubs her head.)* No, everything's fine. I—the play is crap, it fell apart, it's— No. You know what? It's fine. The place is— Listen, Chris. I can't— I can't do this anymore. It isn't fair. No. Listen. I can't keep talking with you about my new place. I can't keep *talking with you.* It's twisted. It's fucked up. It's *not* temporary. I didn't wait nine fucking months for it to be temporary. I'm *not moving back. (Pause.)* I want a divorce. *(Beat.)* Yeah. I'm sorry. I've gotta go. I've gotta—Go. *(She puts down the phone. Closes her computer.)*

(Shift to: The apartment. LAURA walks in. BUTCHY sits against the wall, his eyes closed, axe over his lap. She looks at him, he's not moving.)

LAURA: Butchy? Hey, are you alright, are you— Butchy?

(She shakes him, in a panic.)

BUTCHY: Hey. What's up?

LAURA: Oh.

BUTCHY: I was working on it. I just—

LAURA: No, I was just—

BUTCHY: ...nodded off.

LAURA: You scared me.

BUTCHY: What are you doin' here, it's like two o'clock in the morning.

LAURA: I saw the light on. I was...in the neighborhood.

BUTCHY: I had time between deliveries and I thought I'd—I was working on the molding.

LAURA: I don't need molding.

BUTCHY: You're gonna get molding.

LAURA: You should take a break.

BUTCHY: I can't.

LAURA: You should take care of yourself. Take a day off. Close up for a week.

BUTCHY: I got too much out there, too much on the street.

LAURA: Hire some drivers.

BUTCHY: I tried that. They don't show up. They work enough to make some cash, go fuck off for a while, come back expecting a job. Fuck you. I can do it myself.

LAURA: I see your point.

BUTCHY: One day, that's all it takes, the delivery don't get made? You lose the business. Done. Want some Cheerios? Snack packs.

LAURA: Accident?

BUTCHY: Pennsylvania. 80. *(He takes a swig of milk out of a carton.)* If you drink milk at the same time, it's like eating out of a bowl.

(She takes a Baggie. They sit there side by side, eating them.)

BUTCHY: I started selling things I was fourteen years old. Anything. Screwdrivers. Hooks. Odd lots. By the time I was twenty, I had enough to buy a block in Queens. A full city block. Right on the Sunset Parkway. We have a dry cleaner, a laundromat, a PC Richards...

LAURA: I know that block. You own that?

BUTCHY: A whole building in the city, too... Garment district. Twenty rental units, half empty. I keep it that way. Business loss. I don't *need* to rent this place—

LAURA: I know you don't.

BUTCHY: I see a deal, I can't help it. I gotta pick it up. But I gotta decide. This insurance shit. I gotta be there on a dime. It's too much. But. It's too good. I can't give it up. A few days ago, I got a call. Big load busts up on 95. Little water bottles. Poland Spring. So I pick up the phone. I make two phone calls, one to a ninety-nine cent store, one to another guy with a truck. P.S., I flip the lot for a 900 percent profit without scarcely liftin' a finger. A fuckin phone call. Better odds than the rest of this bullshit. But to do that, I gotta have the infrastructure, I gotta have the route. I gotta decide, but... I can't stop... I can't stop... Listen to me. *(Shaking his head—a revelation.)* I'm like a Jew.

(They both take this in. Beat.)

LAURA: My grandfather worked like you. Woke at three a.m. every morning to go to market.

BUTCHY: What's his racket?

LAURA: Fruits and vegetables.

BUTCHY: In the city?

(She nods.)

LAURA: It started as a little mom and pop store, *his* mom and pop, Hell's Kitchen. He turned it wholesale.

BUTCHY: What's it called?

LAURA: It's gone now. His sons, they ran it into the ground, but— Dom's Market.

BUTCHY: I knew that guy.

LAURA: You *DID*?

BUTCHY: I remember the trucks. White with a big red apple in the center and his name over the top.

LAURA: Yeah, those were his!

BUTCHY: I saw him sometimes, the old guy, up at market. Hunt's Point. I remember him.

(LAURA looks at him, like she could touch her past through him.)

LAURA: That was my grandfather.

BUTCHY: Whatever happened to him?

LAURA: He retired to the suburbs. *(Pause.)* We think that's what killed him.

(BUTCHY chuckles, nods.)

LAURA: Ninth Avenue. They all used to live there. Aunts, cousins, siblings, second cousins, "cousins" you didn't know how they were cousins. So many of them. No one's left. Moved out or died off. Up and out! Why can't we just stay in one place? Why do we always have to *move*? *(Pause.)* Can't afford a place there anymore.

(Beat. He looks at her, for the first time since she got there.)

BUTCHY: You don't look so good.

LAURA: Thanks.

BUTCHY: What are you doin' here, anyhow?

LAURA: I told you, I...I was in the neighborhood.

(He gives her a skeptical look.)

LAURA: I did it. I left him. I left for good.

(He looks at her, approving. He hands her a hammer.)

BUTCHY: C'mon, let's get this done.

(BUTCHY and LAURA continue to work on the apartment, until it's done.)

(Shift to: BRIGID, alone.)

BRIGID: I'm American now. That's what I said when I came here. Not Irish; that was by birth. Not English; that was chance. And Austrian! Well, *that* was by marriage.

Pat joined me, eventually. He did well, at first. Got an agent, started a speaking tour: "Why I Hate my Uncle Adolph"—that was his most popular one. But eventually, they dropped him. The head of the agency, do you know what he said? He thought Pat would have been a loyal Nazi, if his uncle had given him a fat enough paying job! I mean... can you... imagine?

(Beat.)

After that, he signed up to join the army. Declared he'd bomb his uncle himself! March 1944, he was inducted into the United States Navy, newsreel cameras rolling! He looked so good on film, he should have been an actor, you know, he *could* have—

(*Softly.*) Well, he could have.

(*BUTCHY hands LAURA the keys to her apartment. He exits.*)

BRIGID: Do you know what I heard? At Nuremberg, at the trial, Hans Frank—that was Adolph's lawyer—he said that "the Führer" once described us as his most despicable relatives? *That's* a distinction, I think.

(*BRIGID tucks her manuscript under her couch. Flips the swastika pillows to the flower side.*)

BRIGID: Nuremberg. I learned a new word that day: *Sippenhaft.* Blood revenge. What it means is this: if one's relative has been murdered, they can avenge the death on any member of the murderer's blood family.

Over six million people died under Adolph—under *Hitler's* hand. "Hitler."

(*LAURA takes out her computer, begins to type. Fervently.*)

BRIGID: I came to Long Island to forget. For that long finger, pointing out to a future, that's how I saw it. I should have paid more attention to those maps, when Adolph had me cornered. Long Island isn't pointing to any future—any idiot can see that. It's pointing back—to Ireland, to Germany—

LAURA and BRIGID: —to my *past.*

BRIGID: Lately, more and more, I go back to Adolph, to figure it all out, where we came from, how we got here, *why.*

(*BRIGID and LAURA both leaf through copies of* Mein Kampf.*)*

Here. He's talking about the "bourgeoisie" and their disdain for the working classes, but, well, Adolph wrote this, *Adolph*:

LAURA and BRIGID: "For anyone is an upstart who rises by his own efforts from his previous position in life to a higher one.

BRIGID: "Ultimately, this struggle, which is so hard, kills all pity. Our own painful struggle for existence destroys our feeling for the misery of those who have remained behind."

(*Pause.*)

How do we become who we are?

BRIGID and LAURA: A series of little, tiny choices that we make.

(*LAURA stops typing.*)

BRIGID: We changed our name. Brigid Hitler ceased to exist.

(*BRIGID exits.*)

(*LAURA steps through the axed wall, into the rest of her apartment, which includes BRIGID's couch. She carries her plant.*)

(*BUTCHY takes LAURA's number off the meat hook. Puts it in his pocket. The meat hook lifts up out of sight. He pushes the butcher block offstage. The meat prices disappear and become a projection of retro wall paper throughout the whole apartment.*)

(*The phone rings. LAURA looks at caller ID.*)

LAURA: (*Cautious.*) Hello? (*Strange relief.*) Oh, sorry, I thought— Maureen O'Connell. Exactly. This is her number and I thought— No, I'm not a relative. Is she okay? But *you* called *me.* So you found my number; you mean to tell me this was the ONLY number in her entire— Really? Oh. Oh, I see, I...I don't know, Officer. Sorry, *Detective.* I don't know a lot. But. She has a son, I know that. Out on Long Island. Waaaaay out. The very tip. *(Smiling sadly to herself, she stretches out her arm.)* Montauk, I think. He runs a bar.

(The door buzzer rings—loud and metallic.)

LAURA: Listen, I know you can't tell me, but—I mean, will she be okay? Oh. Yeah, I— knew she likes the drink, I just didn't realize...quite how much. Thank you, Offic—sir, and— Could you let me know if you can't find him? I may know someone who can. Thank you, I—

(The buzzer rings again.)

LAURA: *(To the door.)* Wait a minute, I— *(Into the phone, which has gone dead.)* Thanks.

(She looks through the peep hole. She opens the door. BUTCHY enters. He carries a white plastic bag with a smiley face on it; inside are parcels wrapped in butcher paper.)

LAURA: Hey.

BUTCHY: Hey. I got something for ya. *(He holds the package out to her.)*

LAURA: Oh, wow.

BUTCHY: A little... housewarming.

LAURA: Meat. *(She looks up at him, straight in the eye, a little smile on her face.)* Where's it from?

BUTCHY: *(Level.)* The shop.

(Pause. Hesitation. She accepts the bag.)

LAURA: Thanks.

(BUTCHY nods his chin up at her, smiles a little, leaves. LAURA closes the door, puts the bag in the fridge. She notices her hand is wet with meat drippings. She wipes it on her pants. She picks up her plant. And finds the perfect spot for it. She sits on her couch.)

(End of play.)

NAMED

Lucy Thurber

LUCY THURBER is the author of ten plays: *Where We're Born, Ashville, Scarcity, Killers and Other Family, Stay, Bottom of the World, Monstrosity, Dillingham City, The Locus*, and *The Insurgents*. *The Insurgents* was produced at the 2011 Contemporary American Theatre Festival. The Atlantic Theater Company produced *Bottom of the World* and *Scarcity*, and Rattlestick Playwrights Theater has produced three of her plays, *Where We're Born, Killers and Other Family*, and *Stay*. Lucy wrote the text for *Quixote*, conceived and directed by Lear DeBessonet, a site-specific performance with the Psalters made for and with The Broad Street Community; also with Lear DeBessonet and produced by 13P, *Monstrosity*. She was a guest artist at Alaska's Perseverance Theatre twice, where she helped to adapt both *Desire Under the Elms* and *Moby Dick*. She has had readings and workshops at Steam Boat Springs, Manhattan Theatre Club, The New Group, Primary Stages, MCC Theater, Encore Theatre Company, PlayPenn, Williamstown Theatre Festival, The O'Neill with WET, New River Dramatists, Soho Rep, and The Orchard Project. *Scarcity* was published in the December 2007 issue of *American Theatre*. She is published by Dramatists Play Service. Thurber is a member of New Dramatists, 13P, and LAByrinth Theater Company. She has been commissioned by Playwrights Horizons, The Contemporary American Theatre Festival, and Yale Rep. She is the recipient of a Manhattan Theatre Club Playwriting Fellowship, the 1st Gary Bonasorte Memorial Prize for Playwriting 2008, and a Lilly Award. Lucy currently teaches at NYU and Sarah Lawrence College.

VISIBLE SOUL INTERVIEW WITH LUCY THURBER
Conducted by Zack Calhoon, February 26, 2011

How did you get started in theater? What made you start writing plays?

When I was nine my mother and I moved to Western Mass. Before that we moved around a lot. We went South, we went West, we went North and when things got a little too hectic my mother would always take us back to Connecticut to stay with or near my grandparents. During one of our times in Connecticut my mother got involved in a summer theater company run by a woman who worked in the theater department at SUNY Purchase. The company did Shakespeare plays in an amphitheater. It was a ten- to fifteen-minute a walk into the woods. They would put up Tiki torches along the path. It was magic. I played a page in *As You Like It.* I got to sing a song. I ate the same piece of slightly rancid prop meat every night. I loved the words. I loved rehearsals. I loved that a group of people decided to bring a story to life. And I was good at it. I knew I was. I'd found a place where all the stories in my head could come to life. It was nothing but theater for me from that point on.

I can't honestly say why I started writing plays. I like team sports and I like make-believe. I wrote my first play when I was ten. It was a terrible "musical" called "Five Hundred Dollar Bills." I wrote lyrics and then just sang a different tune to them each time I sang them. It made it difficult for the kids in the neighborhood when I cast them to learn the songs. I also got in trouble with some parents because of my play's message. The message was, I guess, or at least I was told, that crime pays and makes people happy and rich.

Tell me about your play, *Named*. What has the process been like? How do you think the play is going?

I was excited to write something tailor made for *Cino Nights* and for Jimmy's. *Named* is about first love, being a girl who likes girls, and shame. I feel like every gay person I know male or female has that one person, that first person who we love enough to admit out loud that we want them. Sometimes it works out but I think more often than not the person we love runs away when we admit how we feel. I remember in high school, laying in bed and "cuddling" with the girl I loved. I wanted to be kissed and touched by her so badly. I felt like a monster. My desire made me feel like a monster. I wanted her to love me. I wanted her to want me. I thought she was "normal," sexually "normal" and I was just wrong because I wasn't. At the same time I was also sure she loved and wanted me. I thought about her all the time. I wanted to have sex with her so badly. It made me angry with her and angry with myself. I wanted to write a play that explored what was spoken and what was unspoken. I wanted to explore how shame, love, desire, and silence can combine into anger and violence.

It's been wonderful. I have a talented, brave, and adventurous cast. My director, Jenna Worsham, is young and talented. I've wanted to get into a room with her for a while. I'm a member of Rising Phoenix Rep so obviously love the company. It's a wild, crazy, beautiful week. It's fun. We're working hard; it's a great adrenaline rush.

You have a very visceral writing and teaching style. What compels you to tell these stories that you tell?

I had a fairly extreme upbringing so, honestly I write what I know and what I think about. Theater is what saved me so I guess I always approach it as a matter of life and death. I believe that after food and shelter the next thing humanity needs is stories.

What kind writing inspires you?

I like honesty. I like work that makes me feel human. I like sweetness. I like integrity. I like explorations of love and violence.

Who or what has been the biggest influence on your work as a playwright thus far?

My mother, Western Mass, and August Wilson.

Named, directed by Jenna Worsham, premiered February 27, 2011, at the Seventh Street Small Stage at Jimmy's No. 43.

CAST LIST

Cora ....Ronete Levenson
Emily .... Sarah Tolan-Mee
Cora 2... Katie Meister
Emily 2... Lila Dupree

Fight Director: Kathryn Ekblad

CHARACTERS

CORA
EMILY
CORA 2
EMILY 2

(A dorm room. Night. CORA sleeps curled up in bed. She is whimpering in her sleep. She wakes with a start. Disoriented, she looks around the room.)

CORA: Emily...?

(No answer.)

CORA: Emily?

(No answer. CORA gets out of bed and crosses to the door. She opens it looks out into the hallway.)

CORA: (A little louder.) Emily...?

(Nothing. She shuts the door and goes back to the bed and sits. She waits. She gets up again and looks for her shoes. She finds them, sits back down on the bed, and puts them on. There is a sweatshirt on the bed. CORA picks it up, holds it to her, and smells it. After a beat, CORA puts the sweatshirt down and crosses to the desk and sits. She reaches under the desk where there is a minifridge and opens it. She takes out a Diet Coke and takes a gulp. As she does, CORA 2 appears and stands behind CORA sitting in the chair. CORA 2 is furious, her fists clenched. CORA gets a piece of paper and a pen and starts to write a note. The door opens and EMILY enters. As she does, EMILY 2 slinks in behind her and stands guiltily in the doorway. CORA 2 stares at EMILY 2.)

CORA: Hi. I was just leaving you a note.

(EMILY goes and flops down on the bed. EMILY 2 steps all the way into the room, shuts the door behind her, and leans against it. EMILY 2 looks at CORA 2. CORA 2 is almost shaking in fury.)

CORA: Where did you go?

EMILY: To see Justin.

CORA: That's what I figured.

EMILY: You were sleeping. But I woke up.

CORA: Restless, huh?

EMILY: Restless. Restless. Restless.

CORA: I get it. You were restless.

EMILY: Hey?

CORA: What?

EMILY: Hey? I'm sensing sarcasm.

CORA: You're so perceptive.

EMILY: Cute.

CORA: Thanks. I am cute.

EMILY: I know you're cute.

CORA: I am cute.

EMILY: I know it. You don't think I know you're cute?

(CORA shrugs.)

EMILY: Oh I see you're playing hard to get.

CORA: What?

EMILY: What's up with the distant act?

CORA: No just it's late and I wish you'd woken me up when you left. I have a lot of work to do.

EMILY: You always have a lot of work to do.

CORA: I have practice in the morning.

EMILY: You always have practice in the morning. Don't leave! Come on—I don't want you to leave...

CORA: Don't start pouting—

(EMILY pouts.)

CORA: Emily don't— Come on you know that's not fair—

(CORA 2 crosses to the door of the room to leave. EMILY 2 blocks her way.)

EMILY 2: I'm sorry.

EMILY: I don't want you to go—I want to talk—I want to cuddle—

(She holds her arms out to CORA.)

EMILY 2: I said I'm sorry.

CORA: Emily if I come over there, I'm never going to leave. I have a shit load of work I have to get done before tomorrow morning.

CORA 2: You're not fucking sorry.

EMILY: Is it my fault you like to over commit yourself? *(Pats the bed.)* Come on. Come here. Come cuddle. *(Holds out her arms.)* Come to me! You know you want to—you know you do.

(CORA crosses to the bed and lets EMILY hug her.)

CORA 2: *(To EMILY 2.)* Move.

(EMILY 2 shakes her head.)

CORA 2: I said move.

EMILY 2: No.

CORA 2: You're a piece of shit.

(EMILY 2 doesn't move.)

CORA 2: You're a fuckin' whore.

(EMILY 2 starts to cry. CORA 2 stands watching her cry, unmoved.)

EMILY 2: Please...please...Cora...don't look at me like that...

CORA 2: I know where you went. I knew the minute I opened my eyes where you went.

EMILY 2: Please. Please—

CORA 2: You left me. You left me.

(EMILY 2 reaches out to touch CORA 2. CORA 2 slaps EMILY 2's hand away. EMILY 2 tries to touch her again and CORA 2 pushes EMILY 2 back against the door and raises her arm to punch

her, stops herself, and moves quickly to the other side of the room. EMILY 2 smiles.)

EMILY: God you feel so good.

CORA: Do I?

EMILY: Turn around. I want to spoon.

(CORA does. EMILY hugs CORA from behind and strokes her stomach. CORA's breathing gets heavier and heavier as the scene goes on. EMILY pulls up CORA's shirt to look at her stomach.)

EMILY: You're in such great shape. I can feel your six pack.

CORA: Girls can't have six packs. We're built differently—we have four packs. I have a four pack.

(EMILY laughs.)

CORA: Don't laugh at me.

EMILY: Relax—

CORA: Why are you laughing at me?

EMILY: God. Don't be so serious. I was fuckin' complimenting you Cora. You're gonna get mad at me for complimenting you?

CORA: No...

EMILY: What?

CORA: No.

(EMILY playfully slaps CORA then cuddles back up to her.)

CORA 2: *(To EMILY 2.)* I'm not doing this.

EMILY: The way you feel is one of my favorite things in the whole world. Justin was wasted.

CORA: Surprise. Surprise.

EMILY: Full-fledged shit-faced.

CORA: Another giant surprise—

EMILY: The party was...

CORA: When is it not?

EMILY: True. True. And he was flirting.

CORA: Sorry.

EMILY: Maybe more than flirting.

CORA: I'm sorry Emily.

EMILY: When I came in Jennifer Kiley was all over him or visa versa...

CORA: It's not to late for me to kill him. I could just walk over there and kill him, if you wanted me too. If you wanted me to I would.

EMILY: He is such a dick! He is such a fuckin' asshole.

CORA: Yeah. Yeah. But you know that Emily. You know he's a dick. You shouldn't have gone over there. You should have just stayed here.

(EMILY is still stroking CORA's stomach. She has her hand under CORA's shirt. CORA whimpers. She is clearly trying not to make sound but can't help herself.)

CORA 2: *(To EMILY 2.)* Move.

(EMILY 2 shakes her head "no.")

CORA 2: I'm not doing this. I'm not doing this. I'm not doing this.

(EMILY 2 laughs at CORA 2. CORA 2 visibly restrains herself from going for EMILY 2.)

CORA 2: It's not funny. You are not funny. I hate you. I hate you. You ruin everything.

(EMILY 2 crosses to the desk and sits.)

CORA 2: I want you out of me. If I could I would reach inside of myself and rip you out of me.

(EMILY alternates between stroking CORA's stomach and back.)

EMILY: He's not always like that. You know that.

(CORA doesn't answer.)

EMILY: I wouldn't be with him if he was like that all the time. You know that don't you, Cora? Cora?

CORA: What?

EMILY: It's important to me that you know that. He's nice when we're alone. He talks when we're alone. I don't know why it's so important to him to pretend he's stupid in public? Cora? Why do you think he pretends to be stupid in public?

(EMILY stops stroking CORA.)

CORA: I don't know... Maybe he's embarrassed...

EMILY: Embarrassed of what?

CORA: You know? His friends...it's not like he hangs out with a crowd that reads.

EMILY: I read.

CORA: I mean besides you. He's a jock Emily. It's in a jock's nature to read in private.

EMILY: You're a jock.

CORA: That's different.

EMILY: You're not a jock?

CORA: You know what I mean. I'm different.

EMILY: I know. I know you're different.

(EMILY resumes stroking CORA's stomach. EMILY 2 opens the minifridge and takes out some chips and salsa. She makes a production of deliberately opening the salsa and chips. She eats. She holds out the bag of chips to CORA 2 offering them to her.)

CORA 2: Fuck you.

EMILY 2: Suit yourself, Cora.

CORA 2: Fuck you.

(EMILY 2 eats chips.)

EMILY: Cora? Cora? You heard me right? I said I know you're different.

CORA 2: You heard me right? You heard me Emily? I said fuck you.

CORA: Okay...

EMILY: I do!

CORA: Okay Emily.

EMILY: Why do you sound mad?

CORA: I don't.

EMILY: You do.

CORA: I'm just tired. I'm just really tired.

(EMILY wraps her arms and legs around CORA from behind her.)

EMILY: But you're too comfortable to move. Aren't you? Aren't you Cora?

(CORA doesn't answer, but she doesn't get up either. CORA closes her eyes. EMILY strokes her. EMILY starts to talk. She talks over the following action between CORA 2 and EMILY 2.)

EMILY: Do you ever feel invisible? I feel invisible a lot of the time. I know you know that about me. Or at least I think you do. I think you do Cora. I walk around the campus. I sit in class. And all these words come at me they just come at me you know? Like darts or razor blades or something. You know Cora? Like zing. Like zing.

(CORA 2 gets up. CORA opens her eyes and looks directly at CORA 2 and EMILY 2. She watches them. EMILY 2 watches her while she puts the cover back onto the salsa container. CORA 2 heads towards the door. EMILY 2 stands up blocking her.)

EMILY: You like it when I talk to you. Really talk.

(EMILY picks up the salsa container and holding it she slams it into CORA 2's shoulder. CORA 2 with one hand knocks the container out of EMILY 2's hand and with the other grabs EMILY 2 by the throat. EMILY 2 puts her hand on CORA 2's privates.)

EMILY: I know what you like.

EMILY 2: I know what you like.

(CORA 2 pulls EMILY 2 into a violent kiss. They go down to the floor. Violent sex. EMILY keeps talking. CORA watches the sex. EMILY keeps talking over it.)

EMILY: They come at me and some of them lodge in my brain. They lodge there. They burrow like—like fuckin' animals or something—they get in there and I can't shake them. I want to. I want to stop thinking. But I can't stop thinking. They make sentences and then the sentences make thoughts. I have thoughts Cora. Beautiful, crazy, big fuckin' thoughts. You know Cora? You know? I watch you sometimes in class. I watch your eyes. You focus in—then focus out—like you're reading something inside your head. Like—Like—you're reading something inside your head—like you're referring to a parchment or something—some ancient piece of text—evaluating and then commenting—commenting to the class—retrieving ancient wisdom from inside your head and then commenting to the class about it. And I wonder does anyone else know the shit that you have going on up there? I wonder do I? Sometimes I just want so bad—

(EMILY 2 comes.)

EMILY: I mean we're so close...you and me we're so close...I just want—something—I don't know—sometimes I look at you and I want so badly. Or late at night—or in the car—or I don't know—I don't know but you know how we are and I—I—I wonder do you see that in me. When you look at me—when you look at me—do you see something ancient in me too?

(CORA 2 comes. EMILY 2 and CORA 2 lay on the floor. CORA watches CORA 2 and EMILY 2. CORA 2 gets up. EMILY 2 tries to stop her but CORA 2 pulls away.)

EMILY 2: Where are you going?

(CORA 2 doesn't answer. She gathers her stuff. EMILY 2 sits up.)

EMILY 2: Where are you going?

(EMILY 2 reaches for CORA 2, who pulls away from her.)

CORA 2: I feel sick.

EMILY 2: Don't—

EMILY: Cora? Cora? Are you sleeping?

CORA: No.

EMILY: What?

CORA: I'm not sleeping. You know I'm not sleeping.

EMILY 2: Cora don't—

CORA: I always listen when you talk.

CORA 2: I feel sick.

EMILY: You understand?

CORA 2: I feel sick.

CORA: I always understand.

EMILY: What?

EMILY: I know...   EMILY 2: Cora...

CORA: What...?   CORA 2: I feel... God...I feel sick—

(CORA 2 exits. CORA watches her go.)

EMILY: I know.

(EMILY 2 exits. CORA watches her go. CORA begins to silently cry.)

EMILY: I know you always listen. Cora? *(Moving so she can see CORA's face.)* Hey? Hey—Oh my goodness. Hey? What's wrong? Why are you crying?

CORA: I'm not crying...

EMILY: You're crying—

CORA: I never cry—

EMILY: Tell me what's wrong—

CORA: I never cry—!

EMILY: There's tears coming out of your eyes—

CORA: I need to leave. I need to get out of here—

(CORA gets up and gathers her stuff.)

EMILY: You always do this—

CORA: What—?

EMILY: Why do you do this—?

CORA: What? What?

EMILY: Why won't you talk to me? I talk to you. I tell you everything—

CORA: I tell you stuff all the time—

EMILY: Cora, please—please—stop and talk to me.

(CORA stops and looks at EMILY.)

EMILY: Talk to me...

(CORA weeps openly now. EMILY goes to her and hugs her. CORA cries harder.)

CORA: I can't bear it—

EMILY: I'm here—

CORA: I can't bear it—I can't bear it—I can't bear it—I can't, I can't—

EMILY: What? What—?

CORA: I can't anymore—

EMILY: Can't what—?

CORA: You know—fuck—fuck—you know—

EMILY: No—

CORA: Us on the bed—

EMILY: What—?

CORA: You—the way you—

EMILY: What? What Cora?

CORA: I love you— You love me— I love you and you love me. Can't we just— can't we just stop now. Can't we just—

EMILY: I don't understand—Cora I don't understand—

(CORA pulls away from EMILY in frustration.)

CORA: Why would you leave me here—?

EMILY: What?

CORA: Why would you leave me here sleeping in your bed to go and fuck someone else—?

EMILY: Wait—? What—what—?

CORA: You know what I'm talking about—

EMILY: I went to see my boyfriend—

CORA: Stop—

EMILY: Stop what? Stop what—?

CORA: Stop it, fuckin' stop it—you know—you know Emily! The way you touch me—the way you touch me—the things you say to me—the way—the way you look at me—you're always looking at me—at me—and I'm tired—tired—

EMILY: Tired...?

CORA: It's like torture—it's torture Emily and I lay here and I think things—I feel things and I want—I want—I want so bad—and the things I think—the things I think and I get so mad—I get so mad at you—the things I think cause I get so mad at you and then I feel sick—sick and ashamed cause of the things I think when I get so mad at you—and—

(EMILY crosses to the bed and sits down.)

CORA: Emily, Emily, I love you—I love you and I wait for you. I wait for you— It's seems like all I do is wait for you— I

wait for you to touch me—to touch me— and I just want us to stop pretending now— Can we just stop pretending now?

(No response.)

CORA: Emily...? Emily...?

(No response.)

CORA: Emily? Emily for God's sake say something? Emily please say something...

EMILY: Like what? Like what Cora? What is it you want me to say?

CORA: I...

EMILY: I mean do you have it scripted? Have you scripted my response?

CORA: What? What? What...?

EMILY: I mean—you've been just—just laying there while I—God—

CORA: What? What—?

EMILY: I mean—I can't believe you'd put me in this position—I can't believe—

CORA: Position—? Position, Emily—?

EMILY: Think about how I feel—

EMILY: So typical— So, so typical— So, fuckin' typical.	CORA: I am. I am. That's the point—how we both feel—how we both feel—and fuck it— fuck it Emily—let's just fuck it all—

CORA: Wait? What?

EMILY: You just lay there while I touch you and you're getting—God Cora you're getting...God—God Cora how could you—?

CORA: Don't—

EMILY: How could you? I made myself so vulnerable to you—I made myself and the whole time—

CORA: Don't—you don't have to—

EMILY: You didn't say anything-

CORA: You don't have to lie—I don't care—I don't care—

EMILY: And I felt so safe with you—so safe and you totally took advantage of that—

CORA: I took advantage—? I took advantage?

EMILY: Of my vulnerability—emotionally—

CORA: Wait? Emotionally? I took advantage of you emotionally?

EMILY: Of my emotional vulnerability, yes.

CORA: Is this a joke—?

EMILY: I think you should go—

CORA: Is this a joke—?

EMILY: I want you to go.

CORA: Really?

(Beat.)

CORA: Really, Emily?

(CORA looks at EMILY. EMILY looks away.)

CORA: You're that scared? I didn't know you were that scared. I knew I was. I knew I was—I just never imagined...

(CORA looks at EMILY.)

CORA: Shit— Shit—fuck—I can't believe it—I thought you were just waiting for me—and I thought I was waiting for you and then I thought fuck it—fuck it I love you and I'm going to be brave—I'm going to be brave because I love you—and I do—I do see all the things you think—and all the ways you move—I love the way you breathe in your sleep. I love the way you wake up in the morning and I love when you laugh and I think you're beautiful when you cry—all the corny stuff—all the corny, stupid, love song stuff. I even love your fear—or I thought I did—I thought I did because I thought your fear was just like mine. I thought you were afraid like me—I thought you loved like me. But you—you—you're not scared like me—you're not scared like me—you're just, you're just...Gosh, gosh that's sad Emily—it's just really sad.

(CORA exits. EMILY sits on the bed. She starts crying but doesn't move.)

(Lights down.)

(End of play.)

ROW AFTER ROW

Jessica Dickey

JESSICA DICKEY made her playwriting debut with her hit one-woman show, *The Amish Project*, a deeply moving multicharacter examination of the 2006 Amish schoolhouse shootings. *The Amish Project* premiered at the New York International Fringe Festival and then transferred to Cherry Lane Theatre before it opened at Rattlestick Playwrights Theater and was greeted with tremendous accolades from audiences and critics alike. *The Amish Project* has since gone on to be produced around the country and the world (recent productions include The American Theater Company in Chicago, the City Theatre in Pittsburgh, and theaters in The Netherlands and South Korea). It is published by Samuel French, and several monologues are in the Smith & Kraus Monologue book (2010). Jessie's play *Charles Ives Take Me Home* is scheduled for production at Rattlestick Playwrights Theater in their 2012-13 season and was nominated for the Susan Smith Blackburn Prize. *Row After Row* premiered in the *Cino Nights* series at Rising Phoenix Repertory and has an upcoming production in Tucson. As an actor Jessie works in TV and theater, recently making her Broadway debut in *Wit*. Special thanks to Abrams Artists, Station 3 Management, and Stone Manners Salners Agency. Big bear hugs to the Rising Phoenix gang!

VISIBLE SOUL INTERVIEW WITH JESSICA DICKEY
Conducted by Zack Calhoon, May 16, 2011

How did you get started in theater? What made you start writing plays?

I was acting in a play by Arthur Laurents and he and I became pen pals and he told me I should write a play, that I could write. So I did and then I did again, and then again, and writing made me so happy that I decided to just keep doing it. But I started writing very young—poetry and short stories, I keep a journal... When I was really little I once designed a magazine from cover to cover! I wrote all the articles and designed all the adds—there was even a quiz! Haha! I really wish I had that little magazine because 1. If I don't have it then who does (and do they have access to the Internet)?!—and 2. I would love to see what my little six-year-old self had to say. It was probably some wretched regurgitation of regular magazine bullshit, like make-up and personality and crap, but who knows—maybe there was some honest little Jessie thoughts in there, and I'd like to read that.

Tell me about your play, *Row After Row*. What has the process been like? How do you think the play is going?

I've been curious about Civil War re-enactors lately, and they are indeed a peculiar, proud, sensitive bunch! Having grown up right next to Gettysburg and the Mason-Dixon Line I have always felt an affinity for the Civil War, and so I enjoyed going back to Gettysburg to research Pickett's Charge (which is the re-enactment that the characters in the play just completed)—it really is such a beautiful little town, and the grounds of the battlefield are profoundly beautiful and complex—trees, boulders, hills... But I wrote the bulk of Row After Row while performing my play *The Amish Project* at the City Theatre in Pittsburgh (just wrapped last week), and it's so nice to be diving in! The crew of talent involved is just awesome—Sevrin Anne Mason, Bjorn Thorstad and Mike Kingsbaker in the cast, and the lovely Stephen Brackett at the helm.

How did you get involved with Rising Phoenix Rep? What do you love most about working with them?

It's hard to summarize what Rising Phoenix means to me—especially as the years go on and they grow to mean more... First of all, as individuals they are the most LOVELIEST people EVER, so there's that. But as a company they are an amazingly talented powerhouse gang, so you know that anything happening with Rising Phoenix is going to be fun, truth-seeking, love-generating, high-quality, deep-magic theater. RPR is a home to professional theater artists—a safe haven to explore their craft and reconnect with their love of the art; nothing has embodied this spirit more than RPR's *Cino Nights*.

What kind writing inspires you?

Because I am also an actor I have the opportunity to encounter all kinds of writing—so I am constantly in contact with storytellers that awaken my understanding of what language can do, what theatrical literature can be… I will always aspire to Arthur Miller for his perfect union of character and plot…and Virginia Woolf for her unflinching inquiry of the mind, the spirit, and the courage to trust us to follow the trail of crumbs her language leaves behind—she was so singular, so true… I also love Marilynn Robinson—her book *Gilead* taught me something about writing that's hard to articulate now, but it had to do with the questions of my own heart, my petty yearnings, and that the pursuit of their true revelation is all the compass I need… and Thornton Wilder—*Our Town* is still one of my favorite fucking plays ever!… Among my fellow playwrights I look to Daniel Talbott, Sheila Callaghan, Dan O'Brien, Annie Baker—there are so many talented writers right now, it's hard to name them all! But you know, and I hope this isn't too lame to confess, I have also been deeply touched by things I wrote a long time ago…a snippet of a poem from my childhood, or a monologue I wrote in college… It touches me to connect to my younger self who picked up the pen and stabbed away at something—I read such things and I feel this delightful recognition, like "There you are!"—Somehow that lightens my spirits as I chip away at my current project—maybe it reminds me that just the act of recording one's inner self, for the stage or even just for the page, is a significant pursuit, is reward in itself.

Who or what has been the biggest influence on your work as a playwright thus far?

My family for sure—they are the bones of everything I write—and with my family I include the landscape of my hometown and rural Pennsylvania. While not everything I write is a rural story, I just know the vocabulary of my heart is that of the woods, a big sky, grass, a quiet space, the smell of skunk—LOL. But yes, my family, and the love and pain that come with them, are imbued in all I make.

Row After Row, directed by Stephen Brackett, premiered May 22, 2011, at the Seventh Street Small Stage at Jimmy's No. 43.

CAST LIST

Cal...Mike Kingsbaker
Tom.. Bjorn Thorstad
Leah..Sevrin Anne Mason

CHARACTERS

LEAH
TOM
CAL

NOTE ABOUT THE TEXT

Slashes (/) indicate overlapping in specific moments, but please also feel free to overlap where it feels natural and aids the humor and chemistry.

Present day. The side room of an old pub in Gettysburg, Pennsylvania. Lots of dark wood. At top, LEAH is sitting at a small table alone with a beer. She is dressed still in her Civil War re-enactment clothes, a gray uniform. After a moment TOM and CAL enter, deep in fraternal, heated discussion.

CAL: All I'm saying is, Pickett's Charge was a mistake, it was a simple mistake—and it could have been prevented.

TOM: That's easy to say because it was such a fucking disaster.

CAL: Well, yes, but that doesn't make it less true. If General Lee had heeded Longstreet's warning that Pickett's Charge would fail, the war might have gone a very different way.

(They stop in their tracks and see LEAH sitting at their table. An awkward moment—what to do?)

CAL: Um, ma'am?

(She doesn't look up.)

CAL: Ma'am?

LEAH: Are you talking to me?

TOM: Uh, yeah—have you been—sitting here long?

LEAH: Um—???

CAL: Did Ron see you come in?

LEAH: I think so...

CAL: Oh he did?/ Cuz—

TOM: What he's trying/—to say—

CAL: Cuz he usually—

LEAH: Yeah, I think he did—I mean I ordered my beer—

TOM: Oh that's fine that's fine, we always sit—um—somewhere else, that's cool.

CAL: No it's not, it's just that we usually sit here.

LEAH: Oh. Uh huh.

TOM: No it's cool, / really—

CAL: I'm sure you understand— *(He indicates their Civil War re-enactment garb.)* We're kind of traditionalists, if you know what I mean/, so—

TOM: Dude, it's cool/, just—

LEAH: Okay.

CAL: Tom, the lady seems to understand, am I right?

LEAH: Yeah, I think so. You usually sit here.

CAL: Exactamundo.

TOM: Yes, we do/, but—

CAL: It's a tradition that every year after Gettysburg we come here and have a beer. Yes.

LEAH: Cool.

CAL: Yes, very. So...

LEAH: So...

(Awkward silence while they wait and see if she'll move. She gestures to the other seats at the table.)

LEAH: Would you care to join me?

(Not what they were expecting.)

CAL: That's—not—exactly—

TOM: Absolutely. That's very kind of you.

(He gives CAL a look, CAL complies; they sit with their beers.)

LEAH: I'm Leah.

TOM: Nice to meet you. I'm Tom, 121st Pennsylvania. And this is my comrade Cal.

CAL: Longstreet's Division. Army of Northern Virginia.

LEAH: Cool.

CAL: What were you?

LEAH: Sorry?

CAL: What infantry were you?

LEAH: Oh, um, I was some Virginia Brigade too. I forget which one. We lost, I know that. Ha ha.

TOM: Oh, uh huh. Yeah. So you're new. *(With a warning to CAL.)* Cal, she's new.

LEAH: Yeah. Very new. I just moved here actually.

TOM: Oh, I see. Where from?

LEAH: New York.

TOM: Huh. A city gal.

LEAH: Sort of, yeah.

TOM: Well, welcome to Gettysburg.

(Awkward sipping of beer.)

CAL: We knew you were new.

TOM: Cal—

LEAH: Oh yeah?

CAL: Yeah, you're farbing all over the place.

TOM: Oh Christ.

CAL: You're what we call FARBTASTIC.

TOM: Calvin.

LEAH: I don't get it.

TOM: It's nothing. Cal, be a gentleman, okay?

CAL: What? I'm sure the little lady is interested.

TOM: Cal, she's new.

CAL: Exactly, so how's she supposed to know?

LEAH: Know what?

CAL: That you're farbing.

LEAH: What's farbing?

(TOM sighs.)

CAL: What's farbing she asks. She willingly asked, you heard it.

TOM: Cal. Uh— Farbing is kind of an inside term.

CAL: YEAH.

TOM: Among us—re-enactors—

CAL: "Us re-enactors." Dude, you act like you're ashamed.

TOM: It's when— What? I do not, I am not, I'm not ashamed, I'm just—

CAL: Okay, don't blow your bayonet, I just thought you sounded ashamed.

TOM: Well, I'm not. I'm not ashamed.

CAL: "Us re-enactors."

TOM: (Ignoring him.) A farb is when your gear or weaponry or uniform— uh— isn't up to—uh—? —par.

LEAH: Par? As in—

TOM: Historical accuracy.

CAL: Yeah, as in WRONG.

LEAH: Oh... You mean... like...

CAL: Yeah, like your nose ring? No way. Your jewelry? Uhn uhn. The color of the wool? Passable, but the thread count? No. More indicative of the mid 1900s, not 1863.

TOM: Okay. Awesome. Now that we've managed to completely alienate our new friend here.

CAL: What? I'm just sayin'.

LEAH: I still don't understand what farbing is.

TOM: A farb is a term used by re-enactors when something in one's uniform or outfit or gear or behavior isn't accurate to the historical context. It's a major concern among re-enactors, who—of course—consider themselves living historians. If you will.

LEAH: So farb is an acronym? Or—?

CAL: No one knows exactly where the term originated. I've heard tell—

TOM: You've heard tell?

CAL: —that it's a combination of the words "fake" and "garb"—thusly— "farb."

TOM: Thusly?! Wow dude. You're really on a roll here.

CAL: (Silencing Tom.) BUT I PREFER— the explanation used by some of us hard core re-enactors that when we see an improper thread count, or a pair of anachronistic eyewear, the re-enactor leans in to the farbing offender and says, "FAR BE IT FROM ME"— to criticize what you're wearing, or whatever... I prefer to think that THAT is where the term "farb" comes from.

LEAH: "Far be it from me."

CAL: Yup.

TOM: "Thusly."

CAL: Farb.

LEAH: Huh.

TOM: Anyway, there are some great resources in the local libraries or whatever, or you can even ask other re-enactors in your brigade for help in making sure your gear is appropriate, they can steer you toward the right vendors or whatever...

CAL: But even if you do get your gear up to historical standards, then there's the fact that you're a woman...

TOM: No, nooooooo, no, that's not a problem.

LEAH: That I'm a woman?

CAL: Yup.

TOM: No it's not. Cal— you know the new rules.

CAL: Oh that is a bunch of mamby pamby bullshit—"Women can be soldiers too"—

TOM: It was just passed this year that women can participate in re-enactment combat, regardless of historical context.

CAL: Oh wah wah wah, I wanna be a soldier, wah wah wah—

TOM: (Plowing forward.) And IN FACT— we now know that there were many women who died in the Civil War, serving as spies, nurses, vivandiéres.

CAL: I wanna sacrifice History so I feel EQUAL—wah wah wah.

TOM: And of course Dr. Mary Walker won the Medal of Honor for her service in the hospitals.

LEAH: Really?

TOM: Yes. Absolutely.

LEAH: Wow, I didn't know that. The Medal of Honor?

TOM: It's true.

CAL: What the fuck is a vivandiére anyway?

TOM: (To CAL.) A vivandiére is a French term for women who provided soldiers with provisions—food, equipment.

CAL: I know what provisions are, Tom.

TOM: Alright, I'm just saying.

CAL: How are we supposed to hold ourselves to historical context if we have skirts running around the battlefield? It's RETARDED.

TOM: Retarded? Oh now we can say retarded? What if there were a retarded person sitting right here, Cal? Huh? What then?

CAL: Oh Christ. You and your freakin'— the school system is making you soft, my friend—

TOM: No really, Cal, this is important, I want you to picture a little retarded boy sitting right here, picture him, picture his eggy eyes and his dropped jaw and lolling tongue and you tell me how it makes him feel to hear you say it's retarded.

CAL: I think that's Downs.

TOM: ...what?

CAL: I think that's Downs.

TOM: What the fuck are you talking about?

CAL: I think when their eyes are sort of big and weird and—sort of—bovine— that it's—it's not retarded—it's called Downs.

TOM: Downs? Like Downs Syndrome?

CAL: Yeah. Drooling lips. The eyes. That's Downs.

TOM: So what is your fucking point?

CAL: That if a little boy of that description were in fact sitting here, he would probably not, well, one: understand what the fuck we mean when we say retarded, and two: necessarily be offended because he's not retarded he just has Downs.

TOM: Oh, he "just" has Downs.

CAL: Well you know what I'm sayin'.

LEAH: (Rather quietly.) I think people with Downs Syndrome are actually considered retarded citizens.

CAL: —Retarded CITIZENS??

TOM: Cal.

LEAH: Yeah—as in—Association of Retarded Citizens—a social program for people who suffer from retardation.

(A beat.)

TOM: Let's move on.

CAL: THE POINT IS—if there WERE a Downs person, who also happened to be retarded, sitting here, then we could take it as an opportunity to *confirm* with them that in fact it IS retarded for a woman to be a soldier on the battlefield when there would not have been a woman on the battlefield (in any traditional sense) at Gettysburg in 1863.

(A beat.)

LEAH: I can kind of see your point on that.

TOM: Wait, about the retarded boy—???

LEAH: No, about women on the battle-field.

TOM: Oh, you don't have to—

CAL: There, see?!

TOM: No, come on— You don't have to agree with him just because he's fragile.

LEAH: No it's cool.

CAL: I'm not fragile.

LEAH: I get it, I do.

TOM: Really?

CAL: Do I seem fragile?

LEAH: If historical accuracy is really important, it's gotta be a bummer to see a woman on the battlefield.

CAL: Yes. Thank you.

LEAH: According to HISTORY, we should be sewing your "freedom flag," or pre-paring the meal over which you discuss your "inalienable rights."

CAL: Thank/ you.

TOM: *(Appreciating her irony.)* That's— huh...

LEAH: I'm sure that IN GENERAL as the rest of the population begins to lobby for equality, if you're part of the group that's always been in power, knowing your time is up must be a BIG FUCKIN' BUZZ KILL.

(Awkward silence.)

TOM: *(Slight clearing of throat.)* So what drew you to Civil War re-enactment?

CAL: Since clearly it wasn't historical accuracy.

LEAH: Well, I'm new to the area and I don't really know anyone, and I saw an ad at the A&P that the whatever brigade of Virginia was seeking new membership for the Gettysburg re-enactment, and I thought, well why not.

TOM: But you do have an interest in history?

LEAH: Yeah, I think history is very interesting—

TOM: *(To CAL.)* See she thinks history is interesting

LEAH: And when I saw the ad at the A&P I thought well let's just get right to it—Gettysburg, Pennsylvania—and I didn't feel like playing the *serving wench* or a *widowed bride* or whatever. So here I am.

TOM: Here you are.

CAL: You know if you wanted to be on a battlefield you could've gone and done the live action fantasy role-playing group they have over in Frederick. They use potions and foam shields and shit.

LEAH: I don't even know what the fuck you're talking about.

CAL: I'm just saying that just because you're new here and you feel like mak-ing friends or whatever doesn't mean you can just show up and ruin what a lot of people—

LEAH: You mean a lot of MEN—

CAL: Have devoted a lot of time and resources to making great and authentic and good.

TOM: Okay, Cal, take it easy, okay? Seriously.

CAL: Farbies, man! It's more than just the outfit, I'm tellin' ya.

LEAH: You know what fuck you. "This is my battlefield and you gotta play by my little rules"—Bullshit.

CAL: It IS my battlefield and the rules are NOT just MINE they belong to HISTORY.

LEAH: Oh my God if I weren't so goddamn desperate to grasp something in life that I can ENJOY I would honestly find this interaction with a bona fide MEATHEAD to be remotely fucking interesting, but unfortunately you caught me in a dark YEAR, so— HISTORY IS JUST THAT. It's HIS-STORY. And you can roll your eyes and call it a feminist battle cry or whatever but it's the truth. Just because your team was the only team with a fucking microphone doesn't mean you were the only ones trying to be HEARD.

(There is a very long, strained silence. TOM has started shredding his napkin.)

CAL: Oh Christ Tom.

TOM: What I'm sorry—

CAL: I hate when you do this dude; it's not, it's not—

TOM: Do what? Do what?

CAL: It's just— It's just not—

TOM: I'm not hurting anyone. This is not hurting anyone.

CAL: Stop it. Just stop. Stop.

TOM: You have issues.

CAL: Fuck yes I have issues, we know this.

TOM: Well okay then, I'm not trying to put you down, I'm just defending the expression of my neurosis.

CAL: You don't see me shredding napkins like a fucking church organist or something.

TOM: I can't help that this kind of conversation makes me uncomfortable.

CAL: What? Why? We're just having a spirited discussion here/, what is there to be so uncomfortable about?

TOM: A church organist? Is that what I am if I shred napkins?

CAL: She seems fine.

LEAH: *(Totally sincere.)* I am actually; I've been told by numerous lovers I have issues with aggression.

(Slight pause.)

CAL: Okay then, there ya go. We're all fine here.

TOM: It's just— The whole men rule the world thing—

LEAH: Men DO rule the world.

CAL: Oh come on.

TOM: See, this—this—weird stratification thing—

LEAH: What? They do.

CAL: Oh okay is that what this awesome feeling is? This nauseous pressure on my chest that I live with every day, no it's not misery, it's just the immeasurable JOY of ruling the world.

LEAH: Well, YOU don't rule the world.

CAL: Oh thank you for the confirmation.

LEAH: So that "awesome feeling" is that fact that men DO rule the world and you DON'T. You're not a general, you're militia.

(Quick, hot beat.)

CAL: I will be eligible for leadership in another five battles.

LEAH: Oh okay.

CAL: *(In her face.)* WHICH IS A PRIVILEGE.

(LEAH suddenly kisses CAL on the mouth really hard. Then she sits back and takes a sip of her beer. There is a moment of stunned silence.)

TOM: WHAT WAS   CAL: Wowza.
THAT??

LEAH: I guess I just wanted you to shut your mouth.

CAL: Oh yeah?

LEAH: Yeah. And the other tactics didn't seem to be working, so...

(CAL would like very much to retaliate in some way—be something other than completely speechless, but that is in fact exactly what he is.)

TOM: *(After a moment.)* Okay. Let's just— Rest ourselves. Chillax.

(A beat.)

CAL: Chillax?

TOM: What, my students say it.

CAL: Don't say chillax.

CAL: *(To LEAH.)* So how was it today?

LEAH: How was what today?

CAL: Being a man. Did you rule the world?

TOM: Okay okay— let's just—ask in another way, okay?

CAL: What dude I'm just talkin' here—

TOM: I realize you two are practically ENJOYING this incredibly tense conversation, but some of us don't have the stomach for so much—

CAL: We're just talkin' here.

TOM: Well, how about "How was your first re-enactment experience?" How's that?

CAL: Fine.

TOM: You know what I'm saying?

CAL: No absolutely, you're right.

TOM: Okay. Yeah, just—you know—

CAL: How was your first re-enactment experience?

TOM: Thank you.

CAL: As a MAN.

TOM: Okay—

CAL: What?

TOM: Calvin—

CAL: How was it?

(TOM sighs.)

LEAH: It was different than I expected.

CAL: *(To TOM.)* See that wasn't so bad. *(To LEAH.)* Say more.

LEAH: It was definitely interesting...

CAL: This is Pickett's Charge, right?

LEAH: Yeah.

CAL: Okay— Interesting—interesting like—

LEAH: I don't know— Stomping through the fields,
the gear clanging against my thighs and back, making an ugly bell sound,
my pack against my shoulders...
All the motion of gear on the body,
all these physical sensations were just immediately interesting to me,
like I couldn't stop feeling my body or something,
which actually I haven't been able to do in a long time...

And my legs—my left and my right,
climbing, the swish of grass,

my left and my right,
gliding next to and then past each
    other...
And even though it's fake, you know?—
you know it's fake—
I still felt scared and excited, a kind of
    sweaty anticipation.

The sun was high.
There were hundreds of us climbing
    across this field, toward the trees
    on the other side...
And suddenly—
there they were—
the *other* hundreds, wearing the *other*
    color,
but the same gear, the same pack, the
    same sweat.

And that's the only clarity there was—
the journey,
the arriving,
seeing them for the first time...
The rest was chaos.

We started through the field—and I
    found myself screaming at the top
    of my lungs,
just hollering like a fucking lunatic!
How often do you get to do that?! Just
    ROAR like a fucking WILD BOAR.
And because you WANT to, not because
    you're in trouble and you have to
    or whatever...
And yet I kept looking around like, what
    the fuck are we doing?
Why are we doing this?

And I kind of loved that—the futility of
    it, you know?
And somewhere near the end of the
    field I got hit and went down.
Just like that.

And then I just lay there and listened.
To my breath, to the other men charg-
    ing around me, sometimes over me,
my chest scratched and hot from the
    charge.
I listened to the earth, the sunshine.

There was a man who went down
    near me,

and I could see his white hand in the
    sun,
extra bright, like coral or a flag.
The gentle curl of his fingers in the
    grass seemed to say,
Touch me;
or— Let me rest;
or— Behold;
or— Soft high five.

(She looks toward the audience.)

And then suddenly I wondered if the
    dead were watching—
watching us.
Sitting in their invisible chairs, in their
    invisible rows,
shaking their heads at these crazy ass-
    holes who actually want to relive
    this terrible moment.

And then I think I took a nap.
The whole thing was more fun—and
    more sad—than I was expecting.

*(TOM and CAL have been really listen-
ing, drawn in.)*

LEAH: But after going through it, I can
see why people come back.

Keep trying—to catch—a *glimpse...*

*(CAL and TOM and LEAH sit in a
thoughtful, brief silence.)*

CAL: That was well said.

TOM: It was.

CAL: Some of your farby points are
reduced for stating an authentic
description of the experience.

LEAH: Thank you.

(CAL notices their glasses are low.)

CAL: I'd say that deserves another
beer. May I?

LEAH: Um, sure. Thanks.

CAL: Tom? You up for another?

TOM: Sure.

CAL: Alright, be right back.

(CAL grabs everyone's glass. He goes. After a beat.)

TOM: I really liked what you said—about it being fake but you still feel it... That's right.

LEAH: Thanks.

(TOM looks at LEAH for a moment, taking her in.)

TOM: You're cool.

LEAH: Thank you!

TOM: You are. You're really cool.

LEAH: Thank you. You're cool too.

TOM: Oh now.

LEAH: You are! I'm very glad you guys sat down.

TOM: Yeah, likewise. And sorry about—

LEAH: Oh no, it's okay.

TOM: Seriously, he's not really like this. I mean, he is, he is like this, but he's not usually so—

He just got through a very bad break-up. Like, VERY bad. So don't— he's actually a really good guy. One of the best I know, really. He's just torn in two right now. But I'm sorry if he—you know—

LEAH: Oh no, that's alright; I can handle him.

TOM: Yes you can!

(They laugh.)

LEAH: So, like, what's your deal?

TOM: What's my deal?

LEAH: Yeah, like, what do you do?

TOM: Oh I'm a teacher.

LEAH: No shit. What do you teach?

TOM: American History.

LEAH: Ahh, yes. Yes you do.

TOM: What does that mean?

LEAH: I don't know, that just makes total sense.

TOM: Really?

LEAH: Totally.

TOM: Huh, well that's nice. I'm teaching a summer class right now.

LEAH: And what're you studying in your class?

TOM: Well, we just finished the Civil War actually—

LEAH: Awesome—

TOM: Uh huh—and now we're discussing the Reconstruction Era.

LEAH: Oooh, bummer—

TOM: Uh, yeah, right? Definitely not a happy time.

LEAH: And what're your students like?

TOM: What you mean, like—?

LEAH: Like, are they smart, do they like class— What do you make of the next generation?

TOM: Oh boy. Well, they didn't give a shit about the Civil War, I know that.

LEAH: Really?

TOM: Well, no, that's not entirely true, some of them gave a shit. But it's like, you know, my favorite topic, like EVER, and they're like, *(Like a douchey kid.)* What kind of name is Pickett??

LEAH: Right.

TOM: They don't really live in this world, kids today, they really don't. They live in a video game, a social network, a media market.

LEAH: Maybe they just have different battlefields. Electronic ones.

TOM: That's what Carrie says. My wife. She's a counselor.

LEAH: Oh yeah?

TOM: Yeah, she says that kids today care just as much, they just have outlets we don't understand.

LEAH: Huh.

TOM: You'd really like Carrie. She's cool like you.

LEAH: Do you guys have kids?

TOM: We're about to!

LEAH: Really?

TOM: Yup. In about another month. A boy.

LEAH: Oh, that's lovely. Congratulations.

TOM: Thanks, we're excited. Do you have kids?

LEAH: Nope.

TOM: Are you married?

LEAH: Nope.

TOM: So you just moved here on your own? You don't know anyone around here?

LEAH: Yup. I put my finger on the map one drunken night about three weeks ago and it landed on Gettysburg, Pennsylvania.

TOM: Wow. That's brave. I've lived here my whole life.

LEAH: Really?

TOM: Yeah, never really lived more than twenty miles from here.

LEAH: There's something brave about that too.

TOM: What do you mean?

LEAH: Just—sticking it out, I guess. Putting your roots down, or keeping your roots down, making a life.

TOM: Well, haven't you done that?

LEAH: I don't think I have. I finally decided that if I didn't leave New York I might die, like seriously die, my heart hurt so much. So I picked a place and here I am. I got a job at the Jo-Ann Fabrics on Route 30—

TOM: Oh yeah, uh huh—

LEAH: Yup, college graduate, now making $11.95 an hour, awesome—

TOM: And what were you, by trade I mean—?

LEAH: I was a modern dancer.

TOM: No kidding.

LEAH: Is that surprising?

TOM: Well sure, you don't meet one of those every day.

LEAH: Yeah, well, for now it just feels better to be away from there.

(CAL reenters with the beers.)

CAL: What did I miss? Any kissing?

TOM: Noooo, no.

LEAH: Tom was just telling me about being a teacher.

CAL: Oh, dude—we haven't even talked about the fuckin' strike.

TOM: It's alright, I don't really wanna talk about it.

LEAH: What strike?

TOM: Oh—it's a long story, but basically tonight I have to decide whether or not I'm gonna sign this paper and agree to the budget cuts, or if I'm gonna go on strike with the other teachers.

LEAH: That sucks.

CAL: The school district is a bunch of assholes.

TOM: Budget cuts.

CAL: Budget cuts. I'd like to know if the superintendent is taking a budget cut.

LEAH: Exactly. I love how there's still a fuckin' aristocracy in this country.

CAL: WORD. So what're you gonna do man? Are you gonna sign?

TOM: Part of me feels like, what's the fuckin' point? It's not like we're gonna win.

CAL: What do you mean? You could win.

TOM: *(Shaking his head.)* Nnnmmm. Part of me just wants to get it over with.

CAL: There is something to be said for fighting the fight even if you might lose.

LEAH: Like Pickett's Charge.

CAL: Exactly. Okay, so dude, so this is what I was trying to say earlier—this just gnawed at me all day.

We're doing the third day of Gettysburg today, which culminated with Pickett's Charge, right? And we know now that it was the turning point of the Civil War—right?

TOM: Right.

CAL: And I don't know why, but all day I just couldn't stop thinking—Pickett's Charge was a mistake, it was just a totally preventable mistake. General Lee made a few bad choices, choices that were totally not like him— And boom—the tide of the war turned.

And Longstreet knew it, he KNEW. He said to Lee, flat out, this charge will fail.

I guess I was just struck by that all day this year—a major event is happening, you're in the thick of it—and someday you're gonna look back and KNOW— know exactly where you went wrong...

TOM: The most amazing thing to me is that the rebel army knew it was going to be bad and they charged anyway. You know what I mean? And at every

moment, every step along the way, they could've turned back, like fuck this. I mean picture it—here's the start point for the Confederates, right? *(He gets up and illustrates Pickett's Charge—sets the space.)*

And like, here's where the Union army is well entrenched, right?— So the rebels walk into this open field, a mile of marching ahead of them—long range artillery firing away, thousands of men waiting on the ridge to kill them—and they make it all the way across Emmittsburg Road, canon fire, death all around, they could've turned back—they pass Cotori farm, around here, they could've turned back—they get all the way to the stone wall, where it turns into a fuckin' blood-bath—bayonets stabbing, guns firing like three feet away, *punching*— And even THEN!...

The courage of that. What makes someone do that? I don't think I could do that.

CAL: Sure you could.

TOM: No, I don't think I could. I come play soldier at Gettysburg because let's face it, I'm gonna go home and have dreams and get up and go teach, and go home and have dreams and get up and go teach, and then have a holiday because it's time to have a holiday, and then go home and have dreams and get up and go teach.

I hate this fucking piece of paper. This piece of paper makes me feel like a piece of shit.

I'm so sick of only having a hundred and sixty-eight dollars extra a month—for anything—a beer or a birthday—I don't need to be rich or anything, but a hundred and sixty-eight dollars? It's no fucking life.

But with a son on the way... When I think of my wife and my son— it makes me want to strike AND sign. Strike because I need more money, and sign because I need my fucking job. And I LIKE my fucking job.

I could totally shove a bayonet into that fucking cheap-ass superintendent.

CAL: What's his name?

TOM: Gerald Leukowski.

LEAH: Fuck that douche bag.

TOM: FUCK THAT DOUCHE BAG.

CAL: Can you imagine actually stabbing someone with a bayonet?

LEAH: Definitely.

(CAL and TOM look at LEAH.)

CAL: You can.

LEAH: *(Dead serious.)* Yeah.

CAL: Really.

LEAH: Yeah.

CAL: A bayonet into another man's *body*...? You could do that...?

LEAH: Yes. I could do that.

CAL: No way.

LEAH: Why do you say that?

CAL: No way.

LEAH: Why not?

CAL: Because that's just not natural. There is nothing natural about shoving a bayonet into another man's body.

LEAH: When your life is in danger? You'd be surprised.

CAL: Well, sure, thousands of soldiers did it, I'm just saying there's nothing natural about it. I mean, not like any of us here would actually know about this because we live in 2011 and we don't really have to fight for our lives on a regular basis or anything.

LEAH: I have fought for my life.

CAL: No, I don't mean like metaphorical, Joseph Campbell kind of shit—

LEAH: Neither do I. I have literally fought for my life.

TOM: Really?

LEAH: Yes.

CAL: Like *really*...

LEAH: Yes Cal.

TOM: What happened?

LEAH: A guy attacked me on the subway.

TOM: Someone attacked you?

LEAH: Yeah. A year ago. I was riding home from a late night catering job, just a money thing I was doing, and he was the only other person on the train with me. He was sitting across from me, like I was here and he was about where that chair is—and at some point he came over to where I was sitting, pretending to look at the map, like here, and he said, "Excuse me do you know which stop is next?" And I said one forty-fifth—and the next thing I knew he was shoving himself on me, like grabbing all over me—and I couldn't breathe, I'm not sure if he had his hands on my throat, or—and he smelled like grapefruit and diesel fuel— And at first I was sort of paralyzed, like I wasn't sure if he fell over cuz the train jerked or something, but then when I couldn't breathe and I felt him, I felt him squeezing my breast hard, like REALLY hard, there was this moment that I understood I was being attacked.

TOM: Holy shit.

LEAH: And I started screaming—or honestly, it was more like roaring, like a mythical PIG LION or something; I fucking kicked and screamed with all my might.

TOM: Jesus Christ.

LEAH: And I think I surprised him or something because he almost immediately backed off, or maybe I actually kicked him off or something—and then he tried to run away, like to the other end of the train, like to here *(She moves the chairs.)* and I just ROARED at him— And then right then the doors opened and he ran out and that was it.

CAL: Jesus Christ.

(They sit stunned for a moment.)

TOM: And that was a year ago?

LEAH: Yeah. And I went to the hospital and got checked out and was basically just badly bruised. Like the next day my legs and arms were all bruised everywhere. And then, like, a month went by, and I realized that something just wasn't right. And it got very very dark in my life. It's been very very dark for what feels like a long time. And here I am.

(After a beat—)

CAL: *(Anguished.)* Jesus. I'm a dick.

TOM: Why do you say that?

CAL: I just... You're more soldier than any of us. And I show up here and I'm like... *(He shakes his head. Deep shame.)* I admire it—what you did.

LEAH: *(Quietly.)* Thanks.

(He is looking downward, downdown-down. After a moment—To LEAH—)

CAL: I was told recently—by someone who knew me really, really well... That I'm a dick. She said— Cal, you hurt people. She said— You stomp through. And you hurt people. And I made some mistakes, mistakes she knows about. She said— You hurt people, and you don't even apologize. So... I'm sorry.

LEAH: *(Very struck.)* Apology accepted.

(A beat. Then—)

CAL: I mean, you thought you were a unit, you know? A union, and then half wants to quit... It's amazing we ever recovered. It's amazing the Mason-Dixon Line doesn't fucking GLOW in the DARK from all that anguish...

(They sit at the table, a long, silent anguish...)

TOM: I feel sick.

CAL: Are you okay?

TOM: Yeah, I just—my stomach is like, in knots.

CAL: Okay.

TOM: I just wanna—eat a Popsicle or something. You know what I mean?

CAL: —? —No.

TOM: Like I wanna just—go home—and have dreams—and get up and do my job—and love my wife—and have a baby—and just be—okay. I just wanna be okay.

CAL: You *are* gonna be okay. You know? You're gonna be okay no matter what.

TOM: Who am I?

(Beat.)

CAL: What?

TOM: Who am I? Who am I?

CAL: *(Gently.)* Come on dude—

TOM: No really, Cal. Who am I? Who am I?

CAL: You're Tom.

TOM: Who's that? Who is Tom?

(CAL doesn't know what to say.)

TOM: Who is Tom? How would I know? I wish I could just—look down and see what color I'm wearing—and then I'd know which direction to march and what I'm fighting for and what I believe in and who my people are. What to kill. What to save. But I look to my left and I look to my right— and there is no army beside me, there is no flag in front of me. I look down and all I see is my shirt from the Gap that my mother-in-law got me for Christmas, and it's got FIVE colors in it. Not one. Five. And they're in some dumbass plaid pattern that screams— "Has No Idea Who He Is—So Shoot At Will."

CAL: Tom. Tom.

(CAL takes TOM's hands and holds them for a moment. They look at each other until TOM feels calmer.)

TOM: I guess I should get home. I got a big day tomorrow.

(CAL nods. TOM gets up to go.)

TOM: Leah, I really liked meeting you.

LEAH: You too, Tom.

TOM: I hope I'll see you around town.

LEAH: Well, you know where to find me. Especially if you need an ugly fabric with American flags on it or whatever.

CAL: *(Who wasn't a part of their earlier conversation.)* Jo-Ann Fabrics on Route 30?

LEAH: Exactly.

(CAL gets up and hugs TOM.)

CAL: Hey— Love ya, buddy.

TOM: Love you too. See you next week.

(They salute.)

CAL: See you next week.

(CAL sits. TOM starts to exit, but then, unheard by LEAH and CAL, he turns back—)

TOM: *(1863.)* I know I'm a piece of shit. I know

for the rest of my life
I'm a piece of shit.
But even if I were to turn back, climb out of this cellar and get back in the line,
I'd just be someone else's piece of shit.
At least
here in the dark
I'm my own piece of shit.
I'm my own.

I wanna see my momma.
Eat so much lingonberry pie I feel sick.
Swim in the creek
catch crawdads.
I wanna sleep on cotton so clean it's a little cool,
smell the magnolia tree—
have good dreams.
I wanna see my pappy
at the table with a Bible,
even if it makes him sore.

Maybe—
the whole goddamn war
will smoke itself out—
The high-up folks
will have their fill—
and the rest of us will—
live.
And we can have our pie.
Our pappy.
Our pretty.
We can have our dreams. *(Exits.)*

(LEAH and CAL sit sipping their beers in silence.)

CAL: He's a good guy.

LEAH: Yeah. He is.

(More silence and sipping.)

CAL: What do you think your spirit animal is?

LEAH: A lion.

CAL: Oh yeah? I'm a bear.

LEAH: Cool.

(Beer finishing.)

LEAH: Well, I guess I should be heading home. I work tomorrow.

CAL: Okay.

LEAH: It was nice meeting you, Cal. And thanks—for—I don't know—for somethin'.

CAL: Hey Leah.

LEAH: Hey yeah.

CAL: I know that, like, I've basically firmly established myself as a meathead douche bag of like, mythic proportion...

LEAH: Mm hmm.

CAL: But—um—there's like, a dance next week, it's like basically a barn dance thing that's to raise money to preserve Civil War barns in Adams County.

LEAH: Okay.

CAL: Anyway, a lot of us re-enactors are going, and I was wondering if you'd like to go with me...?

LEAH: Cal—that's—um—

CAL: I mean, it'll be in full regalia, just to warn you—

LEAH: Full regalia?

CAL: Yeah, like the white gloves and everything.

LEAH: Okay.

CAL: I mean, I don't know if you like to dance, or if you happen to know any of the dances of the era, but like, I could teach you a few—I mean, if—you know...

LEAH: Um—that sounds like a whole lot of seriously geeked-out re-enactor shenanigans.

CAL: Oh it is, it really is. I mean there'll be a full period band and the whole nine.

LEAH: Oh I'm sure.

CAL: So what do you think? You wanna go?

LEAH: Well, I don't know Cal. My farby point status is still pretty bad.

CAL: Yeah, that's a good point. (He thinks for a moment. Like, too long of a moment.)

LEAH: Jesus Christ are you seriously thinking of revoking your invitation (which I have not yet accepted, by the way) because I might not have a fucking HOOP SKIRT??!

CAL: No.

LEAH: Mmm, really?

CAL: Noooo, but I WAS thinking... Well... Maybe I could come by Jo-Ann Fabrics tomorrow and we could pick out a fabric and we could get you a dress made.

LEAH: A dress made. Seriously.

CAL: Well, yeah. My mom is actually really good at that shit and she totally loves it, and like, it'll make her year.

LEAH: You're being serious— A dress— like with a hoop and everything.

CAL: Yeah.

LEAH: Wait, this is not a plot to get me to stop being a soldier on the battlefield, is it? Like if I have a fucking hoop dress I'll wanna stop re-enacting the battles...?

CAL: No. No no no. Seriously. I just thought you might like the dance...

LEAH: And—

CAL: And—I thought—it would be fun to have you.

LEAH: So your mom will make me a hoop dress out of an ugly fabric of my choosing—

CAL: (Quickly, parenthetically.) Which hopefully will be 1863-appropriate—

LEAH: And then you and I will do the fuckin' Schottische, or whatever—

CAL: Oooh, that's a good one, I'm impressed you know that—

LEAH: And then I can put on my Confederate soldier outfit and drink with the boys afterward if I want to.

CAL: Yikes. Okay. Yes.

(She looks at him—considering this scenario.)

LEAH: Okay Cal.

CAL: Okay?

LEAH: Yeah. Okay.

CAL: Wow. Okay!

LEAH: Okay.

CAL: Cool.

LEAH: So… I guess I'll see you at Jo-Ann Fabrics.

CAL: Yes you will. Tomorrow.

LEAH: Okay.

CAL: *(Stands up, and with surprising tenderness—salutes her.)* Good night Leah.

LEAH: *(Touched, salutes back.)* Good night Cal.

(LEAH goes to leave, but just before she does—a voice from another time.)

LEAH: *(1863.)* I've never seen so many men in my life.
They march through town and I cannot look away.
I search their faces for something different,
or bad—
but they just look like sad, dirty men.
Eyes bright from fatigue and home-sickness,
hair matted—
you can smell them
a sharp smell
that makes your tongue move…

And suddenly I have this overwhelming urge to kiss them.
To kiss each and every one of them.
Take the blood
and hunger
and homesickness
into my mouth
and hold it there.
My hands—
their chests, their bellies
Make my own war on them—one after another—
leave a clear, slimy trail across the entire army, both sides!

(She kisses CAL over and over—)

The blue. *(Kiss.)*
The gray. *(Kiss.)*
The rich. *(Kiss.)*
The poor. *(Kiss.)*
The dying. *(Kiss.)*
The dead. *(Kiss.)*

(Suddenly—)

Cannon fire.
Smoke.
The men don't seem to hear.
They march.
And I watch. *(Licks her lips.)*
My gun at the ready. *(Exits.)*

CAL: I cannot sleep. Lee has told me that we will make the charge in the morning,

And that vast open field is heavy on my mind.

I leave my tent and the night is the color of moth dust, and warm,

So I walk down among the tents, ghostly triangles,

Where my men, row after row, are dreaming in the dark.

Long dreams, like rope, pulling them toward the terrible day.

And for just a moment, it's just a pretty summer night…

(He looks right at the audience.)

And suddenly I see them there—

Above the sleeping men, sitting right up, looking right at me—

The future—solemn and serene—they are looking at me.

While my men sleep, their deeper, future selves are alert, like deer.

They look at me expectantly, like they await my command.

Or do I await theirs?

I know not, but here we stand, eye to eye,

The future

And me.

(Still with the audience—a deep, true question.)

Have we done it?

Have we formed a more perfect union?

We must. Right?

Surely we must...

But I cannot read them, their kind, grave faces.

So I return to my tent. My bed.

The long rope of my dreams.

I will grab hold of that rope, and let it pull me toward sunrise,

when the coffee will boil and the wagons will roll.

We will charge that field.

But before I walk back, I raise my hand—

(He raises his hand to the audience, solemnly, like he's taking an oath, or about to wave.)

White in the dark, like coral, or a flag—

And with my hand raised to the future—

I say—

Hello.

Hold.

Help.

I say—

I promise.

I say—

Peace.

I say—

Good night.

(END OF PLAY.)

CLOWN BAR

a clown noir play

Adam Szymkowicz

ADAM SZYMKOWICZ's plays have been produced throughout the United States and in Canada, England, the Netherlands, Germany, and Lithuania. His work has been presented or developed at such places as MCC Theater, Ars Nova, South Coast Rep, Playwrights Horizons, LAByrinth Theater Company, Primary Stages, The New Group, Southern Rep, The Lark, Kitchen Dog, Theatre of Note, Naked Stage, Azuka Theater, and Studio Dante among others. Plays include *Deflowering Waldo, Open Minds, Anne, The Art Machine, Pretty Theft, Food For Fish, Hearts Like Fists, My Base and Scurvy Heart, Herbie, Incendiary, Old Fashioned Cold Fusion, Bee Eater, Temporary Everything, Susan Gets Some Play, Clown Bar, Fat Cat Killers, The Why Overhead, Elsewhere, Where You Can't Follow, The Artist* and *Nerve*. His plays are published by Dramatists Play Service and Samuel French. He received a Playwright's Diploma from the Juilliard School's Lila Acheson Wallace American Playwrights Program and an MFA from Columbia University where he was the Dean's Fellow. Szymkowicz is a two-time Lecomte du Nouy Prize-winner, a member of the Dramatists Guild, Writer's Guild of America, Primary Stages' Dorothy Strelsin New American Writers Group, the MCC Playwright's Coalition, and was a founding member of the Ars Nova Play Group. He served as Playwright in Residence at the William Inge Center, received a grant from the CT Commission on Culture & Tourism, and was commissioned by South Coast Rep. He was the premiere Resident Playwright at The Chance Theater in Anaheim, California, and the first playwright to participate in Bloomington Playwrights Projects' Square One Series. For more, go to www.adamszymkowicz.com.

VISIBLE SOUL INTERVIEW WITH ADAM SZYMKOWICZ
Conducted by Zack Calhoon, June 8, 2011

How did you get started in theater? What made you start writing plays?

I was an actor to start. I was in at least a play a year from first grade on until my senior year of high school when I gave up acting. I had to give it up twice more before it stuck, but I'm definitely done with that now. When I started writing in college, I started writing plays, I think because of being an actor for so long and because I had fallen in love with theater. I was hooked on theater, just not as an actor.

Tell me about your play, *Clown Bar*. What has the process been like? How do you think the play is going?

It's a clown noir play about the seedy underground crime world and what it means to want to be funny and just not be funny enough. It's a comedy and it's pretty dark. We haven't started rehearsals yet. We are frantically casting right now. I'm excited about the whole thing. We're going to give out clown noses at the door. I bought them in bulk.

How did you get involved with Rising Phoenix Rep? What do you love most about working with them?

I've known Daniel for a long time. I love him and his excitement about life and theater and I'm thrilled to work with RPR. They're a great bunch of people and I'm honored to be asked to participate.

What kind writing inspires you?

Good writing.

Who or what has been the biggest influence on your work as a playwright thus far?

Early on it was Chris Durang and Marsha Norman. My senior year of college I wrote, directed and produced a play that was heavily influenced by *The Marriage of Bette and Boo* and *'night, Mother*. It was a comedy about a girl who wanted to commit suicide. Later, I got to study with them both. I don't know if I ever told them how much they influenced me years before I met them.

Since then, there have been many many more, too numerous to name, but the seed is still there between the two of them, the absurdist comedy married with tragic drama.

You are a prolific blogger. What made you decide to start your blog? I am also a huge fan of your Playwright interview series. What compelled you undertake this project?

I kind of just thought it should exist and it didn't so I made it happen. When I started out, I was just interviewing my friends. I wasn't sure I would get to fifty. Then I thought I would stop at a hundred. It's sort of out of my control now and also, I have a list of easily two hundred people I haven't asked yet. I'm nowhere near the ten thousand or so playwrights that are probably seriously writing in the U.S. right now. Not that I'll get that far. Right now I'm thinking I'll stop around four hundred.

Clown Bar, directed by Kip Fagan, premiered June 19, 2011, at the Seventh Street Small Stage at Jimmy's No. 43.

CAST LIST

Happy .... Sam Breslin Wright
Dusty .... Stephen Bel Davies
Giggles .... Dominic Spillane
Twinkles .... Stephen Stout
Shotgun .... Brett Aresco
Timmy .... Alex Anfanger
Petunia .... Jessy Hodges
Popo .... Beth Hoyt
Blinky .... Jessica Pohly
Bobo .... Jamie Effros

Lyrics: Adam Szymkowicz and Adam Overett
Music: Adam Overett
Costumes: Jessica Pabst
Makeup: Erin Kennedy-Lunsford

AUTHOR'S NOTE: Any production is strongly encouraged to use the original music and enhanced lyrics written by Adam Overett for *Clown Bar*. Please contact Adam through Sarah Douglas, Abrams Artists, 275 7th Avenue, 26th Floor, New York, NY 10001; 646-486-4600; sdouglas@dandkartists.com.

CHARACTERS

THE CLOWNS:
GIGGLES
SHOTGUN McGHEE
DUSTY
TIMMY
TWINKLES

THE FORMER CLOWN:
HAPPY MAHONEY

THE LADY CLOWNS:
PETUNIA
POPO
BLINKY

THE CLOWN BOSS:
BOBO

SETTING

The Clown Bar. A bar full of clowns set up like a cabaret. Action takes place in various audience areas and also on the small stage. Audience members are encouraged to dress like clowns. If possible, hand out clown noses to the audience along with their programs. Actors, stagehands, ushers, etc., are all dressed in full clown makeup with bright hair and clown noses. Their outfits could be clowny, or like gangsters from the Thirties, or more recent gangsters. Feel free to make guns as colorful as the clowns. Clowns may hold clip lights to illuminate scenes. On the floor is a chalk outline, like at a crime scene.

TIME

Right fucking now.

(At rise, GIGGLES steps forward. He is a tough clown and talks in a tough-guy accent. He might point to a list of Clown Bar rules on the wall. In an ideal world, the list would be cross-stitch embroidered and framed, like one of those pictures that says "Home Sweet Home." Or perhaps each rule has its own frame.)

GIGGLES: Rule One. There are no rules in a clown bar.

(He walks away. DUSTY, a sad clown, enters and steps onto the small stage.)

DUSTY: Thanks. Thank you for the intro-duction. This song, however needs no introduction. *(Sings sweetly.)*

THE BOZOS ALL ARE BOZING
THE AUDIENCE ARE DOZING
LIKE WRESTING A LAUGH FROM A STONE
THE CLOWNS HAVE ALL GONE HOME

THE BOOZERS ALL ARE BOOZING
THE LOSERS ALL ARE USING
I THINK I'LL DRINK ALONE
THE CLOWNS HAVE ALL GONE HOME

WHEN PRETENDERS TRY PRETENDING
THEIR HEARTS THEY ARE MENDING
BUT LET OUT A VIOLENT MOAN
THE CLOWNS HAVE ALL GONE HOME

WHEN THE SHOOTERS ALL ARE SHOOTING
TO SETTLE THEIR DISPUTING
IT CUTS RIGHT TO THE BONE
THE CLOWNS HAVE ALL GONE HOME

BUT THE HOOKERS KEEP ON HOOKING
THE USERS KEEP ON COOKING
AS THEY SAY, WHEN IN ROME
THE CLOWNS HAVE ALL GONE HOME

WHEN THE CLOWNS FINISH CLOWNING
AT NIGHT THEY DO THEIR DROWNING
THE CLOWN BAR IS THEIR OWN
THE CLOWNS HAVE ALL COME HOME.

Thank you. Thank you. I'm going to get a quick drink.

(DUSTY steps off the stage too close to SHOTGUN McGHEE. Ideally, SHOTGUN wears large clown shoes and DUSTY stumbles over them.)

DUSTY: Excuse me.

SHOTGUN: Did you step on my foot?!

DUSTY: No, I didn't step on your foot.

SHOTGUN: Did you step on my foot?!

DUSTY: No. No. I wouldn't do that.

SHOTGUN: I think you stepped on my foot.

DUSTY: *(Sheepish.)* I mighta stepped on your shoe.

(SHOTGUN takes out a gun and shoots DUSTY in the foot.)

DUSTY: Aaaaaah!

SHOTGUN: Take him outside and beat him, forcefully. If he complains, shoot him in the head.

(GIGGLES and TWINKLES drag DUSTY outside. DUSTY is screaming. HAPPY MAHONEY enters as they exit. HAPPY is not made up as a clown. He probably wears a suit. PETUNIA, a sexy female clown, approaches.)

PETUNIA: Happy Mahoney! As I live and breathe!

HAPPY: Hiya, Petunia. How are ya?

PETUNIA: Same old tricks. What'ya doin' here, Happy?

HAPPY: You know—

PETUNIA: Looking for somebody? Blinky's not here.

HAPPY: *(Sharp.)* Then why are you bringing her up?

PETUNIA: I just thought—

HAPPY: Drop it.

PETUNIA: Sorry. Maybe I can help you. Looking for a date? I'll do a special?

HAPPY: What's that?

PETUNIA: Half off.

HAPPY: Half price?

PETUNIA: No, I'll get you half off for free. If you want me to get you all the way off, it'll cost you.

HAPPY: Naw.

PETUNIA: You sure? I can put on a different wig.

HAPPY: I shouldn't. I work for the other side now. *(HAPPY flashes a badge.)*

PETUNIA: Popo, huh?

SHOTGUN: Popo?

PETUNIA: *(To HAPPY.)* I won't tell if you don't tell.

(Murmurs of "Popo." "Popo." GIGGLES runs in.)

GIGGLES: Popo!

SHOTGUN: Popo's coming?

PETUNIA: No, no. Popo's not coming. Happy's a cop.

SHOTGUN: No Popo?

GIGGLES: False alarm.

(GIGGLES exits hurriedly to finish beating DUSTY.)

PETUNIA: You sure you don't want a little company, anyway? I guess I could give you a discount. You know, for old time's sake.

HAPPY: I can't.

PETUNIA: We can use your handcuffs. Even if they're not funny.

HAPPY: I'm here on business.

PETUNIA: *(Flirting.)* What do you mean? Are you here to arrest me?

HAPPY: Only if you're responsible for Timmy.

PETUNIA: Oh, yeah. Sorry to hear about your brother. It's a shame what happened to him. A damn serious shame.

HAPPY: What did happen to him?

(Enter TIMMY, a clown in white. He stands in front of the chalk outline.)

TIMMY: No! Please! I didn't mean it!

(TIMMY gets shot in slow motion. We hear the shots in slow motion but there is no shooter. He goes down, dead and falls in the chalk outline.)

PETUNIA: Got shot up something fierce. Right over there. It's too bad. I always liked him.

HAPPY: Yeah, he was a good kid. 'Cept when he wasn't.

(TIMMY gets up slowly and exits in slow motion. They watch him go.)

PETUNIA: It's an uncomfortable way to go, death by shooting.

HAPPY: What happened, anyway?

PETUNIA: You mean who done it?

HAPPY: Yeah.

PETUNIA: Oh. I don't know. I was out sick that day. Herpes.

HAPPY: Petunia.

PETUNIA: What?

HAPPY: Just tell me what happened. I'm asking you as a friend.

PETUNIA: Don't go asking me as a friend now. A friend would get friendly with me and then pay me for it. You're just an old acquaintance who's come to stir up trouble.

(Enter TWINKLES and GIGGLES.)

TWINKLES: Happy, how are you?

HAPPY: Twinkles. Hiya Giggles.

(GIGGLES ignores him, walks on by.)

PETUNIA: Don't mind him.

TWINKLES: What's happening, Happy? I haven't seen you since—well, it's been a while.

HAPPY: You look good.

TWINKLE: Thanks. You look like shit. What are you doing here?

HAPPY: Just visiting.

TWINKLES: You shouldn't be here.

HAPPY: That's what Petunia was telling me.

TWINKLES: What's your plan here?

HAPPY: No plan. I'll figure it out extemporaneous.

GIGGLES: (Ready to be upset.) What'd he just say?

SHOTGUN: No. aneous! aneous!

GIGGLES: You stay away from my aneous!

PETUNIA: He says he's here on business.

TWINKLES: Aren't you out of your jurisdiction?

GIGGLES: (Ready to be upset.) What'd he say?

SHOTGUN: No, diction. Diction!

GIGGLES: Fuck you too. I don't take elocution lessons from nobody.

TWINKLES: You're out of your jurisdic-tion.

HAPPY: I put my jurisdiction where I want.

PETUNIA: But he don't want to pay for it.

TWINKLES: I'll buy you a drink but then you got to promise to leave.

HAPPY: I can't do that.

TWINKLES: Then I can't buy you a drink.

HAPPY: I can buy my own drink. (To PETUNIA.) Give me a rye. Make it funny.

(PETUNIA looks at TWINKLES. He nods. She goes off to get the drink.)

TWINKLES: No one here wants any trouble, Happy.

HAPPY: There won't be any trouble. Just let me talk to Bobo. I like to know the truth. I got a certain predilection. (Pronounced prediLICKshun.)

GIGGLES: (Ready to be upset.) What'd he say?

SHOTGUN: Shut up.

TWINKLES: Bobo doesn't want to talk to you.

HAPPY: How do you know, until you ask him?

TWINKLES: It's a standing order.

HAPPY: I deserve a conversation.

TWINKLES: Look, what happened to Timmy was sad. No one is sadder than I am. I liked Timmy a lot, most of the time.

HAPPY: I just want answers.

TWINKLES: What you want is revenge.

HAPPY: What if I do? What's it to you what I want or don't want? You feel like you got to protect Bobo? You gonna live like a lackey all your life?

(PETUNIA returns with his drink.)

PETUNIA: Here you go, Popo. A rye, extra funny.

(Murmurs of "Popo." "Popo.")

SHOTGUN: Popo?

GIGGLES: Where's Popo?

PETUNIA: No Popo. I misspoke.

GIGGLES: You got to stop doing that.

HAPPY: Just tell me. Did he deserve it? What did Timmy do that someone put a bullet in him?

TWINKLES: Come on. We don't need to go into that.

HAPPY: Just tell me this then, was he using again?

TWINKLES: What do I look like, a urine tester?

HAPPY: I remember how it used to be before the drugs. Before he got into the big show.

(Flashback. HAPPY moves to a different space. Maybe a table TIMMY is already sitting at.)

TIMMY: Tell me again, Happy. What was it like?

HAPPY: Then the ringmaster announces us.

TIMMY: What does he say?

HAPPY: "Now the greatest clowns the world has ever seen before your very eyes will perform grand feats of incredulity."

TIMMY: And then what?

HAPPY: Then we do. Giggles drives the clown car. Shotgun rides beside him. The car stops and they get out. Then Twinkles gets out and Lefty and Righty, Bicky, Shorty, Short Bicky, Big Shorty, Petunia, Zeezoo, Dusty, Gobo, then me, then Alice Shortstack, Foolish Todd, then Todd the Fool, Fat Todd, Lolo, Susie Banshee, Garbo The Grape, Tired Sal, Wonder Lu, Hetero Mikey, Gay Mikey, Popo, Slinky, Spanky, Thumbs Walton, Whiskers, Chuckles, Calamity, and Brian.

TIMMY: And then what?

HAPPY: We do our acts. The rusty saw, the runaway kite. Slaps the seal. The overeating iguana. The invisible slug. Trouble at the Sistine Chapel. Nuns in a ballroom. Lolo the kite. Fat foot. Fate. The broom. The classroom. The egg-beater. The old shoe. Existentialism. Soup. Snow. Sleep. The dead mother-in-law. And the gangster.

TIMMY: And—

HAPPY: They eat it up. The crowd loves us. The applause is deafening.

TIMMY: And you bow?

HAPPY: And we bow. And we bow and we bow. Too much we bow. And the audience loves that too. And then the dogs chase us out.

TIMMY: Wow.

HAPPY: Someday, you'll be in the show too, kid, if you work hard and you're funny enough.

TIMMY: Am I funny enough?

HAPPY: Let me see a spit take.

(TIMMY takes a drink.)

HAPPY: The rabbi said, "Yes but are they kosher?"

(TIMMY does a spit take.)

HAPPY: Wait a minute! That's not a milking machine!

(TIMMY does a spit take.)

HAPPY: And the horse said, "I thought this was a donkey show."

(TIMMY does a spit take.)

HAPPY: Yeah, you'll do great. Just don't get involved in the underground clown crime world.

TIMMY: Okay.

HAPPY: No, I'm serious. Promise me. Too many good clowns get killed who got no business picking up a gun.

TIMMY: I promise.

(HAPPY moves back to TWINKLES.)

TWINKLES: He broke that promise.

HAPPY: Sure did. Broke his mama's heart.

TWINKLES: Sorry about your mama.

HAPPY: Thanks, Twink. She went gentle-like. In her sleep.

PETUNIA: That's not such a bad way to go.

HAPPY: So what do you say? Tell Bobo I'm here and I want to talk to him?

TWINKLES: Oh, come on. You're putting me in an awkward position.

HAPPY: You know what an awkward position is? The position my brother died in.

TWINKLES: Oh, come on.

HAPPY: You owe, me Twink. You owe me from way back.

TWINKLES: Don't go bringing that up again.

HAPPY: I was happy to help.

TWINKLES: Come on.

HAPPY: I didn't want you to stay a virgin.

TWINKLES: I could of done it on my own.

HAPPY: You were too shy to ask her.

TWINKLES: I *was* shy.

HAPPY: You were too shy.

TWINKLES: All right. I'll talk to Bobo. But I'm not promising anything.

HAPPY: Thank you, Twinkles.

TWINKLES: Yeah, yeah. *(Exits.)*

GIGGLES: Rule two in a clown bar: You better not try nothing.

SHOTGUN: *(To HAPPY.)* You better not try nothing.

HAPPY: What?

SHOTGUN: I said you better not try nothing.

(SHOTGUN pulls a beer out of his jacket pocket stabs a hole in it and shotguns it.)

HAPPY: Okay. Thanks for the advice, Shotgun.

GIGGLES: I don't think that was advice.

HAPPY: No?

GIGGLES: I think that was a warning. *(Exits.)*

PETUNIA: Don't mind them. They're still angry you left the clown life.

HAPPY: Why aren't you?

PETUNIA: You wasn't built for it, Happy. You wasn't happy as a clown. Not the kind of clowns we was. Anyway, what did you have left here after Blinky—

HAPPY: I don't want to talk about Blinky.

PETUNIA: I'm just sayin' I always understood. Even though I missed you. Timmy, though, he took it hard.

(TIMMY comes to HAPPY.)

TIMMY: What do you mean, you're leaving?

HAPPY: I got to go. Clowning's just not for me anymore. My heart's not in it.

TIMMY: Look, Blinky will come back. It's just a fling.

HAPPY: Stop it. I don't want to hear it.

TIMMY: I'm sorry. *(Beat.)* But you can't leave me.

HAPPY: You'll be fine. You got your own act now, in the big show.

TIMMY: But how can I do it without you there?

HAPPY: You don't need me, Timmy.

TIMMY: But I do. I don't think I'm funny enough.

HAPPY: That's crazy.

TIMMY: It's true. Everybody knows it. With you around they don't mind. Everybody here loves you.

HAPPY: Not everybody.

TIMMY: I need you. You can't go. Not yet.

HAPPY: Listen, kid. I can't be taking care of you forever. I got to take care of me.

TIMMY: Yeah.

HAPPY: I got to follow my own path.

TIMMY: What are you gonna do?

HAPPY: I'm gonna be a cop.

TIMMY: What do you mean a cop? Like a clown cop?

HAPPY: No, like a regular cop. Without any clowning at all.

TIMMY: But you're funny.

HAPPY: So?

TIMMY: You got a gift.

HAPPY: Just because you're good at something doesn't mean you got to do it.

TIMMY: Don't it?

HAPPY: I'm gonna try my hand at something else and maybe I'll be good at that too.

TIMMY: But it's your calling.

HAPPY: Why don't my calling make me happy?

TIMMY: If you keep doing it, maybe you'll get happy again.

HAPPY: I don't think so.

TIMMY: So that's it?

HAPPY: Sorry. I leave in the morning for the academy.

TIMMY: *(Hopeful.)* The clown academy?

HAPPY: No, Timmy. That ship has sailed. Do me a favor. Stay out of trouble. Work on your act. Keep your nose clean.

TIMMY: This nose? *(Takes off one clown nose and puts on another.)* Or this nose?

HAPPY: *(Tousling his hair.)* Oh, Timmy, you scamp!

(They laugh. TIMMY wanders off and the present returns.)

PETUNIA: I liked him.

HAPPY: Yeah.

PETUNIA: He was sweet. And fairly likable.

HAPPY: Yeah.

PETUNIA: Sometimes he bought me drinks. The problem was, he wasn't funny enough.

HAPPY: He wasn't, was he?

PETUNIA: No.

HAPPY: He tried.

PETUNIA: At first he tried. But you know Timmy. He took shortcuts.

HAPPY: You mean he started using.

PETUNIA: A snort here, a needle here, a toke over there. He thought it would make him funnier. And he was right. It worked for a while. But it was unsustainable.

HAPPY: Clowns don't make that kind of money. Not habit-supporting money.

PETUNIA: Not straight up clowns like you were. But unlike you, most of us sideline.

HAPPY: How about him? Did he get into the seedy underbelly of organized clown crime?

PETUNIA: I don't think it's my place to say, Happy.

(GIGGLES runs in.)

GIGGLES: Popo!

SHOTGUN: Popo?

PETUNIA: Popo's coming?

(Murmurs of "Popo." "Popo." Enter POPO, a dangerous clown covered in blood. There is something terrifying about her.)

GIGGLES: Hey, Popo.

SHOTGUN: Hi Popo. You okay? You seem upset.

POPO: Never been better. I just gutted a man like he was a fish and now I'm all zen and shit.

GIGGLES: Oh, so that's what the blood's from.

POPO: *(Crazy.)* Never mind what the blood's from!! That's my business! It's my business! Right?

GIGGLES: It's your business. *(Goes to rules list.)* Rule three: What's your business is your business and what's my business is my business. Don't get in my business.

POPO: Don't get in my business!!

HAPPY: Excuse me, Popo.

POPO: Happy Mahoney, what are you doing here? Last time I saw you, you were looking to get a badge and lock up clowns.

HAPPY: I got my badge.

POPO: Did you, now? How many clowns did you lock up so far?

HAPPY: I'm not looking to lock up clowns.

POPO: How many!!

HAPPY: Five. And every single one haunts me. Each clown I locked up coulda been me if I hadn't veered off the path I was on.

POPO: You proud of yourself?

HAPPY: Not particularly. But it should be said that three of those clowns were Brigham Bill's boys.

POPO: And the other two?

HAPPY: That was Lefty and Righty.

POPO: I knowed it was. I just wanted to hear you say it.

HAPPY: I'm not proud. I just did what I had to do.

POPO: We all got a choice.

HAPPY: That's what I was about to say to you.

POPO: What'd you come here for?

SHOTGUN: He came here asking about Timmy.

POPO: I knew that was gonna happen.

HAPPY: Was it you that gunned him down?

POPO: It wasn't me. You know I'd tell you if it was.

HAPPY: You gonna tell me who it was?

POPO: I don't expect so.

HAPPY: Let me ask you this. What if I was to hire you to kill the man that did it?

POPO: You wearing a wire?

HAPPY: No. Clown Honest Truth.

POPO: Well, Popo will do any job for the right price. But I look at you and I know there's no way you got that kind of money.

HAPPY: Ah. So it's that kind of a situation.

POPO: You're tilting at windmills, Happy. But the kind that tilt back. No skin off my nose to tell you so. If I was you, I'd get back in that piece of shit car you came in and drive away and never come back. Otherwise, my next job might be to erase you.

HAPPY: I appreciate the candor. And the warning. But I think I'll see this thing through.

POPO: I hate to see an honorable man like you die. But what can you do? If you don't mind, I'm gonna go get the money I'm owed.

HAPPY: While you're in there, will you tell Bobo I want to talk to him? My messenger's been gone a long time.

POPO: (Laughing.) Oh, Happy. You always were so funny. Not like your brother. (Exits to the back.)

HAPPY: It was worth a shot.

PETUNIA: She's right, you know. You should get out of here. Nothing you find is going to be pretty from here on out.

HAPPY: I'll take my chances.

PETUNIA: I'm serious, Happy. Take me serious. Don't think I'm joking just cause I'm dressed like a clown. I'd hate for anything to happen to you. It would make me sad. Why don't you come up to my room with me and forget all this nonsense.

HAPPY: Sorry, Petunia. I can't do it.

PETUNIA: At least come back tomorrow. The show's about to start.

HAPPY: You mean—

PETUNIA: You know what I mean.

HAPPY: I guess it's best to face all the demons at once.

PETUNIA: Don't say I didn't warn you.

GIGGLES: Rule four: Don't say I didn't warn you.

HAPPY: I'm not susceptible to warnings.

GIGGLES: Rule five: Whatever will be, will be.

(TIMMY is there, strung out.)

TIMMY: Thanks for coming, Happy.

HAPPY: I got to get back soon. What's going on?

TIMMY: Nothing. I just... Can I borrow some money?

HAPPY: What for?

TIMMY: I got a friend in some trouble who I need to help out.

HAPPY: Who'd you knock up?

TIMMY: No, not like that. Some financial trouble.

HAPPY: I don't really have a lot of money right now.

TIMMY: What do you got? I'll pay you back.

HAPPY: *(Taking out a few bills.)* You're not going to use this for drugs, are you?

TIMMY: No, no. Like I said, it's for my friend.

HAPPY: Look, Timmy. If you need a place to stay, away from the big show...

TIMMY: Naw, naw.

HAPPY: What's going on?

TIMMY: What do you mean?

HAPPY: Tell me what's happening.

TIMMY: Nothin'.

HAPPY: If you don't want to tell me, maybe I'll ask around.

TIMMY: Fine. *(Beat.)* I got canned.

HAPPY: From the show? What happened?

TIMMY: They said I wasn't funny enough.

HAPPY: Come with me. I'll put you up until you're back on your feet.

TIMMY: No, I'm good. I'm getting funnier every day. I'm working on it. I'm gonna show them all. I'm almost there. I just need a little money.

HAPPY: Oh, Timmy.

TIMMY: You don't understand. I'm not like you. I've never been like you. It came so easy to you and you turned your back on it, a clown as funny as you are. You didn't even care.

HAPPY: We're different.

TIMMY: Don't I know it.

HAPPY: Come with me. I'll help you work on your act.

TIMMY: I'm good here. I got some things going on.

HAPPY: What things?

TIMMY: Some things.

HAPPY: You got a girl?

TIMMY: No. Stop it.

HAPPY: What?

TIMMY: I don't want to talk about that stuff.

HAPPY: Look, there are other circuses.

TIMMY: Brigham Bill? That's not a circus.

HAPPY: Well—

TIMMY: You know that ain't a real circus. I'd be competing with monkeys.

HAPPY: Some of those monkeys are real funny, Timmy.

TIMMY: Are you saying I'm not funnier than a monkey?

HAPPY: No, no.

TIMMY: I think that's what you're saying. Thanks for the money. *(Walks off.)*

HAPPY: Timmy! Come on! Timmy!

GIGGLES: Rule six: The past is the past.

(Enter TWINKLES. He sits at the table with HAPPY but says nothing.)

HAPPY: Well?

TWINKLES: Bobo doesn't want to talk to you. He said if you didn't leave, I should shoot you.

HAPPY: You're going to shoot me, Twinkles?

TWINKLES: You going to leave, Happy?

SHOTGUN: I'll shoot him.

(SHOTGUN pulls out a sawed-off shotgun. Before he aims, HAPPY has his gun out. HAPPY shoots SHOTGUN, who falls.)

SHOTGUN: Uuugh.

HAPPY: Tell Bobo I'm not leaving till I talk to him.

GIGGLES: You shot Shotgun. Shotgun, you okay? *(Checks vitals.)* He's dead.

PETUNIA: You killed Shotgun.

GIGGLES: What kind of cop comes in here shooting people?

HAPPY: It was self-defense.

TWINKLES: That it was.

GIGGLES: That's not what I saw. I saw you shoot him in cold blood.

TWINKLES: Who's gonna believe a clown like you?

GIGGLES: *(To PETUNIA.)* Give me a hand.

(GIGGLES and PETUNIA drag SHOTGUN out.)

HAPPY: All right. They left. What are you gonna do? You gonna shoot me?

(They both have their hands on their guns, each watching the other for a sign of movement. DUSTY enters, limping.)

DUSTY: Can I get a ginger ale, funny. Oh, hey, Happy.

HAPPY: How you doing, Dusty?

DUSTY: Not so good. My cat died last week. Thirty-seven years old and died falling off the counter. She was dead before she hit the ground I suspect. I still haven't buried her. I'm too sad about it. I just stuffed her in the freezer and now whenever I want a Popsicle, I see her and I start crying again. On top of that, yesterday, I was sitting on my couch and I noticed a tear in it. I should probably get some thread and stitch it up. It'll just get bigger if you don't do something about it. You know what they say, a stitch in time... something something. Something about stitches. But it applies universally. To all ways of fastening things. Like pull up your zipper now or you'll be cold later. Or take the antibiotics now before you give it to other people. Or like, go to rehab before you OD on cough syrup or PCP or whatever. Or like, take care of your mama. My mama's doing okay. In fact, I was having a pretty good day if I wasn't thinking about the cat or my couch. But then Shotgun shot me in the foot. I'll probably get gangrene. I'm hoping the burlesque show might cheer me up. Hey what are you guys doing?

TWINKLES: We're trying to decide if we should shoot each other.

DUSTY: Ohhh. You shouldn't do that. Then again, a stitch in time...something something.

HAPPY: Saves nine.

DUSTY: What?

HAPPY: A stitch in time saves nine.

DUSTY: Saves nine what?

HAPPY: Stitches.

DUSTY: No. I don't think so. Maybe saves time. A stitch in time saves time. Yeah, that makes more sense. *(Singing.)* "A stitch in time saves time." What do you think?

HAPPY: Very nice.

DUSTY: You think it's in the right key?

HAPPY: Could be.

DUSTY: You sure?

HAPPY: I don't know.

DUSTY: Look, I can't debate this with you right now. I got a song to sing. *(Limps up onto the stage.)*

HAPPY: My brother always liked to hear him sing.

(TIMMY comes out to watch.)

TWINKLES: He did.

HAPPY: You gonna shoot me or what?

TWINKLES: Not until after the song.

HAPPY: On your nose?

TWINKLES: I swear on my nose. Clown's honor.

(The music starts. Sometime during the song, PETUNIA returns.)

DUSTY: This song is dedicated to Happy, who isn't. Women, God's greatest creation. I've known some lookers in my time.

CLEOPATRA, THEY SAY THERE'S NO MATCH FA'
HELEN OF TROY'D USE A MAN LIKE A TOY
THE GODDESS VENUS DOMINATED THE PENIS
MARILYN MONROE GAVE A HELL OF A BLOW
LOIS LANE COULD DRIVE A MAN INSANE

CATHERINE THE GREAT BROKE MORE THAN ONE MATE
BETTE DAVIS WAS SENT TO DEPRAVE US
MAE WEST HAD A HELL OF A CHEST
SOPHIA LOREN'D MAKE YOU FEEL YOUNG AGAIN
LOIS LANE COULD DRIVE A MAN INSANE

GERTRUDE STEIN MADE MEN STAND IN LINE
LAUREN BACALL WAS A WHORE AND A DOLL
GRACE KELLY MAKE YOU JIZZ ON YOUR BELLY
LAURA INGALLS WOULD GIVE YOU THE TINGLES
LOIS LANE COULD DRIVE A MAN INSANE

ANNIE OAKLEY LIKED TO SLURP IT UP VOCALLY
LADY GUINEVERE TOOK IT IN THE EAR
MARLENE DIETRICH MADE MEN SEASICK
JOAN OF ARC WOULD LIGHT UP THE DARK
LOIS LANE COULD DRIVE A MAN INSANE

WELL, I'VE KNOWN ACROBATS, SEXY CATS, AND GIRLS
    WHO MEOW,
BUT NONE OF THEM COMPARE TO BLINKY FATALE.

Blinky Fatale, everyone!

(BLINKY FATALE, a sexy and beautiful clown comes out and does a burlesque act. This goes on for a while. Sometime during her routine, she sees HAPPY and reacts. She finishes her routine, there is applause, and then she steps off the stage to talk to HAPPY.)

HAPPY: *(To TWINKLES.)* You gonna shoot me now?

TWINKLES: Relax. I'll let you have your reunion.

HAPPY: Maybe you should shoot me instead.

(It is at this moment that BLINKY reaches HAPPY.)

BLINKY: Happy, you're a sight that gives me sore eyes.

HAPPY: Oh, hi there, Blinky. I didn't see you come in.

BLINKY: Didn't cha? I was the one spreading my snatch all over the stage.

HAPPY: Oh was that your snatch? It always did spread.

BLINKY: What are you doing back here? As I recall the last time you came, Bobo said he would kill you if you ever returned.

HAPPY: I do recall something like that. Over a girl, wasn't it?

BLINKY: Not just any girl. It was over Blinky Fatale.

HAPPY: Oh yeah, I remember now, the girl who left me for a no good slimy mobster and clown bar owner.

BLINKY: Left you?

HAPPY: That's right. Left me with not so much as a goodbye.

BLINKY: Left you?! Ha! You left me. Bobo claimed me, and you slinked away.

HAPPY: I went to the academy.

BLINKY: Looked a lot like running to me.

HAPPY: Why shouldn't I? You weren't around, anymore. You took off.

BLINKY: That's not how I remember it.

PETUNIA: *(Approaches.)* Is she bothering you, Happy?

BLINKY: Petunia, why don't you go stink up some other room. Your vagina is not needed here.

PETUNIA: Listen here—

BLINKY: No, you listen. Happy and me are catching up. Now buzz off somewhere you can put your legs behind your head before I call Bobo out here to give you what for.

(PETUNIA slinks away.)

HAPPY: You haven't changed.

BLINKY: They say you have.

HAPPY: I had to. I couldn't be who I was.

BLINKY: No one ever stops being a clown. You can take off your makeup and dress up like the beige people but you'll never be one of them.

HAPPY: I am one of them.

BLINKY: You may look like them, but your heart is a clown heart. I can hear it from here. *(Like a heartbeat.)* Honk, honk. Honk, honk.

HAPPY: People can change.

BLINKY: People maybe, not clowns.

HAPPY: I don't believe in fate.

BLINKY: It exists whether you believe it or not. Fate don't care what you think. Why else you think you're back here?

HAPPY: I never knew there was a philosopher in you.

BLINKY: I've had one or two in me.

HAPPY: Look it was good to see you, but I'm here for a reason.

BLINKY: Are you sure you know what that reason is?

HAPPY: I mean—

BLINKY: If you come here to do something, when the time comes to do it, you sure that's something you can do?

HAPPY: What are you talking about?

BLINKY: What do you think I'm talking about?

HAPPY: What do you think I think you're talking about?

BLINKY: You should have fought for me.

HAPPY: What?

BLINKY: You heard me.

HAPPY: You weren't fighting for me.

BLINKY: What was the point if you weren't willing to fight for me? Should I fight for a man that didn't want me?

HAPPY: I wanted you.

BLINKY: Even now, I don't believe you.

HAPPY: What do I got to do to prove it?

BLINKY: Fight for me.

HAPPY: It's too late.

BLINKY: While you're alive, it's not too late.

HAPPY: Can I believe what you're saying to me or are you going to run?

BLINKY: What's that supposed to mean?

HAPPY: Blinky, you were like a very beautiful painting that got up and walked into the next room every time I tried to get a glimpse of you. You were sand through my fingers. You were a speeding freight train I was trying to catch on foot. I never knew you because you never stopped moving long enough to show me who you were. You think I knew what to do with you? You think I ever understood what you wanted? God knows you never told me.

BLINKY: Happy, you are like the most frustrating man that ever lived.

(She kisses him, hard. He kisses back. They start going at it pretty heavily. During this, TWINKLES exits. DUSTY gets on the stage. He sings. They

*make out, rub up against each other.
It is hurried and passionate. They are
too old to be so fervent, but they are
anyway. TIMMY enters and watches the
makeout session and DUSTY singing.)*

DUSTY:

YOUR NOSE—IS THE BEST CLOWN NOSE I HAVE
EVER KNOWN
YOUR TOES—ARE THE BEST CLOWN TOES THAT I HAVE
EVER KNOWN
YOUR EYES—SPARKLE IN THE NIGHT
LIKE A NIGHT—THIS ONE NIGHT-WHERE EVERYTHING
SPARKLES THAT NIGHT
CLOWN LOVE! IT'S LOVE BETWEEN A CLOWN AND A
CLOWN. CLOWN LOVE!
O H H H H H H H H H H H H H H H O O O O O O O O O
OOOOOOOUUUUUUUUUUUUUUU!!!!
CLOWN LOVE! IT'S LOVE BETWEEN A CLOWN AND A
CLOWN. CLOWN LOVE!
O H H H H H H H H H H H H H H H H O O O O O O O
OOOOOOOOOUUUUUUUUUUUUUUUUU!!!!

YOUR LIPS—ARE THE BEST CLOWN LIPS I HAVE
EVER KISSED
YOUR HIPS—ARE THE BEST CLOWN HIPS I HAVE
EVER MISSED
YOUR EYES—SPARKLE IN THE NIGHT
LIKE A NIGHT—THIS ONE NIGHT—WHERE EVERYTHING
SPARKLES THAT NIGHT
CLOWN LOVE! IT'S LOVE BETWEEN A CLOWN AND A
CLOWN. CLOWN LOVE!
O H H H H H H H H H H H H H H H H O O O O O O O
OOOOOOOOOUUUUUUUUUUUUUUUUU!!!!
CLOWN LOVE! IT'S LOVE BETWEEN A CLOWN AND A
CLOWN. CLOWN LOVE!
O H H H H H H H H H H H H H H H H O O O O O O O
OOOOOOOOOUUUUUUUUUUUUUUUUU!!!!

YOUR JUGS—ARE THE BEST CLOWN JUGS I HAVE
EVER RUBBED
YOUR LOVE—IS THE BEST CLOWN LOVE I HAVE
EVER LOVED
YOUR EYES—SPARKLE IN THE NIGHT
LIKE A NIGHT—THIS ONE NIGHT—WHERE EVERYTHING
SPARKLES THAT NIGHT
CLOWN LOVE! IT'S LOVE BETWEEN A CLOWN AND A
CLOWN. CLOWN LOVE!
O H H H H H H H H H H H H H H H O O O O O O O O O O
OOOOOUUUUUUUUUUUUUUU!!!!

CLOWN LOVE! IT'S LOVE BETWEEN A CLOWN AND A
CLOWN. CLOWN LOVE!
O H H H H H H H H H H H H H H H O O O O O O O O O O
OOOOOUUUUUUUUUUUUUUU!!!!

CLOWN LOVE! IT'S LOVE BETWEEN A CLOWN AND A
CLOWN. CLOWN LOVE!
O H H H H H H H H H H H H H H H O O O O O O O O O O
OOOOOUUUUUUUUUUUUUUU!!!!
CLOWN LOVE! IT'S LOVE BETWEEN A CLOWN AND A
CLOWN. CLOWN LOVE!
O H H H H H H H H H H H H H H H H O O O O O O O
OOOOOOOOOUUUUUUUUUUUUUUUUU!!!!

CLOWN LOVE! IT'S LOVE BETWEEN A CLOWN AND A
CLOWN. CLOWN LOVE!
O H H H H H H H H H H H H H H H O O O O O O O O O O
OOOOOUUUUUUUUUUUUUUU!!!!
CLOWN LOVE! IT'S LOVE BETWEEN A CLOWN AND A
CLOWN. CLOWN LOVE!
O H H H H H H H H H H H H H H H H O O O O O O O
OOOOOOOOOUUUUUUUUUUUUUUUUU!!!!

*(The music fades and DUSTY leaves
the stage.)*

BLINKY: Let's get out of here.

HAPPY: Where?

BLINKY: We'll get a room.

HAPPY: Just one night?

BLINKY: You want more?

HAPPY: I want everything. The kids, the
dogs, the picket fence.

BLINKY: Let's run away right now.

HAPPY: I don't know.

BLINKY: You don't know about the me
part or the running away part?

HAPPY: What about Bobo?

BLINKY: What about Bobo?

HAPPY: I have unfinished business.

BLINKY: The past is the past. Let's
leave it there.

HAPPY: I want to. *(Pause.)* But I can't.

BLINKY: Timmy wouldn't want this.

HAPPY: How would you know?

BLINKY: Something he said to me once.

(TIMMY enters.)

BLINKY: Why the sad face, kid?

TIMMY: I can't do it anymore.

BLINKY: What? Work for Bobo?

TIMMY: I mean I understand why he feels like he's got to do what he's gotta do. But he sends me and then he doesn't have to see their faces. To him, it's just a name on a piece of paper.

BLINKY: A name he put on that paper.

TIMMY: I just can't do it. Why does he got to respond with such force? Can't he just let something go?

BLINKY: Nope.

TIMMY: Look, I just need one more fix. I'll get one more and then I'll be funny enough and I'll quit. You got any money, Blinky? I just need it today. Tomorrow, I'll be funny and I won't need it anymore. I can pay you back.

BLINKY: I can't do that.

TIMMY: Please? You want me to keep working for Bobo?

BLINKY: You want to quit, just quit.

TIMMY: I can't do that. Not until I'm funny.

BLINKY: Not everyone can be funny.

TIMMY: But I can. I know I can. You've seen me. On a good day.

BLINKY: On a good day, anybody can be funny. The question is, how many of your days are good days.

TIMMY: Tomorrow will be a good day. I'll show them. I'll show them how funny I can be and they'll have to hire me back.

BLINKY: Look, kid. Isn't there something else you'd like to do? You're not good at killing people and you got fired from clowning.

TIMMY: Once a clown, always a clown.

BLINKY: But you could be a chiropractor or an ornithologist or an air traffic controller. You're a smart kid. You can go back to school and be something if you want. Me, I don't got a lot of options, but you, you could be all sorts of things.

TIMMY: I'm a clown.

BLINKY: Yeah, but—

TIMMY: I'm a clown.

BLINKY: Sure.

TIMMY: I'm a clown.

BLINKY: Yeah.

TIMMY: A clown.

BLINKY: I know.

TIMMY: A clown. A clown clown clown clown clown clown clowny clown.

BLINKY: All right, kid. You do what you want.

TIMMY: I wish I could. (Wanders off.)

HAPPY: So he was doing hits for Bobo.

BLINKY: Bobo paid him just enough to keep him in drugs. But he never got funnier. Actually, I think he was less funny towards the end.

HAPPY: So who killed him?

BLINKY: You know.

HAPPY: I need to hear someone say it.

BLINKY: Then why don't you ask Bobo?

HAPPY: I've been waiting around for him.

BLINKY: Maybe I can get him to come out.

HAPPY: How could you ever be with someone the likes of Bobo.

BLINKY: Bobo treats me good. You don't know what he's like. When it's just the two of us. I know he's a bad person, but he's good to me. I've known a lot of good people who were bad to me. I like it this way better.

HAPPY: Still, you'll help me?

BLINKY: I just said he was good to me. I didn't say I loved him.

HAPPY: Are you saying you love me?

BLINKY: See, that's just like you. Always wanting more. I bring you a gallon of milk and you ask about a cow.

HAPPY: Does that mean the cow's not for sale?

BLINKY: Are you asking me to marry you, Happy Mahoney?

HAPPY: I don't see how I could be any clearer. I got a good job, a nice apartment, a good life. The only thing missing is you.

BLINKY: If I say yes, you walk out of here with me right now and we never look back?

HAPPY: Are you protecting him now?

BLINKY: It can go both ways. I don't want to lose you today.

HAPPY: What about Timmy?

BLINKY: What about Timmy?

HAPPY: He deserves revenge.

BLINKY: Let him rest in peace. Just get him a nice tombstone. It can say, "Here lies Timmy Mahoney, a clown who was funny."

HAPPY: But he wasn't.

BLINKY: What is it with you and the truth?

HAPPY: I don't know. I guess it's just a preoccupation of mine.

BLINKY: It's getting in the way of my happiness.

HAPPY: You and me both.

BLINKY: Run away with me. Forget all this. We'll get married. That's what you're saying, isn't it? I'll be a house-wife. Or I'll do children's birthday parties. Or maybe even take the makeup off to fit in with the other moms at PTA meetings.

HAPPY: PTA?

BLINKY: You want kids, don't you?

HAPPY: I guess.

BLINKY: We'll fill up your apartment with little socks and shoes and shirts.

HAPPY: You'd cook us dinner?

BLINKY: Every night. The clown bar life is a young person's game. I'm getting old.

HAPPY: Not you.

BLINKY: So what do you say?

HAPPY: It sounds nice. Maybe after I talk to Bobo.

BLINKY: It won't just be talking.

HAPPY: No.

BLINKY: You know the rules. Either way, we won't leave.

HAPPY: There's always a way out.

BLINKY: (Defeated.) No. Not for me. I'll never leave. I'll be an old dancer, shoving my gray twat in the faces of old clowns.

HAPPY: No. I'll save you.

BLINKY: How can you?

(GIGGLES enters, gun drawn. HAPPY has his back to him. GIGGLES giggles. It's strange and unsettling. It's the first time we've heard him laugh. HAPPY turns quick and shoots GIGGLES dead.)

BLINKY: Dead?

HAPPY: He better be.

BLINKY: How'd you know he was going for you?

HAPPY: You hear that laugh? He only laughs like that right before he kills someone.

BLINKY: I never heard it before.

HAPPY: If you had, mighta been the last thing you heard. It's a hell of a tell.

BLINKY: So it begins.

HAPPY: What?

BLINKY: That's the second clown you killed within ten minutes.

HAPPY: Both of them was trying to kill me.

BLINKY: You're not going to leave with me, are you?

HAPPY: Not right now.

BLINKY: I'll see if I can get him to come out.

HAPPY: I appreciate it.

BLINKY: Yeah.

HAPPY: Thanks.

BLINKY: Whatever.

HAPPY: I recognize the favor.

BLINKY: This won't end well.

(BLINKY exits. HAPPY sits there. PETUNIA brings him a drink.)

PETUNIA: Here. Extra funny. On the house.

HAPPY: Thanks, Petunia.

(DUSTY steps onstage and sings.)

DUSTY: ONE SUNNY DAY, WHEN I WAS JUST A KID
MY DAD CAME HOME BLOODY AND BEATEN DOWN
I DID MY BEST TO ASK HIM WHAT HE HAD DID
HE SHOOK HIS HEAD AND SAID, WE'RE LEAVING TOWN

I DON'T WANT TO FIND OUT
IF THERE'S A HEAVEN FOR CLOWNS.

ONE RAINY DAY, AFTER I BECAME A DRUNK
I CAME HOME BROKEN AND BEAT DOWN
I DID MY BEST TO FIGURE OUT HOW FAR I'D SUNK
I POPPED SOME PILLS AND KILLED A BOTTLE I FOUND
I WASN'T AFRAID TO FIND OUT
IF THERE'S A HEAVEN FOR CLOWNS.

ONE SUNNY DAY BEFORE PETER'S GATE
I SHOWED UP HUNGOVER AND UNSOUND
I DID MY BEST TO ASK HIM, WHAT WOULD BE MY FATE
HE SIGHED GOODBYE, POINTED AT THE GROUND
I'M AFRAID I'M SAD TO SAY
THERE'S NO HEAVEN FOR CLOWNS

THERE'S NO HEAVEN FOR CLOWNS
THERE'S NO HEAVEN FOR CLOWNS
THERE'S NO HEAVEN FOR CLOWNS
THERE'S NO HEAVEN FOR CLOWNS
THERE'S NO HEAVEN FOR CLOWNS
THERE'S NO HEAVEN...FOR CLOWNS.

HAPPY: You two better get out of here. It's gonna get a bit hairy.

DUSTY: You don't have to tell me twice.

(PETUNIA kisses HAPPY hard on the mouth.)

HAPPY: What was that for?

PETUNIA: Good luck.

(PETUNIA and DUSTY exit. A beat. BOBO, an intimidating clown, enters with BLINKY beside him.)

BOBO: All right. Here I am. You want to talk, we'll talk. But if you want to shoot, you better shoot now. There won't be another opportunity.

HAPPY: I just want to know about my brother.

BOBO: See, you already blew it. A stone cold clown would have already put two in my chest and one in my head and would be spitting on my corpse as we speak. But you never were no stone cold clown.

HAPPY: I guess not.

BOBO: Too bad for you.

(POPO who has entered surreptitiously, now sticks her gun in HAPPY's face.)

POPO: Put the gun on the table, slowly.

HAPPY: Popo.

POPO: What? I warned you, didn't I? On the table.

(HAPPY slowly sets his gun on the table. POPO takes it, keeping her gun trained on him through the rest of the scene.)

BOBO: I always liked you, Happy.

HAPPY: I liked you most of the time till you took my girlfriend away.

BOBO: I didn't hear her complain. But she did ask me not to kill you. But since you seem intent on staying, I agreed to come out.

BLINKY: And not kill him.

BOBO: I didn't say that.

BLINKY: It's what I want.

BOBO: We'll see.

HAPPY: Just tell me what happened to my brother. Did you kill Timmy?

BOBO: I didn't pull the trigger.

HAPPY: But you killed him.

BOBO: Let me tell you something about Timmy.

(Enter TIMMY.)

TIMMY: I'm sorry.

BOBO: You want more money.

TIMMY: Yeah.

BOBO: Then do another hit for me.

TIMMY: I'd prefer not to.

BOBO: But you owe me but you have no plan to pay for the money you owe and you don't want to do any more hits. And now you want more money.

TIMMY: Yeah.

BOBO: Timmy, it's not part of my business plan to support junkies.

TIMMY: I'm not a junkie. I'm just fixing to get funny.

BOBO: What should we do about this?

TIMMY: I'm working on a plan. Just lend me a bit more money until I can get back in the circus.

BOBO: I should shoot you in the head right now. Put you out of your misery.

HAPPY: Is that what you did?

BOBO: You know I don't carry a gun, Happy. Never touch the things. My hands are clean.

HAPPY: But your soul is dirty.

BOBO: I didn't shoot Timmy.

HAPPY: Then what happened?

BOBO: Timmy pleaded with me. "Please," he said. "Please."

TIMMY: Please! Please!

BOBO: Tell you what, Timmy. I'm feelin' generous. You do one more job for me, you don't owe me anything.

HAPPY: He didn't.

TIMMY: Who do you want me to do?

HAPPY: So you're saying he got killed on a job, here in your own bar?

BOBO: Yup.

HAPPY: Who was he supposed to rub out? Someone that worked for you?

BOBO: Yeah.

HAPPY: Shotgun?

BOBO: No.

HAPPY: Giggles?

BOBO: No.

HAPPY: Twinkles?

BOBO: No.

HAPPY: Petunia?

BOBO: No.

HAPPY: Popo?

BOBO: No.

HAPPY: Not Blinky.

BOBO: No.

HAPPY: Thumbs still work for you?

BOBO: It wasn't Thumbs.

HAPPY: Um...

BOBO: It was Dusty.

HAPPY: Dusty?

BOBO: We got into an argument and I was in a mood. I didn't like his new song. It was sappy. Since then, we've mended our ways, but at the time, I told Timmy to whack Dusty.

(Exit TIMMY.)

HAPPY: (Not believing.) Timmy couldn't get the drop on Dusty?

BOBO: Timmy might not be such a good hit man.

HAPPY: Sounds like you told Dusty to kill Timmy, not the other way around.

BOBO: Eh.

HAPPY: Where is Dusty?

BOBO: You already killed two of my clowns. You think I'll let you kill my crooner too?

HAPPY: Yes.

BOBO: I'm a man of my word, Happy.

HAPPY: Are you?

BOBO: And as a man of my word, I have certain declarations I have to live up to.

HAPPY: What?

BOBO: You remember the last thing I said to you the last time I saw you?

HAPPY: That's not important.

BOBO: Oh, but it is. I told you if you ever came back here I would kill you.

HAPPY: Yeah, but—

BOBO: And now here you are.

HAPPY: Sure, but—

BOBO: And not only did you kill two of my employees but I suspect you're trying to take my lady away too.

BLINKY: He loves me!

HAPPY: That's not helping.

BLINKY: Tell him, Happy.

HAPPY: I don't understand how that—

BLINKY: Happy and I are in love.

BOBO: What?

BLINKY: Tell him!

HAPPY: We have feelings for one another.

BOBO: So what do you think? I'll just let you leave with my blessing?

BLINKY: You've always been good to me. Why stop now? If you love something, set it free. If it comes back—

BOBO: You're not coming back. Kill them.

HAPPY: (To BLINKY.) I think you played that wrong.

(POPO is about to shoot. But then TWINKLES enters and shoots POPO's hand. POPO drops the gun. HAPPY retrieves the gun.)

POPO: Ow! Come on Twink! What the fuck?!

BOBO: What the fuck, Twinkles?!

POPO: That's my shooting hand.

TWINKLES: I just thought it was time for a change. *(To HAPPY.)* Your move.

HAPPY: Thanks.

BOBO: So it's like that, huh?

TWINKLES: Yeah.

BOBO: After all I did for you.

HAPPY: I want to talk to Dusty.

BOBO: Dusty?

HAPPY: Get him out here.

POPO: I think I need to go to the hospital. My hand. Are you going to shoot me or can I go to the hospital?

BLINKY: Let her go.

HAPPY: Get out of here.

(Exit POPO, bleeding.)

HAPPY: Get Dusty.

BOBO: Dusty!

(They eye each other as they wait. HAPPY's gun is trained on BOBO.)

BLINKY: I never thought you'd do me like that, Bobo.

BOBO: Dusty!

BLINKY: You deserve whatever happens to you.

BOBO: Dusty!

(DUSTY limps in, casually, carrying a big bunch of balloons.)

DUSTY: Hey, guys. What's going on?

HAPPY: I need to know what happened with Timmy.

DUSTY: Timmy?

HAPPY: I know you killed him.

(DUSTY drops the balloons, which either fall to the ground or float up to the ceiling.)

DUSTY: Me? I couldn't kill anybody. I'm still sad about my cat.

HAPPY: So you're saying Bobo's lying to me?

(BOBO glares.)

DUSTY: *(Backpedaling.)* Oh, no, Bobo would never lie.

HAPPY: What happened with Timmy?

(Enter TIMMY with a gun.)

DUSTY: *(Stepping onstage.)* I was on the stage singing, "When Clowns Get in My Eyes." *(Sings.)*

WHEN CLOWNS GET IN MY EYES.

TIMMY: Hey, Dusty!

DUSTY: I turned and looked. His forty-five was pointed right at me. His finger was itchy on the trigger. It was very unfunny.

TIMMY: I have to kill you. I have to—

DUSTY: Nah, you don't.

TIMMY: I need my fix. I gotta—

DUSTY: Don't shoot me. I'm an innocent. I never done nothing wrong in my life. Killing me would be like breaking a Ming vase or a Rembrandt.

TIMMY: How is it like that?

DUSTY: I am a great artist.

TIMMY: Because you sing?

DUSTY: I make the angels weep.

TIMMY: You're an okay singer.

DUSTY: Okay? Okay?!

TIMMY: Good.

DUSTY: Good?!

TIMMY: But I got to kill you.

DUSTY: No you don't.

TIMMY: I don't have a choice.

DUSTY: There's always a choice. Choose life, Timmy.

TIMMY: I can't. I—

DUSTY: You're not going to shoot me.

TIMMY: I'm not?

DUSTY: No.

TIMMY: Maybe if you turned around so I didn't have to look at your face.

DUSTY: You'd shoot a man in the back?

TIMMY: Yeah, I guess that wouldn't work either. I'm worthless. I'm nothing. I'm not even a clown.

DUSTY: Drop the gun, Timmy.

TIMMY: I'm so—

DUSTY: Drop the gun.

(TIMMY drops the gun. DUSTY takes out a revolver, points it at TIMMY.)

DUSTY: I am a genius! Who do you think you are?

TIMMY: No! Please! I didn't mean it!

DUSTY: You are a philistine! You don't know what art is!

(DUSTY shoots TIMMY in slow motion. TIMMY goes down, dead, and falls in the chalk outline. DUSTY stands there, the gun still in his hand. He looks at it, then at HAPPY. A beat. He aims the gun at HAPPY and pulls the trigger. HAPPY ducks behind something. DUSTY turns over a table on the stage and ducks behind it. TWINKLES grabs BLINKY and they duck behind something else. BOBO also finds cover. A shoot out. HAPPY peeks out and shoots. Then DUSTY peeks and shoots. This goes on for a while. The balloons may pop.)

HAPPY: Stay still.

DUSTY: You stay still.

HAPPY: I'm trying to shoot you.

BLINKY: Shoot him!

DUSTY: *(Fires off a shot in her direction.)* You can't kill me today. Someone has to bury my cat.

HAPPY: I will.

DUSTY: You'll bury my cat?

HAPPY: Sure.

DUSTY: It doesn't matter. You can't kill me! I will never die.

HAPPY: I disagree.

DUSTY: I'm true art! I'm immortal. I'm everlasting! I'm a masterpiece. I'm—uthh! *(DUSTY has been shot. Sings, weakly.)*

THE CLOWNS HAVE ALL COME HOME.

(DUSTY dies.)

BLINKY: Oh! That's sad.

(BOBO pries DUSTY's gun from his dead fingers.)

HAPPY: I had to, didn't I?

(BOBO rises with the gun. HAPPY does not see. TWINKLES is reloading his gun.)

TWINKLES: *(Ducking.)* Watch out!

(But the warning comes too late. BOBO has shot BLINKY. HAPPY runs to her, under cover of TWINKLES shooting. BOBO and TWINKLES shoot back and forth over the next part.)

HAPPY: Baby. Speak to me.

BLINKY: It's okay, Happy. It never would have worked anyway. We're too different.

HAPPY: Don't say that. You're gonna be okay. Everything's gonna be okay.

BLINKY: You'll go back to policing, won't you? Say you won't get sucked into the clown underground again.

HAPPY: We're gonna get you to a hospital.

BLINKY: Don't bother.

(BLINKY dies.)

HAPPY: Nooooo! *(Beat.)* Bobo! You're a dead man!

(HAPPY joins in the gunfight. He shoots BOBO. BOBO falls. HAPPY goes to him.)

BOBO: Don't blame me. I was just following the code. The stone cold clown code.

(BOBO dies. TWINKLES and HAPPY stand there looking at the body. PETUNIA has arrived during this sometime. She goes to the body, takes BOBO's clown nose off and hands it to HAPPY. HAPPY puts on the nose.)

TWINKLES: What now, boss?

(Blackout.)

(END OF PLAY.)

ABOUT RISING PHOENIX REPERTORY

2007 Caffe Cino Fellowship and New York Innovative Theatre Award-winning **RISING PHOENIX REPERTORY** was founded in 1999 by Artistic Director Daniel Talbott. The phoenix takes the energy of the old, combines it with the new, and soars into the future. By learning from the traditions of the past and the teachings of the present, we want to rediscover the craft of a raw and vital living theater. Rising Phoenix Rep started by producing an ongoing reading series of new plays as well as workshops and festivals, and now produces both in the Indie Theatre and Off-Broadway. Upcoming Off-Broadway productions include the world-premieres of *3C* by David Adjmi (produced with Rattlestick and piece by piece productions) and *Analphabet* by Martin Moran (produced with piece by piece and The Barrow Group). Recent productions include the acclaimed, sold-out Off-Broadway runs of *Elective Affinities* (produced with piece by piece and Soho Rep), *Slipping* (produced with piece by piece and Rattlestick) and *Too Much Memory* (also with piece by piece), which transferred to the New York Theatre Workshop's Fourth Street Theatre after winning the FringeNYC award for Outstanding Play in 2008. RPR is currently in the middle of a year-and-a-half-long event called *Cino Nights,* inspired by Joe Cino and his Caffe Cino—one of the original birthplaces of Off-Off-Broadway—for which the company has commissioned nineteen playwrights to write new, full-length plays to be fully produced in the intimate back room of East Village restaurant Jimmy's No. 43 on a shoestring budget. Other recent productions include *Ceremony, Afterclap, Birthday,* and *Don't Pet the Zookeeper* (Seventh Street Small Stage); *365 Days/365 Plays* (Jimmy's No. 43 and The Public Theater); *What Happened When* (HERE Arts Center); *Fall Forward* (part of the Sitelines/River to River festival produced by the Lower Manhattan Cultural Council); *The Telling Trilogy* (including *The Ride,* 2006 NYIT Award Nominee—Outstanding Original Short Script/Crystal Skillman), *Rules of the Universe* (Winner, 2007 NYIT Awards for Outstanding Original Short Script/Daniel Reitz and Director/Daniel Talbott), and *Three Sisters* (Seventh Street Small Stage); *Gift* by Mark Schultz and *Ponies* by Mike Batistick (FringeNYC). Rising Phoenix Rep serves as a home base for a company of theater professionals that encourages an open exchange of work and ideas within the greater theater community. The company is a proud member of the Alliance of Resident Theatres/New York and The Dish. www.RisingPhoenixRep.org.

ABOUT ZACK CALHOON

ZACK CALHOON graduated from NYU's Tisch School of the Arts with a BFA in acting. His plays have been performed and developed by the Orlando Shakespeare Theater, Boomerang Theatre Co., East 3rd Productions, Living Image Arts, Flux Theatre Ensemble, Oberon Theatre Ensemble, New Mummer Group, On the Square Productions, and Dreamscape Theatre. Playwriting credits: *The Weird Sisters* (East 3rd Productions, Orlando Shakespeare Theater's PLAYFEST), *Breaking Ranks* (New Mummer Group), Marlowe, P.I. (Dreamscape), *Violence in the Air* (StageWorks/Hudson), *Krueger, RINO* (Core Creative Productions/Resonance Ensemble production at 2012 Brick Theater Democracy Festival, Resonance Ensemble Play commission), and *Paint* (Semi-Finalist for 2012 Eugene O'Neill Playwrights Conference, Winner of 2010 Georgia Theatre Conference New Play Award, 2010 Semi-Finalist for a Juilliard Playwriting Fellowship). He is currently working on commission for Rising Phoenix Rep. He wrote two episodes for the second season for the award-winning web series, *Then We Got HELP!* (www.thenwegothelp.com). He is an Eagle Scout and a member of the Dramatist Guild, Writers Guild of America, East.

ABOUT THE PUBLISHER

THE NEW YORK THEATRE EXPERIENCE, INC. (NYTE) is a nonprofit New York State corporation. Its mission is to use traditional and new media to foster interest, engagement, and participation in theater and drama and to provide tangible support to theater artists and dramatists, especially emerging artists and artists in the nonprofit sector. The principal activity of NYTE is the operation a free website (www.nytheatre.com) that comprehensively covers the entire New York theater scene. An ongoing program is NYTE Small Press (www.nytesmallpress.com) which publishes yearly anthologies of new plays by worthy underserved playwrights whose work has not yet reached a broad audience. The newest program is Indie Theater Now (www.indietheaternow.com), the digital theater library for the 21st century where academics, students, historians, theater professionals, etc., can immerse themselves in American modern plays of high quality, especially those written by indie playwrights. NYTE received the New York Innovative Theatre Foundation's Stewardship Award in 2008. Information about NYTE can be found at www.nyte.org.